THE AUSTRALIAN
Women's Weekly
100 classic cakes

THE AUSTRALIAN
Women's Weekly

Contents

We've all grown up with the idea of 'a cup of tea and nice piece of cake' – even if our lives today don't easily afford us the opportunity to sit down for a few minutes. I hope that you find a few reminders in this book of just how easy it is to make that nice piece of cake! From traditional dundee cakes to perfect little butterfly cakes… So kick off your shoes and get the kettle on!

Pamela Clark

CLASSIC

Butter cakes

Most of the cakes we know and love are butter
cakes of some sort. We use butter in our recipes
because it will hold the flavour of the cake,
it will keep the texture moist, and the cake will
cut and keep well, but, best of all, it makes
the cakes taste just wonderful.

basic butter cake

prep + cook time 1 hour 30 minutes **serves** 12

250g butter, softened
1 teaspoon vanilla extract
1¼ cups (275g) caster sugar
3 eggs
2¼ cups (335g) self-raising flour
¼ cup (180ml) milk

1 Preheat oven to 180°C/160°C fan-assisted. Grease
deep 22cm-round or 19cm-square cake tin; line base
with baking parchment.
2 Beat butter, extract and sugar in medium bowl with
electric mixer until light and fluffy. Beat in eggs, one at
a time. Stir in sifted flour and milk, in two batches.
3 Spread mixture into tin; bake about 1 hour. Stand
cake in tin 5 minutes before turning, top-side up, onto
wire rack to cool.

marble cake

prep + cook time 1 hour 40 minutes **serves** 12

250g butter, softened
1 teaspoon vanilla extract
1¼ cups (275g) caster sugar
3 eggs
2¼ cups (335g) self-raising flour
¾ cup (180ml) milk
pink food colouring
2 tablespoons cocoa powder
2 tablespoons milk, extra
butter frosting
90g butter, softened
1 cup (160g) icing sugar
1 tablespoon milk

1   Preheat oven to 180°C/160°C fan-assisted. Grease deep 22cm-round or 19cm-square cake tin; line base with baking parchment.
2   Beat butter, extract and sugar in medium bowl with electric mixer until light and fluffy. Beat in eggs, one at a time. Stir in sifted flour and milk, in two batches.
3   Divide mixture among three bowls; tint one mixture pink. Blend sifted cocoa with extra milk in a cup; stir into second mixture; leave remaining mixture plain. Drop alternate spoonfuls of mixtures into tin. Pull a skewer backwards and forwards through cake mixture.
4   Bake cake about 1 hour. Stand cake in tin 5 minutes before turning, top-side up, onto wire rack to cool.
5   Make butter frosting. Spread over top of cake.
butter frosting Beat butter in small bowl with electric mixer until light and fluffy; beat in sifted icing sugar and milk, in two batches.

lemon sour cream cake

prep + cook time 1 hour 15 minutes **serves** 16

250g butter, softened
1 tablespoon finely grated lemon rind
2 cups (440g) caster sugar
6 eggs
¾ cup (180g) soured cream
2 cups (300g) plain flour
¼ cup (35g) self-raising flour
½ cup (80g) pine nuts
1 tablespoon demerara sugar
¼ cup (90g) honey

1 Preheat oven to 180°C/160°C fan-assisted. Grease deep 23cm-square cake tin; line base and two opposite sides with baking parchment, extending paper 5cm over edges.
2 Beat butter, rind and caster sugar in medium bowl with electric mixer until light and fluffy. Beat in eggs, one at a time. Stir in soured cream and sifted flours, in two batches. Spread mixture into tin; bake 15 minutes.
3 Meanwhile, combine pine nuts and demerara sugar in small bowl.
4 Remove cake from oven; working quickly, sprinkle nut mixture evenly over cake, press gently into top. Return cake to oven; bake a further 45 minutes. Stand cake in tin 5 minutes before turning, top-side up, onto wire rack.
5 Meanwhile, heat honey in small saucepan. Drizzle hot cake evenly with hot honey; cool before serving.

orange cake

prep + cook time 50 minutes **serves** 12

150g butter, softened
1 tablespoon finely grated orange rind
⅔ cup (150g) caster sugar
3 eggs
1½ cups (225g) self-raising flour
¼ cup (60ml) milk
¾ cup (120g) icing sugar
1½ tablespoons orange juice

1 Preheat oven to 180°C/160°C fan-assisted. Grease deep 20cm-round cake tin; line base with baking parchment.

2 Beat butter, rind, caster sugar, eggs, flour and milk in medium bowl on low speed with electric mixer until just combined. Increase speed to medium; beat about 3 minutes or until mixture is smooth and pale in colour.

3 Spread mixture into tin; bake about 40 minutes. Stand cake in tin 5 minutes before turning, top-side up, onto wire rack to cool.

4 Meanwhile, combine sifted icing sugar and orange juice in small bowl; stir until smooth. Spread icing over top of cake.

cut & keep butter cake

prep + cook time 1 hour 30 minutes **serves** 10

125g butter, softened
1 teaspoon vanilla extract
1¼ cups (275g) caster sugar
3 eggs
1 cup (150g) plain flour
½ cup (75g) self-raising flour
¼ teaspoon bicarbonate of soda
½ cup (125ml) milk

1 Preheat oven to 180°C/160°C fan-assisted. Grease deep 20cm-round cake tin; line base of tin with baking parchment.
2 Beat ingredients in medium bowl on low speed with electric mixer until just combined. Increase speed to medium; beat about 3 minutes or until mixture is smooth and pale in colour.
3 Spread mixture into tin; bake about 1¼ hours. Stand cake in tin 5 minutes before turning, top-side up, onto wire rack to cool. Dust cake with sifted icing sugar, if desired.

madeira cake

prep + cook time 1 hour 15 minutes **serves** 12

180g butter, softened
2 teaspoons finely grated lemon rind
⅔ cup (150g) caster sugar
3 eggs
¾ cup (110g) plain flour
¾ cup (110g) self-raising flour
⅓ cup (55g) mixed peel
¼ cup (35g) slivered almonds

1 Preheat oven to 160°C/140°C fan-assisted. Grease deep 20cm-round cake tin; line base with baking parchment.
2 Beat butter, rind and sugar in small bowl with electric mixer until light and fluffy; beat in eggs, one at a time. Transfer mixture to large bowl, stir in sifted flours.
3 Spread mixture into tin; bake 20 minutes. Remove cake from oven; sprinkle with mixed peel and almonds. Return to oven; bake about 40 minutes. Stand cake in tin 5 minutes before turning, top-side up, onto wire rack to cool.

cinnamon teacake

prep + cook time 50 minutes **serves** 10

60g butter, softened
1 teaspoon vanilla extract
⅔ cup (150g) caster sugar
1 egg
1 cup (150g) self-raising flour
⅓ cup (80ml) milk
10g butter, extra, melted
1 teaspoon ground cinnamon
1 tablespoon caster sugar, extra

1 Preheat oven to 180°C/160°C fan-assisted. Grease deep 20cm-round cake tin; line base with baking parchment.
2 Beat butter, vanilla extract, sugar and egg in small bowl with electric mixer until light and fluffy. Stir in sifted flour and milk.
3 Spread mixture into tin; bake about 30 minutes. Stand cake in tin 5 minutes before turning, top-side up, onto wire rack. Brush top of cake with melted butter; sprinkle with combined cinnamon and extra sugar. Serve warm with whipped cream or butter.

malt loaf

prep + cook time 2 hours serves 10

4 cups (640g) wholemeal plain flour
½ cup (110g) firmly packed brown sugar
1½ cups (250g) sultanas
1 teaspoon bicarbonate of soda
1 tablespoon hot water
1¼ cups (310ml) milk
1 cup (250ml) liquid malt
½ cup (125ml) treacle

1   Preheat oven to 160°C/140°C fan-assisted. Grease 15cm x 25cm loaf tin; line base with baking parchment.
2   Sift flour into large heatproof bowl; stir in sugar and sultanas.
3   Add soda to the water in medium jug; stir in milk.
4   Place malt and treacle in medium saucepan; stir over low heat until mixture begins to bubble; stir in milk mixture. Stir foaming milk mixture into flour mixture.
5   Spread mixture into prepared tin; bake about 1¾ hours. Stand cake in tin 5 minutes before turning, top-side up, onto wire rack to cool.

tip Liquid malt is a malt extract available from brewing shops and some health-food stores.

cherry almond cake

prep + cook time 1 hour 50 minutes (plus cooling time) **serves** 22

185g butter, softened
1 cup (220g) caster sugar
1 teaspoon almond essence
3 eggs
⅔ cup (140g) red glacé cherries, quartered
1 cup (160g) sultanas
⅔ cup (90g) slivered almonds
1 cup (150g) plain flour
½ cup (75g) self-raising flour
⅓ cup (80ml) milk

1   Preheat oven to 160°C/140°C fan-assisted. Line base and side of deep 20cm-round cake tin with three thicknesses of baking parchment, extending paper 5cm above edge.
2   Beat butter, sugar and essence in small bowl with electric mixer until light and fluffy. Beat in eggs, one at a time. Combine cherries, sultanas and nuts in large bowl; stir in butter mixture, sifted flours and milk.
3   Spread mixture into tin; bake about 1½ hours. Cover tin tightly with foil; cool cake in tin.

tip Cover cake loosely with foil during baking if it starts to overbrown. Give the cake quarter turns several times during baking to help uneven browning.

almond butter cake

prep + cook time 1 hour 20 minutes **serves** 10

250g butter, softened
1 teaspoon almond essence
1 cup (220g) caster sugar
4 eggs
1 cup (150g) self-raising flour
½ cup (75g) plain flour
¾ cup (90g) ground almonds

1 Preheat oven to 180°C/160°C fan-assisted. Grease deep 19cm-square cake tin; line base and two opposite sides with baking parchment, extending paper 5cm over edges.
2 Beat butter, essence and sugar in medium bowl with electric mixer until light and fluffy. Beat in eggs, one at a time. Fold in sifted flours and ground almonds in two batches.
3 Spread mixture into tin; bake for 30 minutes. Reduce oven temperature to 160°C/140°C fan-assisted; bake a further 30 minutes. Stand cake in tin 5 minutes before turning, top-side up, onto wire rack to cool. Serve dusted with icing sugar and toasted flaked almonds, if you like.

greek yogurt cake

prep + cook time 1 hour **serves** 12

125g butter, softened
1 cup (220g) caster sugar
3 eggs, separated
2 cups (300g) self-raising flour
½ teaspoon bicarbonate of soda
¼ cup (40g) finely chopped blanched almonds
1 cup (280g) plain yogurt

1 Preheat oven to 180°C/160°C fan-assisted. Grease 20cm x 30cm traybake tin; line base and long sides with baking parchment, extending paper 5cm over edges.
2 Beat butter and sugar in small bowl with electric mixer until light and fluffy. Add egg yolks, beat well. Transfer mixture to large bowl; stir in sifted flour and soda in two batches, then nuts and yogurt.
3 Beat egg whites in small bowl with electric mixer until soft peaks form. Gently fold egg whites into yogurt mixture in two batches.
4 Spread mixture into tin; bake about 35 minutes. Stand cake in tin 5 minutes before turning, top-side up, onto wire rack to cool. Dust cake with sifted icing sugar, if desired.

quick-mix cupcakes

prep + cook time 40 minutes **makes** 24

125g butter, softened
½ teaspoon vanilla extract
¾ cup (165g) caster sugar
3 eggs
2 cups (300g) self-raising flour
¼ cup (60ml) milk

1   Preheat oven to 180°C/160°C fan-assisted. Line two 12-hole (2 tablespoon/ 40ml) deep flat-based bun tins with paper cases.
2   Beat ingredients in medium bowl on low speed with electric mixer until ingredients are just combined. Increase speed to medium; beat about 3 minutes or until mixture is smooth and pale in colour.
3   Drop rounded tablespoons of mixture into paper cases; bake about 20 minutes. Stand cakes in tins 5 minutes before turning, top-sides up, onto wire racks to cool.
4   Top cakes with icing of your choice.

variations

chocolate & orange
Stir in 1 teaspoon finely grated orange rind and ½ cup (95g) dark chocolate chips at the end of step 2.

passionfruit & lime
Stir in 1 teaspoon finely grated lime rind and ¼ cup (60ml) passionfruit pulp at the end of step 2.

banana & white chocolate chip
Stir in ½ cup overripe mashed banana and ½ cup (95g) white chocolate chips at the end of step 2.

mocha
Blend 1 tablespoon sifted cocoa powder with 1 table-spoon strong black coffee; stir in at the end of step 2.

glacé icing

2 cups (320g) icing sugar
20g butter, melted
2 tablespoons hot water, approximately

1   Place sifted icing sugar in small bowl; stir in butter and enough of the hot water to make a firm paste. Stir over small saucepan of simmering water until icing is spreadable.

variations

chocolate
Stir in 1 teaspoon sifted cocoa powder.

coffee
Dissolve 1 teaspoon instant coffee granules in the hot water.

passionfruit
Stir in 1 tablespoon passionfruit pulp.

butterfly cakes

prep + cook time 50 minutes **makes** 24

125g butter, softened
1 teaspoon vanilla extract
⅔ cup (150g) caster sugar
3 eggs
1½ cups (225g) self-raising flour
¼ cup (60ml) milk
½ cup (160g) jam
300ml whipping cream, whipped

1 Preheat oven to 180°C/160°C fan-assisted. Line two 12-hole (2 tablespoon/40ml) deep flat-based bun tins with paper cases.

2 Beat butter, extract, sugar, eggs, sifted flour and milk in small bowl on low speed with electric mixer until ingredients are just combined. Increase speed to medium; beat about 3 minutes or until mixture is smooth and pale in colour.

3 Drop rounded tablespoons of mixture into cases. Bake about 20 minutes. Stand cakes in tins 5 minutes before turning, top-sides up, onto wire racks to cool.

4 Using sharp pointed vegetable knife, cut a circle from the top of each cake; cut circle in half to make two 'wings'. Fill cavities with jam and whipped cream. Place wings in position on top of cakes. Dust with a little sifted icing sugar before serving, if you like.

upside-down cashew & maple syrup loaf

prep + cook time 1 hour 20 minutes **serves** 10

125g butter
¾ cup (150g) firmly packed brown sugar
2 eggs
1 cup (150g) self-raising flour
½ cup (75g) plain flour
½ teaspoon mixed spice
½ cup (120ml) soured cream
2 tablespoons pure maple syrup
90g butter, extra
½ cup (110g) firmly packed brown sugar, extra
2 tablespoons pure maple syrup, extra
1 cup (150g) unsalted roasted cashews, chopped coarsely

1 Preheat oven to 180°C/160°C fan-assisted. Grease 15cm x 25cm loaf tin; line base and long sides with baking parchment, extending paper 5cm above the edges.
2 Beat butter, sugar, eggs, sifted flours and spice, cream and syrup in medium bowl on low speed with electric mixer until combined. Increase speed to medium; beat about 3 minutes or until mixture is smooth and pale in colour.
3 Beat extra butter, sugar and syrup in small bowl with wooden spoon until smooth; spread over base of tin. Sprinkle with cashews; spread with cake mixture. Bake about 1 hour. Stand cake in tin 5 minutes before turning out onto wire rack to cool.

ginger cake

prep + cook time 1 hour 45 minutes serves 24

1½ cups (330g) firmly packed brown sugar
1½ cups (225g) plain flour
1½ cups (225g) self-raising flour
½ teaspoon bicarbonate of soda
1 tablespoon ground ginger
2 teaspoons ground cinnamon
1 teaspoon ground nutmeg
250g butter, softened
2 eggs
1 cup (250ml) buttermilk
½ cup (175g) golden syrup
lemon frosting
60g butter, softened
2 teaspoons finely grated lemon rind
2 tablespoons lemon juice
2 cups (320g) icing sugar

1   Preheat oven to 160°C/140°C fan-assisted. Grease deep 23cm-square cake tin; line base with baking parchment.
2   Sift dry ingredients into large bowl; add remaining ingredients. Beat mixture on low speed with electric mixer until ingredients are combined. Increase speed to medium; beat mixture about 3 minutes or until mixture is smooth and pale in colour.
3   Spread mixture into tin; bake about 1½ hours. Stand cake in tin 10 minutes before turning, top-side up, onto wire rack to cool.
4   Meanwhile, make lemon frosting. Spread cold cake with frosting.
lemon frosting Using a wooden spoon, beat butter and rind in small bowl; gradually beat in juice and sifted icing sugar.

coconut cake

prep + cook time 1 hour 5 minutes **serves** 20

125g butter, softened
½ teaspoon coconut essence
1 cup (220g) caster sugar
2 eggs
½ cup (40g) desiccated coconut
1½ cups (225g) self-raising flour
1¼ cups (300g) soured cream
⅓ cup (80ml) milk
coconut ice frosting
2 cups (320g) icing sugar
1⅓ cups (100g) desiccated coconut
2 egg whites, beaten lightly
pink food colouring

1 Preheat oven to 180°C/160°C fan-assisted. Grease deep 23cm-square cake tin; line base with baking parchment.
2 Beat butter, essence and sugar in small bowl with electric mixer until light and fluffy. Beat in eggs, one at a time. Transfer mixture to large bowl; stir in coconut, sifted flour, soured cream and milk, in two batches.
3 Spread mixture into tin; bake about 40 minutes. Stand cake in tin 5 minutes before turning, top-side up, onto wire rack to cool.
4 Meanwhile, make coconut ice frosting. Drop alternate spoonfuls of white and pink frosting onto cake; marble over top of cake.
coconut ice frosting Sift icing sugar into medium bowl; stir in desiccated coconut and egg white. Place half the mixture in small bowl; tint with pink colouring.

kisses

prep + cook time 40 minutes **makes about** 40

125g butter, softened
½ cup (110g) caster sugar
1 egg
⅓ cup (50g) plain flour
¼ cup (35g) self-raising flour
⅔ cup (100g) cornflour
¼ cup (30g) custard powder
vienna cream
60g butter, softened
¾ cup (120g) icing sugar
2 teaspoons milk

1 Preheat oven to 180°C/160°C fan-assisted. Grease two baking trays.
2 Beat butter and sugar in small bowl with electric mixer until smooth and creamy; beat in egg. Stir in sifted dry ingredients in two batches.
3 Spoon mixture into piping bag fitted with 1cm tube. Pipe 3cm-diameter rounds of mixture, about 3cm apart, onto trays. Bake about 10 minutes or until browned lightly. Loosen cakes; cool on trays.
4 Meanwhile, make vienna cream. Sandwich cold cakes with vienna cream; dust with a little extra sifted icing sugar, if desired.
vienna cream Beat butter until as white as possible. Gradually beat in half the sifted icing sugar; beat in milk. Gradually beat in remaining icing sugar.

cream cheese lemon cake

prep + cook time 1 hour 15 minutes **serves** 10

125g butter, chopped
125g cream cheese, chopped
3 teaspoons finely grated lemon rind
1 cup (220g) caster sugar
2 eggs
¾ cup (110g) self-raising flour
½ cup (75g) plain flour
lemon glacé icing
1 cup (160g) icing sugar
10g butter, melted
2 tablespoons hot water approximately
½ teaspoon finely grated lemon rind

1 Preheat oven to 180°C/160°C fan-assisted. Grease 20cm savarin tin (or grease deep 20cm-round cake tin and line base and side with baking parchment).
2 Beat ingredients in medium bowl on low speed with electric mixer until combined. Increase speed to medium; beat about 3 minutes or until mixture is smooth and pale in colour.
3 Spread mixture into tin; bake about 55 minutes. Stand cake in tin 5 minutes before turning onto wire rack to cool. Spoon icing over cold cake.
lemon glacé icing Sift icing sugar into small heatproof bowl; stir in butter and enough of the water to make a firm paste. Stir over small saucepan of simmering water until icing is spreadable. Stir in rind.

pound cake

prep + cook time 1 hour 20 minutes **serves** 12

250g butter, softened
1 cup (220g) caster sugar
1 teaspoon vanilla extract
4 eggs
½ cup (75g) self-raising flour
1 cup (150g) plain flour

1 Preheat oven to 180°C/160°C fan-assisted.
Grease deep 20cm-round cake tin; line base with
baking parchment.
2 Beat butter, sugar and extract in small bowl with
electric mixer until light and fluffy. Beat in eggs, one
at a time. Transfer mixture to large bowl; fold in sifted
flours in two batches.
3 Spread mixture into tin; bake about 1 hour. Stand
cake in tin 5 minutes before turning, top-side up, onto
wire rack to cool.
4 If you like, serve the cake with whipped cream and
strawberries, and dust with sifted icing sugar.

coffee walnut streusel cake

prep + cook time 1 hour **serves** 12

1 tablespoon instant coffee granules
¼ cup (60ml) boiling water
125g butter, softened
1cup (220g) caster sugar
1 teaspoon vanilla extract
2 eggs
⅔ cup (160g) soured cream
1¼ cups (185g) plain flour
¼ cup (35g) self-raising flour
¼ teaspoon bicarbonate of soda
walnut streusel
⅔ cup (100g) self-raising flour
⅔ cup (150g) firmly packed brown sugar
100g cold butter, chopped
1 cup (110g) coarsely chopped walnuts, roasted

1 Preheat oven to 180°C/160°C fan-assisted. Grease 20cm x 30cm traybake tin; line base and long sides with baking parchment, extending paper 5cm over edges.
2 Combine coffee and the water in small bowl; stir until coffee dissolves. Cool 5 minutes.
3 Make walnut streusel.
4 Beat butter, sugar and extract in medium bowl with electric mixer until light and fluffy; beat in eggs, one at a time. Stir in soured cream and sifted flours and soda, in two batches. Stir in coffee mixture.
5 Spread mixture into tin; sprinkle walnut streusel over top of mixture. Sprinkle over remaining walnuts. Bake about 30 minutes.
walnut streusel Combine flour and sugar in medium bowl; rub in butter, using fingertips, until mixture resembles coarse breadcrumbs. Stir in half the walnuts.

CLASSIC
Sponge cakes

❦

Eggs are the star ingredients in sponge cakes,
they are responsible for the light airy textures
and the melt-in-the mouth appeal. A quick light
touch is needed when the other ingredients
are combined with the beaten egg mixture.
These cakes can be challenging to make,
but are worth the effort.

best-ever sponge cake

prep + cook time 50 minutes **serves** 8

4 eggs
¾ cup (165g) caster sugar
1 cup (150g) self-raising flour
1 tablespoon cornflour
10g butter, softened
⅓ cup (80ml) hot water
⅓ cup (115g) lemon curd
⅓ cup (180ml) whipping cream, whipped
1 tablespoon icing sugar

1 Preheat oven to 180°C/160°C fan-assisted. Grease two deep 20cm-round cake tins; line base with baking parchment.
2 Beat eggs in small bowl with electric mixer about 10 minutes or until thick and creamy. Gradually add sugar, beating until dissolved between additions. Triple-sift flours; fold into egg mixture. Pour combined butter and the water down side of bowl; using one clean hand, fold through egg mixture.
3 Pour mixture evenly into pans; bake about 25 minutes. Immediately turn sponges, top-side up, onto baking-parchment-covered wire rack to cool.
4 Sandwich sponges with lemon curd and cream. Serve dusted with sifted icing sugar.

génoise sponge

prep + cook time 1 hour **serves** 8

4 eggs
½ cup (110g) caster sugar
⅔ cup (100g) plain flour
60g butter, melted, cooled
300ml whipping cream
1 tablespoon icing sugar
¼ cup (80g) strawberry jam, warmed
500g strawberries, sliced thinly
1 tablespoon icing sugar, extra

1　Preheat oven to 180°C/160°C fan-assisted. Grease deep 20cm-round cake tin; line base with baking parchment.

2　Combine eggs and sugar in large heatproof bowl, place over saucepan of simmering water (do not allow water to touch base of bowl); beat with electric mixer about 10 minutes or until mixture is thick and creamy. Remove bowl from saucepan; beat mixture until it returns to room temperature.

3　Sift half the flour over egg mixture; carefully fold in flour. Sift remaining flour into bowl, fold into mixture. Working quickly, fold in melted butter.

4　Pour mixture into tin; bake about 20 minutes. Turn immediately, top-side up, onto baking-parchment-covered wire rack to cool.

5　Beat cream and sifted icing sugar in small bowl with electric mixer until soft peaks form. Split sponge in half; place one half, cut-side up, on serving plate. Spread with jam and cream; top with the strawberries, then remaining sponge. Decorate cake with extra sifted icing sugar, and strawberries, if you like.

jam roll

prep + cook time 30 minutes **serves** 10

3 eggs, separated
½ cup (110g) caster sugar
2 tablespoons hot milk
¾ cup (110g) self-raising flour
¼ cup (55g) caster sugar, extra
½ cup (160g) jam, warmed

1 Preheat oven to 200°C/180°C fan-assisted. Grease 25cm x 30cm swiss roll tin; line base and long sides with baking parchment, extending paper 5cm over sides.
2 Beat egg whites in small bowl with electric mixer until soft peaks form; gradually add sugar, 1 tablespoon at a time, beating until sugar is dissolved between additions. With motor operating, add egg yolks, one at a time, beating about 10 minutes or until mixture is thick and creamy.
3 Pour hot milk down side of bowl; add triple-sifted flour. Working quickly, use plastic spatula to fold milk and flour through egg mixture. Spread mixture into tin; bake about 8 minutes.
4 Meanwhile, place a piece of baking parchment cut the same size as the tin on worktop; sprinkle with extra sugar. Turn hot sponge onto parchment; peel away lining paper. Cool; trim all sides of sponge.
5 Roll sponge from short side; unroll, spread evenly with jam. Re-roll cake, from same short side, by lifting parchment and using it as a guide. Serve jam roll with whipped cream, if desired.

honey spice sponge cake

prep + cook time 30 minutes **serves** 6

2 eggs
½ cup (110g) caster sugar
⅓ cup (50g) cornflour
1½ tablespoons custard powder
1 teaspoon mixed spice
½ teaspoon cream of tartar
¼ teaspoon bicarbonate of soda
300ml whipping cream
2 tablespoons honey
1 tablespoon icing sugar

1 Preheat oven to 180°C/160°C fan-assisted. Grease 25cm x 30cm swiss roll tin; line base and long sides with baking parchment, extending paper 5cm over sides.

2 Beat eggs and ⅓ cup of the sugar in small bowl with electric mixer about 10 minutes or until thick and creamy.

3 Meanwhile, triple-sift dry ingredients; fold into egg mixture. Spread mixture into tin; bake 10 minutes.

4 Place a piece of baking parchment cut the same size as the tin on worktop; sprinkle evenly with remaining sugar. Turn hot sponge onto parchment; peel away lining paper. Cool; trim all sides of sponge.

5 Beat cream and honey in small bowl with electric mixer until firm peaks form.

6 Cut sponge widthways into three equal-sized rectangles. Place one piece of sponge on serving plate; spread with half the cream mixture. Top with second piece of sponge and remaining cream. Finish with remaining sponge piece then dust with sifted icing sugar.

featherlight sponge cake

prep + cook time 40 minutes **serves** 10

4 eggs
¾ cup (165g) caster sugar
⅔ cup (100g) cornflour
¼ cup (30g) custard powder
1 teaspoon cream of tartar
½ teaspoon bicarbonate of soda
⅓ cup (110g) apricot jam
300ml whipping cream, whipped

1 Preheat oven to 180°C/160°C fan-assisted. Grease and flour two deep 22cm-round cake tins; shake away excess flour.
2 Beat eggs and sugar in small bowl with electric mixer until mixture is thick and creamy and sugar is dissolved; transfer to large bowl.
3 Triple-sift dry ingredients; fold gently into egg mixture. Divide sponge mixture between prepared tins; bake about 20 minutes. Turn sponges, top-side up, onto baking-parchment-covered wire rack to cool.
4 Sandwich sponges with jam and whipped cream.

strawberry powder puffs

prep + cook time 40 minutes **makes** 36

2 eggs
⅓ cup (75g) caster sugar
2 tablespoons cornflour
2 tablespoons plain flour
2 tablespoons self-raising flour
½ cup (125ml) whipped cream
2 tablespoons icing sugar
½ cup (65g) finely chopped strawberries

1 Preheat oven to 180°C/160°C fan-assisted. Grease and flour three 12-hole shallow (1-tablespoon/20ml) round-based bun tins; shake away excess flour.
2 Beat eggs and sugar in small bowl with electric mixer about 4 minutes or until thick and creamy. Triple-sift flours; fold into egg mixture.
3 Drop 1 teaspoon of mixture into bun tray holes. Bake about 7 minutes; turn immediately onto wire racks to cool.
4 Beat cream and half the sifted icing sugar in small bowl with electric mixer until firm peaks form; fold in strawberries. Sandwich puffs with strawberry cream just before serving. Dust with remaining sifted icing sugar.

tip If you don't have three bun trays, just wash, grease and flour the tray again, and continue using until all the mixture is baked.

victoria sponge sandwich

prep + cook time 50 minutes **serves** 10

250g butter
1 teaspoon vanilla extract
1 cup (220g) caster sugar
4 eggs
⅓ cup (80ml) milk
2 cups (300g) self-raising flour
⅓ cup (110g) raspberry jam, warmed

1   Preheat oven to 180°C/160°C fan-assisted. Grease two deep 20cm-round cake tins; line bases with baking parchment.

2   Beat butter, extract and sugar in small bowl with electric mixer until light and fluffy. Beat in eggs, one at a time. Add milk and beat well. Transfer mixture to large bowl. Stir in half the sifted flour, then remaining sifted flour; stir until mixture is smooth.

3   Divide mixture evenly between tins; bake about 30 minutes.

4   Turn cakes, top-sides up, onto baking-parchment-covered wire rack to cool. Sandwich cakes together with jam; dust with sifted icing sugar, if you like.

strawberry jelly cakes

prep + cook time 50 minutes (plus refrigeration time) **makes** 15

6 eggs
⅔ cup (150g) caster sugar
⅓ cup (50g) cornflour
½ cup (75g) plain flour
⅓ cup (50g) self-raising flour
80g packet strawberry jelly crystals
2 cups (160g) desiccated coconut
300ml whipping cream, whipped

1 Preheat oven to 180°C/160°C fan-assisted. Grease 20cm x 30cm traybake tin; line base and long sides with baking parchment, extending paper 5cm over sides.
2 Beat eggs in large bowl with electric mixer about 10 minutes or until thick and creamy; gradually add sugar, beating until dissolved between additions. Triple-sift flours; fold into egg mixture.
3 Spread mixture into baking tin; bake about 35 minutes. Turn cake immediately onto baking-parchment-covered wire rack to cool.
4 Meanwhile, make jelly as per packet instructions; refrigerate until set to the consistency of unbeaten egg white.
5 Trim all sides of cake. Cut cake into 15 squares; dip squares into jelly, drain off excess. Place coconut into medium bowl; toss squares in coconut. Refrigerate 30 minutes. Halve cakes horizontally; sandwich cakes with whipped cream.

chocolate coconut squares

prep + cook time 50 minutes **makes** 16

6 eggs
⅔ cup (150g) caster sugar
⅓ cup (50g) cornflour
½ cup (75g) plain flour
⅓ cup (50g) self-raising flour
2 cups (160g) desiccated coconut
chocolate icing
4 cups (640g) icing sugar
½ cup (50g) cocoa powder
15g butter, melted
1 cup (250ml) milk

1 Preheat oven to 180°C/160°C fan-assisted. Grease 20cm x 30cm traybake tin; line base and long sides with baking parchment, extending paper 5cm over sides.
2 Beat eggs in large bowl with electric mixer about 10 minutes or until thick and creamy; gradually add sugar, beating until dissolved between additions. Triple-sift flours; fold into egg mixture.
3 Spread mixture into tin; bake about 35 minutes. Turn cake immediately onto baking-parchment-covered wire rack to cool.
4 Meanwhile, make chocolate icing.
5 Cut cake into 16 squares; dip each square into icing, drain off excess. Place coconut into medium bowl; toss squares in coconut. Place on wire rack to set.
chocolate icing Sift icing sugar and cocoa into medium heatproof bowl; stir in butter and milk. Set bowl over medium saucepan of simmering water; stir until icing is of a coating consistency.

chocolate sponge

prep + cook time 40 minutes (plus standing time) **serves** 10

3 eggs
½ cup (110g) caster sugar
¼ cup (35g) cornflour
¼ cup (35g) plain flour
¼ cup (35g) self-raising flour
2 tablespoons cocoa powder
300ml whipping cream, whipped
coffee icing
3 teaspoons instant coffee granules
2 tablespoons milk
1½ cups (240g) icing sugar
1 teaspoon softened butter

1 Preheat oven to 180°C/160°C fan-assisted. Grease deep 22cm-round cake tin; line base with baking parchment.
2 Beat eggs in small bowl with electric mixer about 10 minutes or until thick and creamy; gradually add sugar, beating until dissolved between additions; transfer mixture to large bowl. Triple-sift dry ingredients; fold into egg mixture.
3 Spread mixture into tin; bake about 25 minutes. Turn sponge immediately onto baking-parchment-covered wire rack to cool.
4 Make coffee icing.
5 Split sponge in half; sandwich with cream. Spread top with coffee icing; stand until set before cutting.
coffee icing Combine coffee and milk in small bowl; stir until dissolved. Sift icing sugar into small bowl; stir in butter and enough of the coffee mixture to give a firm paste. Stir over hot water until icing is spreadable; do not over-heat. Use immediately.

passionfruit curd sponge cakes

prep + cook time 40 minutes (plus refrigeration time) **serves** 12

3 eggs
½ cup (110g) caster sugar
¾ cup (110g) self-raising flour
20g butter
¼ cup (60ml) boiling water
passionfruit curd
⅓ cup (80ml) passionfruit pulp
½ cup (110g) caster sugar
2 eggs, beaten lightly
125g unsalted butter, chopped coarsely

1 Make passionfruit curd.

2 Preheat oven to 180°C/160°C fan-assisted. Grease 12-hole (½-cup/125ml) mini muffin tin; dust lightly with flour.

3 Beat eggs in small bowl with electric mixer about 10 minutes or until thick and creamy. Gradually add sugar, beating until dissolved between additions. Transfer mixture to a large bowl. Fold in sifted flour then combined butter and the boiling water.

4 Divide mixture among flan tin holes; bake about 12 minutes. Working quickly, loosen edges of cakes from tin using a small knife; turn immediately onto baking-parchment-covered wire racks to cool.

5 Split cooled cakes in half. Spread cut-sides with curd; replace tops. Dust lightly with sifted icing sugar before serving, if you like.

passionfruit curd Combine ingredients in medium heatproof bowl; stir over pan of simmering water about 10 minutes or until mixture coats the back of a wooden spoon (do not allow the water to touch base of bowl). Cover; refrigerate for 3 hours.

chocolate coconut roll

prep + cook time 45 minutes (plus refrigeration time) **serves** 10

3 eggs
½ cup (110g) caster sugar
¾ cup (110g) self-raising flour
2 tablespoons hot milk
¾ cup (60g) desiccated coconut
butter cream filling
90g unsalted butter, softened
1 teaspoon vanilla extract
1 cup (160g) icing sugar
1 tablespoon milk
chocolate icing
1 cup (160g) icing sugar
¼ cup (25g) cocoa powder
1 teaspoon softened butter
2 tablespoons milk

1 Preheat oven to 180°C/160°C fan-assisted.
Grease 26cm x 32cm swiss roll tin; line base and
long sides with baking parchment, extending paper
5cm over sides.
2 Beat eggs in small bowl with electric mixer about
10 minutes or until thick and creamy; gradually add
sugar, beating until dissolved between additions.
Fold in sifted flour and milk, in two batches; pour into
tin. Bake about 12 minutes.
3 Place a piece of baking parchment cut the same size
as the tin on worktop; sprinkle evenly with a third of
the coconut. Turn hot sponge onto parchment; peel
away lining paper. Using parchment as a guide, loosely
roll sponge from long side. Stand 2 minutes; unroll.
Cool; trim all sides of sponge.
4 Make butter cream filling. Make chocolate icing.
5 Spread filling over sponge. Using parchment as a
guide, roll sponge from long side. Place on wire rack set
over tray; pour icing over roll. Press remaining coconut
onto roll; refrigerate 30 minutes or until set.
butter cream filling Beat butter and extract in small
bowl with electric mixer until pale and creamy.
Gradually beat in sifted icing sugar and milk until light
and fluffy.
chocolate icing Sift icing sugar and cocoa into small
heatproof bowl; stir in butter and milk. Place bowl over
small pan of simmering water; stir until icing reaches a
pouring consistency.

ginger sponge

prep + cook time 40 minutes **serves** 10

5 eggs, separated
¾ cup (165g) caster sugar
1 tablespoon golden syrup
⅓ cup (50g) self-raising flour
⅓ cup (50g) cornflour
3 teaspoons ground ginger
1 teaspoon ground cinnamon
2 teaspoons cocoa powder
300ml whipping cream, whipped

1 Preheat oven to 180°C/160°C fan-assisted. Grease two deep 20cm-round cake tins; line bases with baking parchment.
2 Beat egg whites in medium bowl with electric mixer until soft peaks form; gradually add sugar, beating until sugar is dissolved between additions. Beat in egg yolks and golden syrup. Triple-sift dry ingredients; fold into egg mixture.
3 Pour mixture into tins; bake about 18 minutes. Immediately turn sponges, top-side up, onto baking-parchment-covered wire rack to cool.
4 Sandwich sponges with whipped cream. Serve dusted with sifted icing sugar.

angel food cake

prep + cook time 50 minutes (plus standing time) **serves** 10

½ cup (75g) plain flour
½ cup (75g) cornflour
1¼ cups (275g) caster sugar
¼ teaspoon salt
12 egg whites
1 teaspoon cream of tartar
1 teaspoon vanilla extract

note It is essential to use the correct tin for this recipe. A tube tin is a round cake tin with tall, smooth sides and a hollow metal tube in the centre. The tube (which may be higher than the outside of the tin) helps give a more even baking in the centre of the cake. If you cannot locate a suitable tin in your high-street cook shop, there are many specialist bakeware suppliers on the Internet.

1 Preheat oven to 180°C/160°C fan-assisted.
2 Sift flours, ¼ cup of the sugar and the salt together six times.
3 Beat egg whites in large bowl with electric mixer until foamy; beat in cream of tartar. Gradually add remaining sugar to egg mixture, beating until completely dissolved between additions. Add extract; beat until firm peaks form. Transfer egg mixture to a larger bowl; use a whisk to gently fold in flour mixture.
4 Spread mixture into ungreased 25cm tube tin; bake about 30 minutes.
5 Place a piece of baking parchment cut larger than the tin on worktop; turn tin upside down onto bench over baking parchment (the tin should rest on its 'feet', or the tube, above the paper) – do not move tin until cake is cold (the cake will drop from the tin when cold). If necessary, use a metal spatula to release the cold cake from the dome and base. Decorate with fresh berries, if you like.

CLASSIC
Chocolate cakes

~⚬~

When in doubt about what kind of cake to make,
make it chocolate, you won't go wrong.
Chocolate cakes range in density from extremely
rich and moist like mud cakes, flourless cakes and
brownies through to light, fluffy, spongy chiffon
cakes and everything in between.

one-bowl chocolate cake

~⚬~

prep + cook time 1 hour 20 minutes **serves** 20

125g butter, softened
1 teaspoon vanilla extract
1¼ cups (275g) caster sugar
2 eggs
1⅓ cups (200g) self-raising flour
½ cup (50g) cocoa powder
⅔ cup (160ml) water
chocolate icing
90g dark eating chocolate, chopped coarsely
30g butter, softened
1 cup (160g) icing sugar
2 tablespoons hot water

1 Preheat oven to 180°C/160°C fan-assisted. Grease deep 20cm-round cake tin; line with baking parchment.
2 Beat butter, extract, sugar, eggs, sifted flour and cocoa, and the water in large bowl with electric mixer on low speed until ingredients are combined. Increase speed to medium; beat about 3 minutes or until mixture is smooth and pale in colour.
3 Spread mixture into tin; bake about 1 hour. Stand cake in tin 5 minutes before turning, top-side up, onto wire rack to cool.
4 Make chocolate icing. Spread cold cake with icing.
chocolate icing Melt chocolate and butter in small heatproof bowl over small saucepan of simmering water (do not allow water to touch base of bowl); gradually stir in sifted icing sugar and the water, stirring until icing is spreadable.

mississippi mud cake

prep + cook time 1 hour 45 minutes (plus cooling & standing time) serves 16

250g butter, chopped
150g dark eating chocolate, chopped
2 cups (440g) caster sugar
1 cup (250ml) hot water
⅓ cup (80ml) coffee liqueur
1 tablespoon instant coffee granules
1½ cups (225g) plain flour
¼ cup (35g) self-raising flour
¼ cup (25g) cocoa powder
dark chocolate ganache
½ cup (125ml) double cream
200g dark eating chocolate, chopped coarsely

1   Preheat oven to 160°C/140°C fan-assisted. Grease deep 20cm-round cake tin; line base and side with baking parchment.
2   Combine butter, chocolate, sugar, the water, liqueur and coffee granules in medium saucepan. Using wooden spoon, stir over low heat until chocolate melts.
3   Transfer mixture to large bowl; cool 15 minutes. Whisk in combined sifted flours and cocoa, then egg. Pour mixture into prepared tin.
4   Bake cake about 1½ hours. Stand cake in tin 30 minutes before turning, top-side up, onto wire rack to cool.
5   Meanwhile, make dark chocolate ganache; spread over top of cake before serving.
dark chocolate ganache Bring cream to the boil in small saucepan. Pour hot cream over chocolate in medium heatproof bowl; stir until smooth. Stand at room temperature until spreadable.

devil's food cake

prep + cook time 1 hour **serves** 10

180g butter, softened
1¾ cups (385g) caster sugar
3 eggs
1½ cups (225g) self-raising flour
½ cup (75g) plain flour
½ teaspoon bicarbonate of soda
⅔ cup (70g) cocoa powder
3 teaspoons instant coffee granules
½ cup (125ml) water
½ cup (125ml) milk
½ teaspoon red food colouring
300ml whipping cream, whipped
rich chocolate frosting
60g dark eating chocolate, chopped
60g butter, chopped

1   Preheat oven to 180°C/160°C fan-assisted. Grease two deep 20cm-round cake tins; line bases with baking parchment.
2   Beat butter and sugar in small bowl with electric mixer until light and fluffy; beat in eggs, one at a time.
3   Transfer mixture to large bowl; fold in sifted flours, soda and cocoa powder with combined coffee, the water, milk and colouring, in two batches.
4   Pour mixture into tins; bake about 45 minutes. Stand cakes in tins 5 minutes before turning, top-side up, onto wire racks to cool.
5   Make rich chocolate frosting.
6   Sandwich cold cakes with whipped cream; top with frosting.
rich chocolate frosting Combine chocolate and butter in small heatproof bowl over small saucepan of simmering water (do not allow water to touch the base of the bowl); stir until smooth. Remove from heat. Cool at room temperature, stirring occasionally, until frosting is spreadable.

sacher torte

prep + cook time 1 hour 10 minutes (plus cooling & standing time) **serves** 10

150g dark eating chocolate, chopped
1 tablespoon water
150g butter, softened
½ cup (110g) caster sugar
3 eggs, separated
1 cup (150g) plain flour
2 tablespoons caster sugar, extra
1 cup (320g) apricot jam, warmed, strained
chocolate icing
125g dark eating chocolate, chopped
125g butter, softened

chocolate icing Melt chocolate and butter in small heatproof bowl over small saucepan of simmering water (do not allow water to touch base of bowl). Cool at room temperature until spreadable, stirring occasionally; this can take up to 2 hours.

1 Preheat oven to 180°C/160°C fan-assisted. Grease 22cm-round cake tin; line base with baking parchment.
2 Melt chocolate in small heatproof bowl over pan of simmering water (do not allow water to touch base of bowl); stir in the water; cool to room temperature.
3 Cream butter and sugar with electric mixer until light and fluffy. Add yolks one at a time, beating until combined. Stir in chocolate mixture, then sifted flour.
4 Beat egg whites in small bowl until soft peaks form, gradually beat in extra sugar, beating until dissolved between each addition; fold into chocolate mixture.
5 Spread mixture into tin. Bake about 30 minutes. Stand cake in tin 5 minutes before turning onto wire rack to cool; leave cake upside down.
6 Meanwhile, make chocolate icing.
7 Split cake in half; place one half, cut-side up, on serving plate. Brush with warmed jam, top with other cake half. Brush all over with remaining jam. Stand about 1 hour at room temperature or until jam has set. Spread icing over cake; leave to set.

lemon & lime white chocolate mud cake

prep + cook time 2 hours 10 minutes (plus cooling and refrigeration time) **serves** 12

250g butter, chopped
2 teaspoons finely grated lemon rind
2 teaspoons finely grated lime rind
180g white eating chocolate, chopped coarsely
1½ cups (330g) caster sugar
¾ cup (180ml) milk
1½ cups (225g) plain flour
½ cup (75g) self-raising flour
2 eggs
coconut ganache
140ml can coconut cream
360g white eating chocolate, chopped finely
1 teaspoon finely grated lemon rind
1 teaspoon finely grated lime rind

1 Preheat oven to 170°C/150°C fan-assisted. Grease deep 20cm-round cake tin; line base with baking parchment.
2 Stir butter, rinds, chocolate, sugar and milk in medium saucepan over low heat until smooth. Transfer mixture to large bowl; cool 15 minutes.
3 Stir sifted flours and eggs into mixture; pour into tin.
4 Bake about 1 hour 40 minutes. Cool cake in tin.
5 Meanwhile, make coconut ganache.
6 Turn cake, top-side up, onto serving plate; spread ganache over cake.
coconut ganache Bring coconut cream to the boil in small saucepan. Place chocolate and rinds in medium bowl, add hot cream; stir until smooth. Cover; refrigerate, stirring occasionally, about 30 minutes or until ganache is spreadable.

chocolate buttermilk cake

prep + cook time 1 hour 20 minutes (plus refrigeration time) **serves** 10

180g butter, softened
1 teaspoon vanilla extract
1½ cups (330g) caster sugar
4 eggs, separated
¾ cup (110g) self-raising flour
⅓ cup (35g) cocoa powder
¾ cup (180ml) buttermilk
chocolate filling
400g dark eating chocolate, melted
250g butter, melted
½ cup (80g) icing sugar

1 Preheat oven to 180°C/160°C fan-assisted. Grease deep 20cm-round cake tin; line base with baking parchment.
2 Beat butter, extract and sugar in small bowl with electric mixer until light and fluffy; beat in egg yolks, one at a time, until just combined. Transfer mixture to large bowl; stir in sifted dry ingredients and buttermilk.
3 Beat egg whites in clean small bowl with electric mixer until soft peaks form; fold into cake mixture in two batches. Pour mixture into tin. Bake about 1 hour. Cool cake in tin.
4 Meanwhile, make chocolate filling. Reserve about 1 cup of filling.
5 Split cake into three layers; place one layer on serving plate, spread thinly with some of the chocolate filling. Repeat layering with remaining cake layers and filling. Spread reserved filling all over cake. Refrigerate cake 3 hours before serving.
chocolate filling Combine chocolate and butter in medium bowl; stir in sifted icing sugar. Cool filling to room temperature; beat with wooden spoon until thick and spreadable.

chocolate fudge cake

prep + cook time 50 minutes **serves** 12

250g dark eating chocolate, chopped
125g butter, chopped
⅔ cup (150g) caster sugar
⅔ cup (100g) self-raising flour
4 eggs, lightly beaten

1 Preheat oven to 180°C/160°C fan-assisted. Grease 19cm x 29cm traybake tin; line base and long sides with baking parchment, extending paper 5cm above sides.
2 Stir chocolate and butter in medium heatproof bowl over medium saucepan of simmering water (do not allow the water to touch base of bowl); cool.
3 Combine chocolate mixture and remaining ingredients in medium bowl; beat on low speed with electric mixer until ingredients are combined. Increase speed to medium; beat about 3 minutes or until mixture is changed in colour and smooth.
4 Pour mixture into tin; bake about 30 minutes. Stand cake 5 minutes before turning, top-side up, onto wire rack to cool. Serve dusted with sifted icing sugar, if desired.

flourless chocolate hazelnut cake

prep + cook time 1 hour 30 minutes **serves** 8

⅓ cup (35g) cocoa powder
⅓ cup (80ml) hot water
150g dark eating chocolate, melted
150g butter, melted
1⅓ cups (295g) firmly packed brown sugar
1 cup (100g) ground hazelnuts
4 eggs, separated
1 tablespoon cocoa powder, extra

1 Preheat oven to 180°C/160°C fan-assisted. Grease deep 20cm-round cake tin; line base and side with baking parchment.
2 Blend cocoa with the water in large bowl until smooth. Add chocolate, butter, sugar, ground hazelnuts and egg yolks; stir until combined.
3 Beat egg whites in small bowl with electric mixer until soft peaks form; fold into chocolate mixture in two batches.
4 Pour mixture into tin; bake about 1 hour. Stand cake in tin 15 minutes before turning, top-side up, onto wire rack to cool. Dust with sifted extra cocoa before serving.

chocolate fudge brownies

prep + cook time 1 hour 20 minutes **makes** 16

150g butter, chopped
300g dark eating chocolate, chopped
1½ cups (330g) firmly packed brown sugar
3 eggs
1 teaspoon vanilla extract
¾ cup (110g) plain flour
¾ cup (140g) dark chocolate chips
½ cup (120g) soured cream
¾ cup (110g) roasted macadamias, chopped coarsely

1 Preheat oven to 180°C/160°C fan-assisted. Grease 19cm x 29cm traybake tin; line base and sides with baking parchment, extending paper 5cm above long sides.
2 Combine butter and chocolate in medium saucepan; stir over low heat until smooth. Cool 10 minutes.
3 Stir in sugar, eggs and extract, then sifted flour, chocolate chips, soured cream and nuts. Spread mixture into prepared tin; bake 40 minutes. Cover tin with foil; bake a further 20 minutes. Cool in tin before cutting into 16 pieces.
4 Dust brownies with sifted cocoa powder, if desired.

chocolate chiffon cake

prep + cook time 1 hour 30 minutes **serves** 16

½ cup (50g) cocoa powder
¾ cup (180ml) boiling water
2 cups (300g) self-raising flour
1½ cups (330g) caster sugar
7 eggs, separated
½ cup (125ml) vegetable oil
1 teaspoon vanilla extract
walnut praline
1 cup (220g) caster sugar
½ cup (50g) walnuts
60g dark eating chocolate, chopped
brandied butter cream
190g butter, softened
3 cups (480g) icing sugar
¼ cup (25g) cocoa powder
¼ cup (60ml) brandy

1   Preheat oven to 180°C/160°C fan-assisted. Grease deep 22cm-round cake tin; cover base and side with baking parchment.
2   Blend cocoa with the water in small bowl; cool. Sift flour and sugar into large bowl; add cocoa mixture, egg yolks, oil and extract. Beat with electric mixer until smooth and mixture is changed in colour.
3   Beat egg whites in large bowl with electric mixer until soft peaks form; fold into cocoa mixture in four batches.
4   Pour mixture into tin; bake about 1 hour or until firm. Stand cake 5 minutes before turning, top-side up, onto wire rack to cool.
5   Make walnut praline; make brandied butter cream.
6   Split cold cake into three layers; join layers with some of the butter cream. Spread cake evenly with remaining butter cream. Decorate with walnut praline.
walnut praline Place sugar in heavy-based frying pan; cook over heat, without stirring, until sugar is melted and golden brown. Add nuts; pour onto greased oven tray; cool. Blend or process praline with chocolate until finely chopped.
brandied butter cream Cream butter in small bowl with electric mixer until as white as possible; beat in sifted icing sugar and cocoa, then brandy.

chocoholic's chocolate cake

prep + cook time 2 hours 35 minutes (plus standing and refrigeration time) **serves** 16

250g butter, chopped
1 tablespoon instant coffee granules
1½ cups (375ml) water
2 cups (440g) caster sugar
1 teaspoon vanilla extract
100g dark eating chocolate, chopped coarsely
2 eggs
1½ cups (225g) self-raising flour
1 cup (150g) plain flour
¼ cup (25g) cocoa powder
180g white eating chocolate, melted
2 x 45g packets Maltesers™
chocolate ganache
100g dark eating chocolate, chopped coarsely
⅓ cup (80ml) double cream

1 Preheat oven to 150°C/130°C fan-assisted. Grease deep 19cm-square cake tin; line base and sides with baking parchment.
2 Heat butter, coffee, the water, sugar, extract and dark chocolate in large saucepan, stirring until smooth. Transfer mixture to large bowl; cool 20 minutes. Stir in eggs and sifted dry ingredients, in two batches. Pour mixture into tin.
3 Bake cake about 1 hour 50 minutes. Stand cake in tin 15 minutes; turn, top-side up, onto wire rack to cool.
4 Meanwhile, make chocolate ganache.
5 Spread white chocolate into 15cm x 20cm rectangle onto baking parchment; stand until just set. Using 3cm- and 5cm-star cutter, cut as many stars as possible from chocolate. Stand about 30 minutes or until firm.
6 Spread cake with ganache; decorate with stars and Maltesers™.

chocolate ganache Stir ingredients in small saucepan over low heat until smooth. Cover; refrigerate 1 hour or until spreadable.

fudge-frosted chocolate cupcakes

prep + cook time 1 hour 10 minutes **makes** 24

2 cups (500ml) hot water
¼ cup (75g) cocoa powder, sifted
250g butter, softened
2 cups (440g) caster sugar
2 teaspoons vanilla extract
3 eggs
1½ cups (225g) plain flour
1 cup (150g) self-raising flour
½ teaspoon bicarbonate of soda
silver cachous
fudge frosting
50g butter, softened
¼ cup (60ml) milk
1 teaspoon vanilla extract
¼ cup (25g) cocoa powder
2 cups (320g) icing sugar

1 Preheat oven to 180°C/160°C fan-assisted. Line two 12-hole (⅓-cup/80ml) muffin tins with paper cases.
2 Whisk the water and cocoa together in a medium size bowl.
3 Beat butter, sugar and vanilla in large bowl with electric mixer until light and fluffy. Beat in eggs, one at a time. Fold in half of the combined sifted flours and soda then half of the cocoa mixture; stir in remaining flour mixture and cocoa mixture until just combined.
4 Divide mixture among paper cases; bake about 25 minutes. Cool cakes in tins 5 minutes before turning onto wire racks to cool.
5 Meanwhile, make fudge frosting. Spread frosting over cakes; decorate with cachous.
fudge frosting Beat butter in medium bowl with electric mixer until light and fluffy. Add milk, extract, sifted cocoa and half the sifted icing sugar; beat about 5 minutes or until light and fluffy. Add remaining sifted icing sugar; beat a further 5 minutes.

CLASSIC
Fruit cakes

Fruit – dried, fresh, frozen or canned, along
with some vegetables like carrot and courgette,
all go to make up ever-popular fruit cakes.
The more fruit-packed the cakes are, the better
they will keep. Store them airtight in a cool
dark cupboard, or, if the weather is steamy,
in the refrigerator.

one-bowl sultana loaf

prep + cook time 1 hour 45 minutes **serves** 8

125g butter, melted
750g sultanas
½ cup (110g) firmly packed brown sugar
2 tablespoons marmalade
2 eggs, lightly beaten
¼ cup (60ml) sweet sherry
¾ cup (110g) plain flour
¼ cup (35g) self-raising flour
30g blanched almonds
2 tablespoons apricot jam

1 Preheat oven to 150°C/130°C fan-assisted. Grease 15cm x 25cm loaf tin; line base with baking parchment.
2 Beat butter, sultanas, sugar, marmalade, egg, sherry and flours in large bowl using a wooden spoon until combined.
3 Spread mixture into tin; decorate top with blanched almonds. Bake about 1½ hours. Cover cake with foil; cool in tin. Brush top of cold cake with warmed sieved apricot jam.

banana cake

prep + cook time 1 hour 15 minutes **serves** 10

You will need 2 large (460g) overripe bananas to get the amount of mashed banana needed for this recipe.

125g butter, softened
¾ cup (165g) caster sugar
2 eggs
1 cup mashed banana
1 teaspoon bicarbonate of soda
2 tablespoons hot milk
1 cup (150g) plain flour
⅔ cup (100g) self-raising flour
icing sugar, to dust

1 Preheat oven to 180°C/160°C. Grease deep 20cm-round cake tin; line base and side with baking parchment.
2 Beat butter and sugar in small bowl with electric mixer until light and fluffy. Beat in eggs, one at a time. Transfer to large bowl; stir in banana. Combine soda and milk in small jug; stir into banana mixture then stir in sifted flours.
3 Spread mixture into tin; bake about 50 minutes. Stand cake in tin 5 minutes before turning, top-side up, onto wire rack to cool. Dust with sifted icing sugar to serve.

hummingbird cake

prep + cook time 1 hour 10 minutes **serves** 12

You need two large overripe (460g) bananas for this recipe.

450g can crushed pineapple in syrup
1 cup (150g) plain flour
½ cup (75g) self-raising flour
½ teaspoon bicarbonate of soda
½ teaspoon ground cinnamon
½ teaspoon ground ginger
1 cup (220g) firmly packed brown sugar
½ cup (40g) desiccated coconut
1 cup mashed banana
2 eggs, beaten lightly
¾ cup (180ml) vegetable oil
cream cheese frosting
30g butter, softened
60g cream cheese, softened
1 teaspoon vanilla extract
1½ cups (240g) icing sugar

1 Preheat oven to 180°C/160°C fan-assisted. Grease deep 23cm-square cake tin; line base with baking parchment.
2 Drain pineapple over medium bowl, pressing with spoon to extract as much syrup as possible. Reserve ¼ cup (60ml) of the syrup.
3 Sift flours, soda, spices and sugar into large bowl. Using wooden spoon, stir in the drained pineapple, reserved syrup, coconut, banana, egg and oil.
4 Pour mixture into tin; bake about 40 minutes. Stand cake in tin 5 minutes before turning, top-side up, onto wire rack to cool.
5 Meanwhile, make cream cheese frosting; spread cake with frosting.
cream cheese frosting Beat butter, cream cheese and vanilla extract in small bowl with electric mixer until light and fluffy; gradually beat in sifted icing sugar.

boiled whisky fruit cake

prep + cook time 3 hours 35 minutes (plus standing and cooling time) **serves** 16

1½ cups (220g) raisins, chopped
1½ cups (210g) dried pitted dates, chopped
1½ cups (250g) pitted prunes, chopped
1½ cups (250g) sultanas
⅓ cup (70g) red glacé cherries, quartered
⅓ cup (55g) mixed peel
2 tablespoons caster sugar
30g butter
½ cup (125ml) whisky
250g butter, chopped, extra
1 cup (220g) firmly packed dark brown sugar
½ teaspoon bicarbonate of soda
½ cup (70g) slivered almonds
2 cups (300g) plain flour
2 teaspoons mixed spice
5 eggs
¼ cup (60ml) whisky, extra

1 Combine raisins, dates, prunes, sultanas, cherries and mixed peel in large bowl.
2 Place caster sugar in large heavy-based saucepan over medium heat; move pan occasionally until sugar is melted. Add butter and whisky to pan; stir over low heat until smooth.
3 Add extra butter, brown sugar and fruit to pan. Stir over heat until butter melts; bring to the boil. Remove from heat; stir in soda. Transfer to large bowl, cover; stand overnight at room temperature.
4 Preheat oven to 150°C/130°C fan-assisted. Grease deep 19cm-square cake tin; line base and sides with two layers of brown paper then baking parchment, extending paper 5cm over edges.
5 Add nuts, sifted flour and spice, and eggs to fruit mixture; stir until combined.
6 Spoon mixture into corners of tin then spread remaining mixture into tin. Drop tin from a height of about 15cm onto worktop to settle mixture into tin and to break any large air bubbles; level surface of cake with wet spatula. Bake about 3 hours.
7 Brush hot cake with extra whisky. Cover hot cake tightly with foil; cool in tin.

sticky date cake with butterscotch sauce

prep + cook time 1 hour 10 minutes **serves** 20

3¾ cups (525g) dried pitted dates
3 cups (750ml) hot water
2 teaspoons bicarbonate of soda
185g butter, softened
2¼ cups (500g) firmly packed brown sugar
6 eggs
3 cups (450g) self-raising flour
½ cup (60g) coarsely chopped walnuts
½ cup (60g) coarsely chopped pecans
butterscotch sauce
2 cups (440g) firmly packed brown sugar
500ml whipping cream
250g butter, chopped

1 Preheat oven to 180°C/160°C fan-assisted. Grease 26cm x 36cm baking tin; line base and long sides of dish with two layers baking parchment, extending paper 5cm above edges.
2 Combine dates and the water in medium saucepan; bring to the boil. Remove from heat; stir in soda. Stand 5 minutes then blend or process date mixture until smooth.
3 Beat butter and sugar in large bowl with electric mixer until light and fluffy. Beat in eggs, one at a time. Stir date mixture and sifted flour into egg mixture; spread mixture into tin. Sprinkle with nuts; bake about 50 minutes. Stand cake in tin 10 minutes before turning, top-side up, onto wire rack to cool.
4 Meanwhile, make butterscotch sauce.
5 Brush surface of hot cake with ⅓ cup of the hot butterscotch sauce. Serve with remaining sauce.
butterscotch sauce Stir ingredients in medium saucepan over heat, without boiling, until sugar dissolves; bring to the boil. Reduce heat; simmer 3 minutes.

apple streusel cake

prep + cook time 1 hour 15 minutes (plus freezing time) **serves** 16

200g butter, softened + 25g butter, extra
2 teaspoons finely grated lemon rind
⅔ cup (150g) caster sugar
3 eggs
1 cup (150g) self-raising flour
½ cup (75g) plain flour
⅓ cup (80ml) milk
5 medium apples (750g)
⅓ cup (75g) firmly packed brown sugar
streusel
½ cup (75g) plain flour
¼ cup (35g) self-raising flour
⅓ cup (75g) firmly packed brown sugar
½ teaspoon ground cinnamon
80g cold butter, chopped finely

streusel Process flours, sugar and cinnamon until combined. Add butter; process until ingredients come together. Wrap in cling film; freeze 1 hour or until firm.

1 Preheat oven to 180°C/160°C fan-assisted. Grease deep 23cm-round cake tin; line base with baking parchment.
2 Make streusel.
3 Beat butter, rind and caster sugar in small bowl with electric mixer until light and fluffy. Beat in eggs, one at a time. Transfer to large bowl; stir in sifted flours and milk, in two batches. Spread into tin; bake 25 minutes.
4 Meanwhile, peel, core and quarter apples; slice thinly. Melt extra butter in large frying pan, add apple; cook, stirring, about 5 minutes or until browned lightly. Add brown sugar; cook, stirring, about 5 minutes or until mixture thickens slightly. Set aside.
5 Remove cake from oven. Working quickly, top cake with apple mixture then coarsely grate streusel over apple. Return cake to oven; bake about 25 minutes. Stand cake in tin 10 minutes before turning, top-side up, onto wire rack to cool. Serve cake warm or cold.

pecan & raisin loaf

prep + cook time 45 minutes (plus cooling time) **serves** 8

⅓ cup (50g) raisins
90g butter, chopped
½ cup (110g) firmly packed brown sugar
⅓ cup (80ml) water
½ teaspoon bicarbonate of soda
2 eggs, beaten lightly
½ cup (60g) coarsely chopped pecans
½ cup (75g) plain flour
½ cup (75g) self-raising flour

1   Combine raisins, butter, sugar and the water in medium saucepan; bring to the boil. Remove from heat; stir in soda. Transfer mixture to medium bowl; cool 15 minutes.

2   Preheat oven to 150°C / 130°C fan-assisted. Grease 8cm x 25cm cake tin; line base of tin with baking parchment.

3   Stir egg and nuts into raisin mixture; stir in sifted flours. Pour mixture into tin; bake about 35 minutes. Stand cake in tin 5 minutes before turning, top-side up, onto wire rack to cool.

lumberjack cake

prep + cook time 1 hour 40 minutes **serves** 12

2 large apples (400g), peeled, cored, chopped finely
1 cup (150g) finely chopped pitted dried dates
1 teaspoon bicarbonate of soda
1 cup (250ml) boiling water
125g butter, softened
1 teaspoon vanilla extract
1 cup (220g) caster sugar
1 egg
1½ cups (225g) plain flour
coconut topping
60g butter, chopped
½ cup (110g) firmly packed brown sugar
½ cup (125ml) milk
⅔ cup (50g) shredded coconut

1   Preheat oven to 180°C/160°C fan-assisted. Grease deep 23cm-square cake tin; line base and sides with baking parchment.
2   Combine apple, dates and soda in large bowl, stir in the water; cover bowl with cling film, stand 10 minutes.
3   Meanwhile, beat butter, extract, sugar and egg in small bowl with electric mixer until light and fluffy. Add butter mixture to apple mixture; stir to combine. Add sifted flour; stir to combine. Pour mixture into tin; bake about 50 minutes.
4   Meanwhile, make coconut topping.
5   Remove cake carefully from oven to worktop. Using metal spatula, carefully spread warm topping evenly over cake; return to oven, bake about 20 minutes or until topping is browned.
6   Stand cake in tin 5 minutes before turning, top-side up, onto wire rack to cool.
coconut topping Combine ingredients in medium saucepan; using wooden spoon, stir mixture over low heat until butter melts and sugar dissolves.

date & walnut rolls

prep + cook time 1 hour 10 minutes **serves** 20

60g butter, chopped
1 cup (250ml) boiling water
1 cup (150g) finely chopped pitted dried dates
½ teaspoon bicarbonate of soda
1 cup (220g) firmly packed brown sugar
2 cups (300g) self-raising flour
½ cup (60g) coarsely chopped walnuts
1 egg, beaten lightly

note It is essential to use the correct tin for this recipe. A nut roll tin is a cylindrical cake tin with removable ends top and bottom. If you cannot locate a suitable tin in your high-street cook shop, there are many specialist bakeware suppliers on the Internet.

1 Adjust oven shelves to fit upright tins.
2 Preheat oven to 180°C / 160°C fan-assisted. Grease two 8cm x 19cm nut roll tins; line bases of tins with baking parchment. Place tins upright on oven tray.
3 Combine butter and the water in medium saucepan; stir over low heat until butter melts.
4 Transfer mixture to large bowl; stir in dates and soda, then sugar, sifted flour, nuts and egg.
5 Spoon mixture into tins; replace lids. Bake rolls, tins standing upright, about 50 minutes.
6 Stand rolls 5 minutes, remove ends (top and bottom); shake tins gently to release nut rolls onto wire rack to cool.

yogurt fruit loaf

prep + cook time 2 hours **serves** 10

100g butter, softened
2 teaspoons finely grated orange rind
¾ cup (165g) caster sugar
2 eggs
2 cups (320g) wholemeal self-raising flour
1 cup (280g) plain yogurt
⅓ cup (80ml) orange juice
1 cup (200g) finely chopped dried figs
1 cup (160g) coarsely chopped raisins

1   Preheat oven to 180°C/160°C fan-assisted. Grease 14cm x 21cm loaf tin.
2   Beat butter, rind, sugar, eggs, sifted flour, yogurt and juice in medium bowl with electric mixer, on low speed, until just combined. Stir in figs and raisins.
3   Pour mixture into tin; cover with foil. Bake 1¼ hours; remove foil, bake about 15 minutes. Stand loaf in tin 10 minutes before turning, top-side up, onto wire rack to cool. Serve at room temperature, or toasted, with butter.

apple custard tea cakes

prep + cook time 50 minutes (plus cooling time) **makes** 12

90g butter, softened
½ teaspoon vanilla extract
½ cup (110g) caster sugar
2 eggs
¾ cup (110g) self-raising flour
¼ cup (30g) custard powder
2 tablespoons milk
1 unpeeled large apple (200g), cored, sliced finely
30g butter, extra, melted
1 tablespoon caster sugar, extra
½ teaspoon ground cinnamon
custard filling
1 tablespoon custard powder
1 tablespoon caster sugar
½ cup (125ml) milk
¼ teaspoon vanilla extract

1 Make custard filling.
2 Preheat oven to 180°C / 160°C fan-assisted. Line 12-hole (⅓ cup / 80ml) muffin tin with paper cases.
3 Beat butter, extract, sugar, eggs, sifted flour and custard powder, and milk in small bowl with electric mixer, on low speed, until ingredients are just combined. Increase speed to medium, beat until mixture is pale in colour.
4 Divide half the mixture among paper cases; top with custard, then add remaining cake mixture, spread mixture to cover custard. Top with apple, pressing slightly into cakes. Bake about 30 minutes.
5 Turn cakes, top-side up, onto wire rack. Brush hot cakes with extra butter, then sprinkle with combined extra sugar and cinnamon. Serve warm or cold.
custard filling Blend custard powder and sugar with milk and extract in small saucepan; stir over heat until mixture boils and thickens. Remove from heat; cover surface with cling film, cool to room temperature.

raspberry coconut slice

prep + cook time 1 hour **makes** 16

90g butter, softened
½ cup (110g) caster sugar
1 egg
¼ cup (35g) self-raising flour
⅔ cup (100g) plain flour
1 tablespoon custard powder
⅔ cup (220g) raspberry jam
coconut topping
2 cups (160g) desiccated coconut
¼ cup (55g) caster sugar
2 eggs, beaten lightly

1 Preheat oven to 180°C/160°C fan-assisted. Grease 20cm x 30cm traybake tin; line base and long sides with baking parchment, extending paper 5cm above sides.
2 Beat butter, sugar and egg in small bowl with electric mixer until light and fluffy. Transfer to medium bowl; stir in sifted flours and custard powder. Spread dough evenly into tin; spread with jam.
3 Make coconut topping; sprinkle topping over jam.
4 Bake about 40 minutes; allow slice to cool in tin before cutting.
coconut topping Combine ingredients in small bowl.

dutch ginger & almond slice

prep + cook time 50 minutes **makes** 20

1¾ cups (260g) plain flour
1 cup (220g) caster sugar
⅔ cup (150g) coarsely chopped glacé ginger
½ cup (80g) blanched almonds, chopped coarsely
1 egg
185g butter, melted
2 teaspoons icing sugar

1 Preheat oven to 180°C/160°C fan-assisted.
Grease 20cm x 30cm traybake tin; line base and
long sides with baking parchment, extending paper
5cm above sides.
2 Combine sifted flour, sugar, ginger, nuts and
egg in medium bowl; stir in butter.
3 Press mixture into tin; bake about 35 minutes.
Stand slice in tin 10 minutes before lifting onto wire
rack to cool. Dust slice with a little sifted icing sugar
before cutting.

citrus poppy seed friands

prep + cook time 45 minutes **makes** 12

6 egg whites
185g butter, melted
1 cup (120g) ground almonds
1½ cups (240g) icing sugar
½ cup (75g) plain flour
1 tablespoon poppy seeds
2 teaspoons finely grated orange rind
1 teaspoon finely grated lemon rind

1 Preheat oven to 200°C / 180°C fan-assisted. Grease 12 x ½-cup (125ml) friand or muffin tins; place on oven tray.
2 Place egg whites in medium bowl; whisk lightly with fork until combined. Stir in remaining ingredients.
3 Divide mixture among tins; bake about 25 minutes. Stand cakes in tins 5 minutes before turning, top-side up, onto wire rack to cool. Serve cakes dusted with a little extra sifted icing sugar, if desired.

note A friand is a small densely-textured sponge cake, popular in Australia and New Zealand and similar to a French Financier. Traditionally baked in oval shapes, they are made with butter, ground almonds and a variety of flavourings. If you can't get hold of the traditional oval tins, then deep muffin tins work just as well.

berry muffins

prep + cook time 30 minutes **makes** 12

2½ cups (375g) self-raising flour
90g cold butter, chopped
1 cup (220g) caster sugar
1¼ cups (310ml) buttermilk
1 egg, beaten lightly
200g fresh or frozen mixed berries

1 Preheat oven to 180°C/160°C fan-assisted. Grease 12-hole (⅓-cup/80ml) muffin tin.
2 Sift flour into large bowl; rub in butter. Stir in sugar, buttermilk and egg. Do not overmix – the mixture should be lumpy. Add the berries and stir gently through the mixture.
3 Spoon mixture into tin holes; bake about 20 minutes. Stand muffins in tin 5 minutes before turning, top-side up, onto wire rack to cool.

celebration fruit cake

prep + cook time 3 hours 50 minutes (plus standing & cooling time) serves 24

3 cups (500g) sultanas
1¾ cups (300g) raisins, halved
1¾ cups (300g) dried dates, chopped finely
1 cup (150g) currants
⅔ cup (110g) mixed peel
⅔ cup (150g) glacé cherries, halved
¼ cup (50g) coarsely chopped glacé pineapple
¼ cup (60g) coarsely chopped glacé apricots
½ cup (125ml) dark rum
250g butter, softened
1 cup (220g) firmly packed brown sugar
5 eggs
1½ cups (225g) plain flour
⅓ cup (50g) self-raising flour
1 teaspoon mixed spice
2 tablespoons dark rum, extra

1   Combine fruit and rum in large bowl, mix well; cover tightly with cling film. Store mixture in a cool, dark place overnight, or for up to a week, stirring every day.
2   Preheat oven to 150°C / 130°C fan-assisted. Line deep 22cm-round cake tin with three layers of baking parchment, extending paper 5cm above the edge.
3   Beat butter and sugar in small bowl with electric mixer until just combined. Beat in eggs, one at a time.
4   Add butter mixture to fruit mixture; mix well. Mix in sifted dry ingredients; spread mixture evenly into prepared tin. Bake about 3½ hours.
5   Brush cake with extra rum. Cover hot cake tightly with foil; cool in tin.

tip If cake starts to brown too much during baking, cover loosely with foil.

last-minute fruit cake

prep + cook time 2 hours 20 minutes (plus cooling time) serves 20

1½ cups (250g) sultanas
1 cup (150g) raisins, chopped coarsely
1 cup (150g) currants
½ cup (85g) mixed peel
⅓ cup (70g) glacé cherries, halved
2 tablespoons coarsely chopped glacé pineapple
2 tablespoons coarsely chopped glacé apricots
185g butter, chopped
¾ cup (165g) firmly packed brown sugar
⅓ cup (80ml) brandy
⅓ cup (80ml) water
2 teaspoons finely grated orange rind
1 teaspoon finely grated lemon rind
1 tablespoon treacle
3 eggs, beaten lightly
1¼ cups (185g) plain flour
¼ cup (35g) self-raising flour
½ teaspoon bicarbonate of soda
½ cup (80g) blanched almonds

1 Combine fruit, butter, sugar, brandy and the water in medium saucepan, stir over medium heat until butter is melted and sugar is dissolved; bring to the boil. Remove from heat; transfer to large bowl. Cool to room temperature.
2 Preheat oven to 150°C/130°C fan-assisted. Line base and side of deep 20cm-round cake tin with three thicknesses of baking parchment, extending paper 5cm above edge.
3 Stir rinds, treacle and egg into fruit mixture then stir in sifted dry ingredients. Spread mixture into tin; decorate with nuts. Bake about 2 hours.
4 Cover hot cake tightly with foil; allow to cool in tin overnight.

rich sherried fruit cake

prep + cook time 3 hours 45 minutes (plus cooling and standing time) **serves** 20

250g butter, softened
2 tablespoons plum jam
2 teaspoons finely grated orange rind
1¼ cups (275g) firmly packed brown sugar
5 eggs
¾ cup (180ml) sweet sherry
1½ cups (225g) plain flour
½ cup (75g) self-raising flour
2 teaspoons mixed spice
1kg (5 cups) mixed dried fruit
½ cup (125ml) sweet sherry, extra, warmed

1   Preheat oven to 150°C/130°C fan-assisted. Line base and side of deep 22cm-round cake tin with four thicknesses of baking parchment, extending paper 5cm above edge.
2   Beat butter, jam, rind and sugar in medium bowl with electric mixer until just combined. Beat in eggs, one at a time.
3   Stir in ½ cup of the sherry, sifted dry ingredients and fruit; mix well.
4   Spread mixture into tin. Bake about 3¼ hours.
5   Brush top of hot cake with remaining ¼ cup of sherry, cover hot cake with foil; cool in tin overnight.
6   Remove cake from tin, peel paper away from cake. Brush cake all over with 2 tablespoons of the warmed extra sherry each week for 3 weeks.

boiled pineapple rum cake

prep + cook time 2 hours 20 minutes (plus cooling time) **serves** 20

450g can crushed pineapple in syrup
1kg (5 cups) mixed dried fruit
250g butter, chopped coarsely
1 cup (220g) firmly packed brown sugar
2 tablespoons orange marmalade
2 tablespoons dark rum
4 eggs, beaten lightly
1⅔ cups (250g) plain flour
⅓ cup (50g) self-raising flour
½ teaspoon bicarbonate of soda
1 tablespoon dark rum, extra

1 Drain pineapple over large jug; discard ½ cup of the syrup.
2 Combine pineapple, remaining syrup, fruit, butter, sugar, marmalade and rum in large saucepan. Using wooden spoon, stir over heat until butter melts and sugar dissolves; bring to the boil. Reduce heat; simmer, covered, 10 minutes. Cool to room temperature.
3 Preheat oven to 150°C/130°C fan-assisted. Line base and side of deep 20cm-round cake tin with three thicknesses baking parchment, extending paper 5cm above edges.
4 Using wooden spoon, stir egg and sifted dry ingredients into fruit mixture. Pour mixture into tin; bake about 2 hours.
5 Brush hot cake with extra rum. Cover tin tightly with foil; cool cake in tin.

rock cakes

prep + cook time 30 minutes **makes** 18

2 cups (300g) self-raising flour
¼ teaspoon ground cinnamon
⅓ cup (75g) caster sugar
90g cold butter, chopped
1 cup (160g) sultanas
1 egg, beaten lightly
½ cup (125ml) milk
1 tablespoon caster sugar, extra

1 Preheat oven to 200°C/180°C fan-assisted. Grease oven trays.
2 Sift flour, cinnamon and sugar into medium bowl; rub in butter. Stir in sultanas, egg and milk. Do not overmix.
3 Drop rounded tablespoons of mixture about 5cm apart onto trays; sprinkle with extra sugar. Bake about 15 minutes; cool cakes on trays.

carrot cake with lemon cream cheese frosting

prep + cook time 1 hour 45 minutes **serves** 12

You need three large carrots (540g) for this recipe.

1 cup (250ml) vegetable oil
1⅓ cups (295g) firmly packed brown sugar
3 eggs
3 cups firmly packed, coarsely grated carrot
1 cup (110g) coarsely chopped walnuts
2½ cups (375g) self-raising flour
½ teaspoon bicarbonate of soda
2 teaspoons mixed spice
lemon cream cheese frosting
30g butter, softened
80g cream cheese, softened
1 teaspoon finely grated lemon rind
1½ cups (240g) icing sugar

1   Preheat oven to 180°C/160°C fan-assisted. Grease deep 22cm-round cake tin; line base with baking parchment.
2   Beat oil, sugar and eggs in small bowl with electric mixer until thick and creamy. Transfer mixture to large bowl; stir in carrot, nuts then sifted dry ingredients.
3   Pour mixture into tin; bake about 1¼ hours. Stand cake in tin 5 minutes before turning, top-side up, onto wire rack to cool.
4   Meanwhile, make lemon cream cheese frosting. Spread cake with frosting.
lemon cream cheese frosting Beat butter, cream cheese and rind in small bowl with electric mixer until light and fluffy; gradually incorporate the sifted icing sugar.

upside-down toffee banana cake

prep + cook time 1 hour 10 minutes **serves** 10

You need four bananas for this recipe; two large overripe bananas weighing about 460g to make 1 cup of mashed banana, and two medium bananas.

1 cup (220g) caster sugar
1 cup (250ml) water
2 medium bananas (400g), sliced thinly
2 eggs, beaten lightly
⅔ cup (160ml) vegetable oil
¾ cup (165g) firmly packed brown sugar
1 teaspoon vanilla extract
⅔ cup (100g) plain flour
⅓ cup (50g) wholemeal self-raising flour
2 teaspoons mixed spice
1 teaspoon bicarbonate of soda
1 cup mashed banana

1 Preheat oven to 180°C/160°C fan-assisted. Grease deep 22cm-round cake tin; line base with baking parchment.
2 Stir caster sugar and the water in medium saucepan over heat, without boiling, until sugar dissolves; bring to the boil. Boil, uncovered, without stirring, about 10 minutes or until caramel in colour. Pour toffee into prepared tin; top with sliced banana.
3 Combine egg, oil, brown sugar and extract in medium bowl. Stir in sifted dry ingredients, then add the mashed banana.
4 Pour mixture into tin; bake about 40 minutes. Turn cake onto serving plate; peel off baking parchment. Serve cake, warm or at room temperature, with thick cream, if desired.

dundee cake

prep + cook time 3 hours 20 minutes (plus cooling time) **serves** 15

180g butter, softened
¾ cup (165g) caster sugar
5 eggs, lightly beaten
1½ cups (225g) plain flour
½ cup (75g) self-raising flour
½ teaspoon mixed spice
⅔ cup (80ml) milk
1¼ cups (200g) raisins, chopped coarsely
1½ cups (250g) currants
1¼ cups (200g) sultanas
⅔ cup (70g) red glacé cherries, chopped coarsely
2 tablespoons mixed peel
½ cup (80g) blanched almonds
1 tablespoon brandy

1 Preheat oven to 150°C/130°C fan-assisted. Line deep 19cm-square cake tin with three layers of baking parchment, extending paper 5cm above edges.
2 Beat butter, sugar, egg, sifted dry ingredients and milk in large bowl with electric mixer on medium speed about 3 minutes or until mixture becomes pale in colour. Stir in the fruit and half the nuts.
3 Spread mixture into tin; decorate top with remaining nuts. Bake about 2 hours. Brush hot cake with brandy; cover tightly with foil, cool in tin.

siena cake

prep + cook time 1 hour 30 minutes (plus cooling and standing time) **serves** 8

¾ cup (120g) blanched almonds, roasted, chopped coarsely
1 cup (140g) coarsely chopped roasted hazelnuts
¼ cup (80g) finely chopped glacé apricots
¼ cup (55g) finely chopped glacé pineapple
⅓ cup (55g) mixed peel, chopped finely
⅔ cup (100g) plain flour
2 tablespoons cocoa powder
1 teaspoon ground cinnamon
⅓ cup (75g) caster sugar
½ cup (180g) honey
60g dark eating chocolate, melted

1   Preheat oven to 170°C/150°C fan-assisted. Grease deep 20cm-round cake tin; line base and side with baking parchment.
2   Combine nuts, apricots, pineapple, mixed peel, and sifted flour, cocoa and cinnamon in large bowl; mix well.
3   Place sugar and honey in medium saucepan; stir over low heat until sugar dissolves, brushing down side of pan to dissolve any sugar crystals. Bring to the boil; reduce heat, simmer, uncovered, about 5 minutes or until syrup forms a soft ball when a few drops of the syrup are dropped into a glass of cold water.
4   Add syrup and chocolate to fruit and nut mixture; mix well. Spread mixture quickly into tin; bake about 35 minutes. Cool cake in tin. Turn out cake; remove paper. Wrap cake in foil; stand overnight.

courgette walnut loaf

prep + cook time 1 hour 30 minutes **serves** 10

You need 3 medium courgettes (360g), for this recipe.

3 eggs
1½ cups (330g) firmly packed brown sugar
1 cup (250ml) vegetable oil
1½ cups finely grated courgettes
1 cup (110g) coarsely chopped walnuts
1½ cups (225g) self-raising flour
1½ cups (225g) plain flour

1 Preheat oven to 180°C/160°C fan-assisted. Grease 15cm x 25cm loaf tin; line base and long sides with baking parchment, extending paper 5cm above edges.
2 Beat eggs, sugar and oil in large bowl with electric mixer until combined. Stir in courgettes, walnuts and sifted flours in two batches.
3 Spread mixture into tin; bake about 1¼ hours. Stand cake in tin 5 minutes before turning, top-side up, onto wire rack to cool. Serve the cake with butter if you prefer.

CLASSIC
Syrup cakes

❧

Syrup-soaked cakes are at their best served warm,
either just as they are with a good cup of tea or
coffee, or as a dessert with a dollop of cream
and maybe some fresh fruit that ties in with the
flavour of the cake. Slices of cake can be reheated
gently in a microwave oven.

mixed berry cake with vanilla syrup

prep + cook time 1 hour **serves** 8

125g butter, softened
1 cup (220g) caster sugar
3 eggs
½ cup (75g) plain flour
¼ cup (35g) self-raising flour
½ cup (60g) ground almonds
⅓ cup (80g) soured cream
1½ cups (225g) frozen mixed berries
½ cup (100g) drained canned pitted black cherries
vanilla syrup
½ cup (125ml) water
½ cup (110g) caster sugar
2 vanilla pods

1 Preheat oven to 180°C/160°C fan-assisted. Grease 21cm savarin tin thoroughly.
2 Beat butter and sugar in small bowl with electric mixer until light and fluffy. Beat in eggs, one at a time. Transfer mixture to large bowl; stir in sifted flours, ground almonds, soured cream, berries and cherries. Pour mixture into tin; bake about 40 minutes.
3 Meanwhile, make vanilla syrup.
4 Stand cake in tin 5 minutes before turning onto wire rack set over tray. Pour hot syrup over hot cake.
vanilla syrup Combine the water and sugar in small saucepan. Split vanilla pods in half lengthways; scrape seeds into pan then place pods in pan. Stir over heat, without boiling, until sugar dissolves. Simmer, uncovered, without stirring, 5 minutes. Using tongs, remove pods from syrup.

lemon syrup cake

prep + cook time 1 hour 10 minutes **serves** 12

250g butter, softened
1 tablespoon finely grated lemon rind
1 cup (220g) caster sugar
3 eggs
1 cup (250ml) buttermilk
⅓ cup (80ml) lemon juice
2 cups (300g) self-raising flour
lemon syrup
⅓ cup (80ml) lemon juice
¼ cup (60ml) water
¾ cup (165g) caster sugar

1 Preheat oven to 180°C/160°C fan-assisted. Grease 24cm savarin tin (or grease deep 22cm-round cake tin and line base and side with baking parchment).
2 Beat butter, rind and sugar in small bowl with electric mixer until light and fluffy. Beat in eggs, one at a time. Transfer mixture to large bowl; fold in buttermilk, juice and sifted flour, in two batches.
3 Spread mixture into tin; bake about 50 minutes if using savarin tin or bake about 1 hour if using round tin. Cover cake with foil if browning too quickly.
4 Meanwhile, make lemon syrup.
5 Stand cake in tin 5 minutes before turning onto wire rack set over tray. Pour hot syrup over hot cake; serve warm.
lemon syrup Combine ingredients in small saucepan; stir over heat, without boiling, until sugar dissolves. Simmer, uncovered, without stirring, 5 minutes.

orange syrup cake

prep + cook time 1 hour 35 minutes **serves** 12

1 large orange (300g)
2 cups (500ml) water
2 cups (440g) caster sugar
⅔ cup (160ml) brandy
250g unsalted butter, softened
1 cup (220g) caster sugar, extra
4 eggs
1½ cups (225g) self-raising flour
2 tablespoons cornflour

1 Preheat oven to 160°C/140°C fan-assisted. Grease deep 22cm-round cake tin; line base and side with baking parchment.

2 Peel orange. Chop peel and flesh of orange finely; discard pips. Stir orange flesh and peel in medium saucepan with the water, sugar and brandy, over medium heat, until sugar dissolves; bring to the boil. Reduce heat; simmer, uncovered, about 15 minutes or until orange skin is tender. Strain syrup into heatproof jug; reserve orange solids separately.

3 Beat butter and extra sugar in small bowl with electric mixer until light and fluffy. Beat in eggs, one at a time. Transfer mixture to large bowl. Stir in combined sifted flours, and reserved orange solids. Pour mixture into tin; bake about 50 minutes.

4 Meanwhile, simmer reserved syrup over heat in small saucepan until thickened slightly.

5 Stand cake in tin 5 minutes before turning, top-side up, onto wire rack set over tray. Pour hot syrup over hot cake; serve warm.

banana butterscotch syrup cake

prep + cook time 1 hour 15 minutes **serves** 9

You will need 2 large overripe bananas (460g) for this recipe.

125g butter, softened
¾ cup (165g) caster sugar
2 eggs
1 cup mashed banana
¾ cup (110g) self-raising flour
¾ cup (110g) plain flour
½ teaspoon bicarbonate of soda
¾ cup (110g) hazelnuts, roasted, chopped finely
butterscotch syrup
½ cup (110g) firmly packed brown sugar
30g butter, chopped
¾ cup (180ml) water

1   Preheat oven to 180°C/160°C fan-assisted. Grease deep 19cm-square cake tin; line base with baking parchment.
2   Beat butter and sugar in medium bowl with electric mixer until light and fluffy. Beat in eggs, one at a time. Stir in banana, then combined sifted flours and soda, and nuts. Spread mixture into tin; bake about 1 hour.
3   Meanwhile, make butterscotch syrup.
4   Stand cake in tin 5 minutes before turning, top-side up, onto wire rack set over tray. Drizzle hot syrup over hot cake.
butterscotch syrup Combine sugar and butter in small saucepan; stir over heat until butter melts. Add the water and bring to the boil, stirring; remove from heat.

semolina & yogurt lemon-syrup cake

prep + cook time 1 hour 10 minutes **serves** 8

250g butter, softened
1 tablespoon finely grated lemon rind
1 cup (220g) caster sugar
3 eggs, separated
1 cup (150g) self-raising flour
1 cup (180g) semolina
1 cup (280g) plain yogurt
lemon syrup
1 cup (220g) caster sugar
⅓ cup (80ml) lemon juice

lemon syrup Combine ingredients in small pan; stir over heat, without boiling, until sugar dissolves. Bring to the boil, without stirring, then remove from heat.

1 Preheat oven to 180°C/160°C fan-assisted. Grease 20cm savarin tin (or grease deep 20cm-round cake tin and line base and side with baking parchment).
2 Beat butter, rind and sugar in small bowl with electric mixer until light and fluffy. Beat in egg yolks. Transfer mixture to large bowl; stir in sifted flour, semolina and yogurt.
3 Beat egg whites in small bowl with electric mixer until soft peaks form; fold egg whites into cake mixture, in two batches. Spread mixture into tin; bake about 50 minutes.
4 Meanwhile, make lemon syrup.
5 Stand cake in tin 5 minutes before turning onto wire rack set over tray. Pierce cake all over with skewer; pour hot lemon syrup over hot cake.

espresso syrup cake

prep + cook time 1 hour **serves** 8

3 teaspoons instant espresso coffee granules
1 tablespoon hot water
3 eggs
¾ cup (165g) caster sugar
1 cup (150g) self-raising flour
1 tablespoon cocoa powder
150g butter, melted
espresso syrup
¾ cup (165g) caster sugar
¾ cup (180ml) water
3 teaspoons instant espresso coffee granules

1 Preheat oven to 180°C/160°C fan-assisted. Grease 20cm savarin tin (or grease deep 20cm-round cake tin and line base and side with baking parchment).
2 Combine coffee and the water in small jug; stir until dissolved.
3 Beat eggs in small bowl with electric mixer about 8 minutes or until thick and creamy; gradually add sugar, beating until dissolved between additions. Fold in sifted flour and cocoa, then butter and coffee mixture. Pour mixture into tin; bake about 40 minutes.
4 Meanwhile, make espresso syrup.
5 Stand cake in tin 5 minutes before turning onto wire rack set over tray. Reserve ¼ cup espresso syrup; drizzle remaining hot syrup over hot cake. Serve with reserved syrup.

espresso syrup Combine ingredients in small saucepan; stir over heat, without boiling, until sugar dissolves. Bring to the boil then remove from heat.

cinnamon & walnut syrup cake

prep + cook time 1 hour **serves** 12

3 eggs
¾ cup (165g) caster sugar
¾ cup (110g) self-raising flour
3 teaspoons ground cinnamon
185g butter, melted
¾ cup (80g) coarsely chopped walnuts
sugar syrup
1 cup (220) caster sugar
¾ cup (180ml) water

1 Preheat oven to 180°C/160°C fan-assisted. Grease 23cm-square traybake tin; line base with baking parchment.
2 Beat eggs in small bowl with electric mixer until thick and creamy. Gradually add sugar, beating until dissolved between additions. Beat in sifted flour and cinnamon, in two batches; beat in butter then stir in nuts. Pour mixture into tin; bake about 30 minutes.
3 Meanwhile, make sugar syrup.
4 Stand cake in tin 5 minutes before turning onto wire rack set over tray. Pour hot syrup over hot cake. Serve cake warm or cold.
sugar syrup Combine ingredients in small saucepan; stir constantly over heat without boiling until sugar is dissolved. Bring to the boil; reduce heat, simmer, uncovered, 5 minutes.

lime syrup buttermilk cake

prep + cook time 1 hour 30 minutes **serves** 8

250g butter, softened
1 tablespoon finely grated lime rind
1 cup (220g) caster sugar
3 eggs, separated
2 cups (300g) self-raising flour
1 cup (250ml) buttermilk
lime syrup
⅓ cup (80ml) lime juice
¾ cup (165g) caster sugar
¼ cup (60ml) water

1   Preheat oven to 180°C/160°C fan-assisted. Grease 20cm savarin tin (or grease deep 20cm-round cake tin and line base and side with baking parchment).
2   Beat butter, rind and sugar in small bowl with electric mixer until light and fluffy; beat in egg yolks, one at a time, until combined. Transfer mixture to large bowl; stir in sifted flour, and buttermilk, in two batches.
3   Beat egg whites in small bowl with electric mixer until soft peaks form; fold into flour mixture, in two batches. Spread mixture into tin; bake about 1 hour.
4   Meanwhile, make lime syrup.
5   Stand cake in tin 5 minutes before turning onto serving plate. Gradually pour hot lime syrup evenly over hot cake. Serve cake sprinkled with thinly sliced lime rind, if desired.
lime syrup Combine ingredients in small saucepan; stir over heat, without boiling, until sugar is dissolved. Bring to the boil; remove from heat.

glacé fruit cake

prep + cook time 2 hours 50 minutes (plus cooling time) **serves** 12

185g butter, softened
½ cup (110g) caster sugar
3 eggs
1 cup (250g) finely chopped glacé apricot
½ cup (80g) finely chopped glacé orange
½ cup (90g) finely chopped glacé ginger
¾ cup (210g) finely chopped glacé fig
1½ cups (225g) plain flour
½ cup (75g) self-raising flour
½ cup (125ml) milk
¼ cup (60ml) ginger wine

ginger syrup
¼ cup (60ml) ginger wine
¼ cup (60ml) water
¼ cup (55g) caster sugar
2 teaspoons lemon juice

1   Preheat oven to 150°C / 130°C fan-assisted. Line base and long sides of 14cm x 21cm loaf tin with baking parchment, extending paper 5cm above sides.
2   Beat butter and sugar in small bowl with electric mixer until just combined. Beat in eggs, one at a time. Transfer mixture to large bowl; stir in fruit then combined sifted flours, and combined milk and wine, in two batches. Spread mixture into tin; bake about 2½ hours.
3   Meanwhile, make ginger syrup.
4   Pour hot ginger syrup over hot cake in tin. Cover cake with foil; cool in tin.
ginger syrup Stir ingredients in small saucepan over low heat, without boiling, until sugar dissolves; bring to the boil. Boil, uncovered, without stirring, about 2 minutes or until syrup thickens slightly.

tip Ginger wine, a beverage that is 14% alcohol by volume, has the piquant taste of fresh ginger. You can substitute it with dry (white) vermouth, if you prefer.

almond orange halva cake

prep + cook time 1 hour 15 minutes **serves** 10

125g butter, softened
2 teaspoons finely grated orange rind
½ cup (110g) caster sugar
2 eggs
1 teaspoon baking powder
1 cup (180g) semolina
1 cup (120g) ground almonds
¼ cup (60ml) orange juice
orange & brandy syrup
1 cup (250ml) orange juice
½ cup (110g) caster sugar
1 tablespoon brandy

1   Preheat oven to 180°C/160°C fan-assisted. Grease deep 20cm-round cake tin; line base and side with baking parchment.
2   Cream butter, rind and sugar in small bowl with electric mixer until light and fluffy. Beat in eggs, one at a time, until combined. Transfer mixture to large bowl; stir in dry ingredients and juice in two batches. Spread mixture into tin; bake about 40 minutes.
3 Meanwhile, make orange and brandy syrup.
4   Turn cake, top-side up, onto wire rack set over oven tray; brush half the hot syrup over hot cake. Bake (on wire rack) a further 5 minutes. Remove from oven; brush with remaining hot syrup. Serve cake warm or cold.
orange & brandy syrup Combine juice and sugar in small saucepan; stir constantly over heat, without boiling, until sugar is dissolved. Bring to the boil; reduce heat, simmer, uncovered, without stirring, 5 minutes. Stir in brandy.

whole tangelo cake

prep + cook time 1 hour 5 minutes **serves** 12

2 medium tangelos (420g)
125g butter, softened
1½ cups (330g) caster sugar
2 eggs
1 cup (150g) self-raising flour
½ cup (75g) plain flour
½ cup (45g) desiccated coconut
tangelo syrup
1 cup (220g) caster sugar
rind of 1 tangelo, sliced thinly
⅔ cup (160ml) tangelo juice
⅓ cup (80ml) water

note Tangelos – a citrus fruit that's a cross between a tangerine and grapefruit – have a fairly short season. If you can't get them, use the same weight in either oranges or mandarins.

1 Place tangelos in medium saucepan; cover with cold water. Bring to the boil; drain. Repeat process twice; cool to room temperature.
2 Preheat oven to 180°C/160°C fan-assisted. Grease deep 22cm-round cake tin; line base and side with baking parchment.
3 Halve tangelos; discard seeds. Blend or process tangelo until pulpy; transfer to large bowl.
4 Beat butter, sugar and eggs in small bowl with electric mixer until light and fluffy. Stir butter mixture into tangelo pulp. Stir in sifted flours and coconut. Pour mixture into tin.
5 Bake cake about 45 minutes. Stand cake in tin 5 minutes; turn, top-side up, onto wire rack over tray.
6 Make tangelo syrup; pour hot syrup over hot cake. Serve cake warm.

tangelo syrup Stir ingredients in small saucepan over heat, without boiling, until sugar dissolves; bring to the boil. Reduce heat; simmer, uncovered, without stirring, 2 minutes.

CLASSIC
Dessert cakes

Forget the diet, think luscious indulgence.
Most dessert cakes take a little time and effort to make,
but usually they can be made at least a day ahead of serving.
Leave any assembling, filling and decorating until the
last minute for maximum effect.

black forest cake

prep + cook time 2 hours 25 minutes (plus cooling time) **serves** 12

250g butter, chopped
1 tablespoon instant coffee granules
1½ cups (375ml) hot water
200g dark eating chocolate, chopped
2 cups (440g) caster sugar
1½ cups (225g) self-raising flour
1 cup (150g) plain flour
¼ cup (25g) cocoa powder
2 eggs
2 teaspoons vanilla extract
¼ cup (60ml) kirsch
600ml whipping cream, whipped
2 x 425g cans pitted black cherries, drained, halved
2 teaspoons cocoa powder, extra

1 Preheat oven to 150°C/130°C fan-assisted. Grease deep 22cm-round cake tin, line base and side with baking parchment.
2 Melt butter in medium saucepan; stir in combined coffee and hot water, then chocolate and sugar. Stir over low heat, without boiling, until smooth. Transfer mixture to large bowl, cool to warm.
3 Beat chocolate mixture on low speed with electric mixer; gradually beat in sifted dry ingredients, in three batches. Beat in eggs, one at a time, then extract.
4 Pour mixture into tin; bake about 1¾ hours. Stand cake in tin 5 minutes before turning, top-side up, onto wire rack to cool.
5 Trim top of cake to make it flat. Split cake into three even layers. Place one layer onto serving plate; brush with half of the kirsch, top with half of the whipped cream and half of the cherries. Repeat layering, then top with cake top. Dust with extra sifted cocoa.

apple cake with brandy butterscotch sauce

prep + cook time 1 hour 10 minutes **serves** 8

125g butter, softened
½ cup (110g) caster sugar
2 eggs
⅔ cup (100g) self-raising flour
⅓ cup (50g) plain flour
1 tablespoon milk
3 medium green-skinned apples (450g)
½ cup (160g) apricot jam, warmed
brandy butterscotch sauce
½ cup (100g) firmly packed brown sugar
½ cup (125ml) whipping cream
100g butter, chopped
2 tablespoons brandy

1   Preheat oven to 160°C/140°C fan-assisted. Grease two 8cm x 25cm bar cake tins; line bases and long sides with baking parchment, extending paper 5cm above sides.
2   Beat butter and sugar in small bowl with electric mixer until light and fluffy. Beat in eggs, one at a time. Stir in sifted flours and milk; spread mixture into tins.
3   Peel, core and halve apples; slice each half thinly. Push apple slices gently into surface of cake mixture. Brush apple with jam; bake about 40 minutes.
4   Make brandy butterscotch sauce.
5   Stand cakes in tins 10 minutes before turning out, top-sides up, onto wire racks to cool. Serve pieces of warm apple cake drizzled with the brandy butterscotch sauce.

brandy butterscotch sauce Combine ingredients in small saucepan. Stir over heat, without boiling, until sugar dissolves; bring to the boil. Reduce heat; simmer, uncovered, without stirring, about 3 minutes **or** until mixture thickens slightly.

vanilla pear almond cake

prep + cook time 2 hours 45 minutes (plus cooling time) **serves** 8

8 firm pears (800g)
2½ cups (625ml) water
1 strip lemon rind
1¾ cups (385g) caster sugar
1 vanilla pod, halved lengthways
125g butter, softened
3 eggs
⅔ cup (160g) soured cream
⅔ cup (100g) plain flour
⅔ cup (100g) self-raising flour
¼ cup (40g) blanched almonds, roasted, chopped coarsely
40g dark eating chocolate, chopped
½ cup (60g) ground almonds

1 Peel pears, leaving stems intact.
2 Combine the water, rind and 1 cup of the sugar in medium pan. Scrape vanilla seeds into pan, then add pod. Stir over heat, without boiling, until sugar dissolves. Add pears; bring to a boil. Reduce heat; simmer, covered, about 30 minutes until pears are just tender. Transfer pears to a bowl; bring syrup to the boil. Boil, uncovered, until syrup reduces by half. Using tongs, remove vanilla pod. Cool syrup completely.
3 Preheat oven to 200°C/180°C fan-assisted. Insert base of 23cm springform tin upside down in tin to give a flat base; grease tin.
4 Beat butter and remaining sugar in medium bowl with electric mixer until light and fluffy. Beat in eggs, one at a time. Add soured cream; beat until just combined. Stir in 2 tablespoons of the syrup, then combined sifted flours, nuts, chocolate and ground almonds.
5 Spread mixture into tin; place pears upright around edge of tin, gently pushing pears to the bottom. Bake about 1 hour 35 minutes. Stand cake 10 minutes before removing from tin.
6 Serve cake warm, brushed with remaining syrup.

plum & almond upside-down cake

prep + cook time 1 hour 15 minutes **serves** 9

50g butter, chopped
½ cup (110g) firmly packed brown sugar
12 small plums (900g), halved, stones removed
125g butter, softened
1 teaspoon vanilla extract
1¼ cups (275g) caster sugar
3 eggs
¾ cup (110g) self-raising flour
¾ cup (110g) plain flour
¾ cup (180ml) milk
1 cup (120g) ground almonds
⅓ cup (25g) flaked almonds, toasted

1   Preheat oven to 180°C/160°C fan-assisted. Grease 19cm-square cake tin; line with baking parchment.
2   Combine butter and brown sugar in a small saucepan, stir over low heat until smooth; pour into base of cake tin. Place plums, cut side down, over caramel mixture.
3   Beat butter, extract and caster sugar in medium bowl with electric mixer until light and fluffy. Beat in eggs, one at a time. Stir in both sifted flours, and milk, in two batches. Stir in ground almonds.
4   Spread mixture into tin; bake about 50 minutes. Stand cake in tin 15 minutes before turning onto wire rack to cool. Serve sprinkled with flaked almonds and a dollop of cream.

banana caramel layer cake

prep + cook time 1 hour 10 minutes **serves** 8

You need two large overripe bananas (460g) for this recipe.

185g butter, softened
1¼ cup (175g) caster sugar
3 eggs
2¼ cups (335g) self-raising flour
½ teaspoon bicarbonate of soda
1¼ cups mashed banana
⅓ cup (80ml) milk
380g dulce de leche (caramel sauce)
¾ cup (180ml) whipping cream, whipped
1 large (230g) banana, sliced thinly

1 Preheat oven to 180°C/160°C fan-assisted. Grease 24cm savarin tin or 24cm patterned silicone tube tin.
2 Beat butter and sugar in small bowl with electric mixer until light and fluffy. Beat in eggs, one at a time. Transfer mixture to large bowl; stir in sifted dry ingredients, mashed banana and milk.
3 Spread mixture into prepared tin; bake about 40 minutes. Stand cake in tin 5 minutes before turning onto wire rack to cool.
4 Split cake into three layers. Spread bottom layer of cake with half the caramel, top with half the cream then half the banana slices. Repeat next layer using remaining caramel, cream and banana slices. Replace top of cake and dust with icing sugar before serving.

chocolate roulade with coffee cream

prep + cook time 30 minutes (plus cooling & refrigeration time) **serves** 8

200g dark eating chocolate, chopped coarsely
¼ cup (60ml) hot water
2 teaspoons instant coffee granules
4 eggs, separated
½ cup (110g) caster sugar
1 tablespoon caster sugar, extra
coffee cream
2 teaspoons instant coffee granules
1 teaspoon hot water
300ml whipping cream
2 tablespoons coffee-flavoured liqueur
1 tablespoon icing sugar

coffee cream Dissolve coffee granules in the hot water in small bowl. Add cream, liqueur and sifted icing sugar; beat with electric mixer until firm peaks form.

1   Preheat oven to 180°C/160°C fan-assisted. Grease 25cm x 30cm swiss roll tin; line base and sides with baking parchment, extending paper 5cm above sides.
2   Combine chocolate, the water and coffee granules in large heatproof bowl. Stir mixture over large saucepan of simmering water until smooth (do not allow water to touch base of bowl); remove from heat.
3   Beat egg yolks and caster sugar in small bowl with electric mixer until thick and creamy; fold egg mixture into warm chocolate mixture.
4   Beat egg whites in small bowl with electric mixer to soft peaks; fold egg whites into chocolate mixture, in two batches. Spread into tin; bake about 10 minutes.
5   Meanwhile, place piece of baking parchment cut the same size as tin on worktop; sprinkle with extra caster sugar. Turn hot cake onto paper; peel lining paper away. Cool, then trim sides of cake. Cover cake with tea-towel.
6   Make coffee cream.
7   Spread cake evenly with coffee cream. Using paper as a guide, roll cake from long side. Cover roll; refrigerate 30 minutes before serving.

soft-centred mocha puddings

prep + cook time 40 minutes **makes** 6

150g dark chocolate, chopped
125g butter, chopped
3 teaspoons instant coffee granules
2 eggs
2 egg yolks
⅓ cup (75g) caster sugar
¼ cup (35g) plain flour
2 teaspoons cocoa powder

1 Preheat oven to 200°C/180°C fan-assisted. Grease six-hole (¾-cup/180ml) large muffin tin well with softened butter.
2 Stir chocolate, butter and coffee in small saucepan, over low heat, until smooth; cool 10 minutes. Transfer mixture to a large bowl.
3 Beat eggs, egg yolks and sugar in small bowl with electric mixer until thick and creamy. Gently fold egg mixture and sifted flour into barely warm chocolate mixture.
4 Divide mixture among tin holes; bake, in oven, 12 minutes. Gently turn puddings, top-side down, onto serving plates. Serve immediately, dusted with sifted cocoa powder.

torta di mamma

prep + cook time 1 hour 50 minutes (plus refrigeration time) **serves** 12

280g packet sponge cake mix
1 cup (250ml) strong black coffee
⅓ cup (80ml) coffee liqueur
⅓ cup (80ml) brandy
1 tablespoon caster sugar
custard filling
½ cup (75g) cornflour
½ cup (60g) custard powder
½ cup (110g) caster sugar
2½ cups (625ml) milk
1½ cups (375ml) double cream
2 teaspoons vanilla extract
30g butter
2 egg yolks
90g dark eating chocolate, melted

1 Preheat oven to 160°C/140°C fan-assisted. Grease deep 22cm-round cake tin; line base with baking parchment.
2 Make sponge cake according to the directions on packet; pour mixture into tin. Bake about 35 minutes. Turn cake onto wire rack to cool.
3 Meanwhile, make custard filling.
4 Combine cold coffee, liqueur, brandy and sugar in small jug; mix well. Split cold cake into four layers. Place first layer on serving plate; brush well with coffee mixture.
5 Spread half the plain custard over cake. Top custard with second layer of cake; brush with coffee mixture. Spread a third of the chocolate custard over cake. Place third layer of cake on top of custard; brush with coffee mixture then spread with remaining plain custard. Top with fourth layer of cake; brush with coffee mixture.
6 Using a large spatula, spread remaining chocolate custard over top and side of cake; refrigerate 3 hours or overnight.
custard filling Combine cornflour, custard powder and sugar in medium saucepan. Gradually add combined milk, cream and extract; stir over low heat until mixture boils and thickens. Add butter; simmer, stirring, 3 minutes. Remove pan from heat; stir in egg yolk. Place custard in large bowl; cover with cling film. Cool. Divide custard mixture between two bowls. Stir melted chocolate into one bowl. Leave remaining custard plain.

flourless chocolate dessert cake

prep + cook time 1 hour (plus refrigeration time) **serves** 6

100g dark eating chocolate, chopped
100g butter, chopped
½ cup (110g) caster sugar
2 tablespoons marsala
⅔ cup (80g) ground almonds
1 tablespoon instant coffee granules
1 tablespoon hot water
3 eggs, separated
strawberry coulis
250g strawberries
¼ cup (40g) icing sugar

1 Preheat oven to 180°C/160°C fan-assisted. Grease deep 20cm-round cake tin; line base and side with baking parchment.
2 Melt chocolate and butter in small saucepan, over low heat, stirring, until mixture is combined.
3 Combine chocolate mixture with sugar, marsala, ground almonds and combined coffee and the water in a large bowl; beat in egg yolks, one at a time.
4 Beat egg whites in small bowl with electric mixer until soft peaks form; gently fold into chocolate mixture, in two batches.
5 Pour mixture into tin; bake about 45 minutes. Cool cake in tin, cover; refrigerate several hours or overnight.
6 Make strawberry coulis.
7 Carefully turn cake onto board; cut into slices with a hot knife. Serve cake with strawberry coulis. Dust with sifted icing sugar and serve with whipped cream, if you like.
strawberry coulis Blend or process ingredients until mixture is smooth.

rich truffle mud cake

prep + cook time 1 hour 15 minutes (plus cooling and refrigeration time) **serves** 12

6 eggs
½ cup (110g) firmly packed brown sugar
400g dark eating chocolate, melted
1 cup (250ml) thick cream (48% fat content)
⅓ cup (80ml) Cointreau

1   Preheat oven to 180°C/160°C fan-assisted. Grease deep 22cm-round cake tin; line base and side with baking parchment.
2   Beat eggs and sugar in large bowl with electric mixer until thick and creamy. With motor operating, gradually beat in barely warm melted chocolate until combined. Using metal spoon, gently fold in combined cream and liqueur.
3   Pour mixture into tin. Place tin in baking dish; pour enough boiling water into dish to come halfway up side of tin. Bake about 30 minutes. Cover tin loosely with foil; bake about 30 minutes. Discard foil; remove tin from dish, cool cake in tin.
4   Turn cake onto serving plate, cover; refrigerate overnight. Serve dusted with a little sifted cocoa, if desired.

tip Goes well served with a raspberry coulis and fresh raspberries.

opera gateau

prep + cook time 1 hour (plus cooling and refrigeration time) **serves** 24

4 eggs
1¼ cups (150g) ground almonds
1 cup (160g) icing sugar, sifted
⅓ cup (50g) plain flour
25g unsalted butter, melted
4 egg whites
1 tablespoon caster sugar
coffee buttercream
¼ cup (60ml) milk
¼ cup (55g) brown sugar
2 teaspoons instant coffee granules
1 egg yolk
125g unsalted butter, softened
coffee syrup
⅓ cup (80ml) boiling water
2 tablespoons caster sugar
1 tablespoon instant coffee granules
ganache
160g dark eating chocolate, chopped coarsely
⅓ cup (80ml) double cream
glaze
50g unsalted butter, chopped
75g dark eating chocolate

1 Preheat oven to 220°C/200°C fan-assisted. Grease two 25cm x 30cm swiss roll tins; line bases with baking parchment, extending paper 5cm over long sides.
2 Beat eggs, ground almonds and icing sugar in small bowl with electric mixer until creamy; beat in flour. Transfer to large bowl; stir in butter. Beat egg whites in small bowl with electric mixer until soft peaks form; add caster sugar, beating until sugar dissolves. Fold into almond mixture, in two batches. Divide mixture between tins. Bake 7 minutes. Cool.
3 Make coffee buttercream, coffee syrup, and ganache.
4 Place one of the large cake rectangles on baking-parchment-lined tray; brush with half the coffee syrup then spread cake with half the buttercream. Chill 10 minutes. Top buttercream with the two small cake rectangles, side-by-side. Brush tops with the remaining coffee syrup then spread with ganache. Top with remaining cake; chill 10 minutes. Spread remaining buttercream over top of cake; chill 3 hours.
5 Make glaze.
6 Quickly spread glaze evenly over cake. Refrigerate 30 minutes or until set.
coffee buttercream Stir milk, sugar and coffee in small saucepan, over low heat, until sugar dissolves. Whisk yolk in small bowl; gradually whisk in hot milk mixture. Return custard to pan; stir over heat, without boiling, about 5 minutes or until thickened slightly. Cool. Beat butter in small bowl with electric mixer until light and fluffy; beat in custard.
coffee syrup Combine ingredients in small bowl.
ganache Stir ingredients in small heatproof bowl over small saucepan of simmering water until smooth. Refrigerate until spreadable.
glaze Stir ingredients in small heat-proof bowl over small pan of simmering water until smooth. Use while still warm.

rum baba

prep + cook time 40 minutes (plus standing time) **serves** 6

7g sachet dry yeast
¼ cup (35g) plain flour
¼ cup (60ml) warm milk
¾ cup (110g) plain flour, extra
2 tablespoons caster sugar
2 eggs, beaten lightly
60g butter, melted
rum syrup
1½ cups (330g) caster sugar
1 cup (250ml) water
2 tablespoons dark rum

1 Grease six ½-cup (125ml) moulds.
2 Mix yeast with flour and milk in small bowl; cover, stand in warm place about 10 minutes or until mixture is frothy.
3 Sift extra flour and sugar into large bowl; stir in yeast mixture, egg and butter. Beat about 3 minutes with a wooden spoon until batter is smooth. Place batter in large greased bowl, cover; stand in warm place about 40 minutes or until batter has doubled in size.
4 Preheat oven to 200°C/180°C fan-assisted.
5 Beat batter again. Divide batter between moulds; stand, uncovered, until batter rises three-quarters of the way up side of moulds. Place moulds on oven tray; bake about 15 minutes.
6 Meanwhile, make rum syrup.
7 Turn babas onto wire rack set over tray; pour hot rum syrup over hot babas. Place babas on serving plates; pour syrup from tray over babas until all syrup has been absorbed.
rum syrup Combine sugar and the water in small saucepan; stir over heat, without boiling, until sugar is dissolved. Bring to the boil; boil, uncovered, without stirring, 2 minutes. Remove from heat, stir in rum.

brandied apricot chocolate cake

prep + cook time 1 hour 20 minutes (plus refrigeration time) **serves** 10

125g dark eating chocolate, chopped
½ cup (125ml) water
125g butter, softened
1 cup (220g) firmly packed brown sugar
2 eggs
½ cup (125ml) soured cream
1⅓ cups (200g) plain flour
⅓ cup (35g) self-raising flour
¼ cup (80g) apricot jam
1 tablespoon brandy
½ cup (125ml) whipping cream, whipped
chocolate icing
90g dark eating chocolate, chopped
15g butter, chopped

1   Preheat oven to 160°C/140°C fan-assisted. Grease deep 20cm-round cake tin; line base with baking parchment.
2   Stir chocolate and the water in small saucepan, over low heat, until smooth; cool chocolate mixture.
3   Cream butter and sugar in small bowl with electric mixer until light and fluffy. Beat in eggs, one at a time. Transfer mixture to large bowl, stir in chocolate mixture, soured cream and sifted flours in two batches.
4   Spread mixture into tin; bake about 1 hour. Stand cake in tin 5 minutes before turning, top-side up, onto wire rack to cool.
5   Meanwhile make chocolate icing.
6   Split cake in half. Combine jam and brandy. Sandwich cake with jam mixture and cream. Spread cake with icing, refrigerate until set.
chocolate icing Stir chocolate and butter in small bowl set over small saucepan of simmering water until smooth (do not allow water to touch base of bowl); cool.

rich mocha gâteau

prep + cook time 1 hour 15 minutes (plus standing & refrigeration time) **serves** 12

½ cup (125ml) Cointreau
2 teaspoons finely grated orange rind
150g milk chocolate, melted
90g unsalted butter, melted
6 eggs, separated
¾ cup (110g) self-raising flour
⅓ cup (75g) caster sugar
rich mocha filling
2 teaspoons instant coffee granules
2 tablespoons hot water
300g dark eating chocolate, melted
6 egg yolks
chocolate butter cream
2 tablespoons instant coffee granules
¼ cup (60ml) hot water
200g dark eating chocolate, melted
4 egg yolks
¼ cup (55g) caster sugar
185g unsalted butter, softened

1 Preheat oven to 180°C/160°C fan-assisted. Grease deep 22cm-round cake tin; line base with baking parchment.

2 Stand liqueur and rind in small bowl for 30 minutes. Strain; reserve rind and liqueur separately.

3 Combine chocolate, butter and rind in large bowl. Stir in 3 teaspoons of the liqueur along with the egg yolks and sifted flour.

4 Beat egg whites in large bowl with electric mixer until soft peaks form; gradually add sugar, beating until dissolved between additions. Fold whites into chocolate mixture, in two batches.

5 Pour mixture into tin; bake about 35 minutes. Stand cake in tin 5 minutes before turning, top-side up, onto wire rack to cool.

6 Meanwhile, make rich mocha filling and chocolate butter cream.

7 Split cake into three layers. Place first layer on serving plate; spread with half the mocha filling. Refrigerate 15 minutes. Top with second layer; spread with remaining mocha filling. Top with third layer; refrigerate 30 minutes. Spread butter cream over top and side of cake; refrigerate 30 minutes.

rich mocha filling Combine coffee and the water in large bowl; stir in melted chocolate, then yolks and ⅓ cup of the remaining liqueur. Refrigerate until set.

chocolate butter cream Combine coffee and the water in large bowl; stir in the chocolate and remaining liqueur. Beat yolks and sugar in small bowl with electric mixer until thick and creamy; beat in butter in several batches until smooth. Gradually beat in chocolate mixture; refrigerate 10 minutes or until spreadable.

italian ricotta cheesecake

prep + cook time 1 hour 40 minutes (plus refrigeration & cooling time) **serves** 16

90g butter, softened
¼ cup (55g) caster sugar
1 egg
1¼ cups (185g) plain flour
¼ cup (35g) self-raising flour
ricotta filling
1kg ricotta cheese
1 tablespoon finely grated lemon rind
¼ cup (60ml) lemon juice
1 cup (220g) caster sugar
5 eggs
¼ cup (40g) sultanas
¼ cup (80g) finely chopped glacé fruit salad

1 Grease 28cm springform cake tin.
2 Beat butter, sugar and egg in small bowl with electric mixer until combined. Stir in half the sifted flours, then work in remaining flours by hand. Lightly knead pastry on floured surface until smooth; wrap in cling film; refrigerate for 30 minutes.
3 Press pastry over base of tin; prick with fork. Place on oven tray; refrigerate 30 minutes.
4 Preheat oven to 200°C/180°C fan-assisted.
5 Cover pastry with baking parchment, fill with beans or rice; bake 10 minutes. Remove parchment and beans; bake 15 minutes or until browned lightly. Cool. Reduce oven temperature to 160°C/140°C fan-assisted.
6 Meanwhile, make ricotta filling.
7 Pour filling into tin; bake about 50 minutes. Cool cheesecake in oven with door ajar.
8 Refrigerate cheesecake 3 hours or overnight. Serve cheesecake dusted with sifted icing sugar, if desired.
ricotta filling Process cheese, rind, juice, sugar and eggs until smooth; stir in fruit.

new york cheesecake

prep + cook time 2 hours (plus refrigeration & cooling time) **serves** 12

250g plain sweet biscuits
125g butter, melted
cream cheese filling
750g cream cheese, softened
2 teaspoons finely grated orange rind
1 teaspoon finely grated lemon rind
1 cup (220g) caster sugar
3 eggs
¾ cup (180g) soured cream
¼ cup (60ml) lemon juice
soured cream topping
1 cup (240g) soured cream
2 tablespoons caster sugar
2 teaspoons lemon juice

1   Process biscuits until fine. Add butter, process until combined. Press mixture over base and side of 24cm springform cake tin. Place tin on oven tray; chill 30 minutes.
2   Preheat oven to 180°C/160°C fan-assisted.
3   Meanwhile make cream cheese filling.
4   Pour filling into tin; bake 1¼ hours. Remove from oven; cool 15 minutes.
5   Meanwhile make soured cream topping. Spread topping over the cheesecake. Bake 20 minutes. Cool in oven with door ajar.
6   Refrigerate cheesecake 3 hours or overnight.
cream cheese filling Beat cheese, rinds and sugar in medium bowl with electric mixer until smooth. Beat in eggs, one at a time, then soured cream and juice.
soured cream topping Combine ingredients together in small bowl.

chocolate mocha dacquoise terrine

prep + cook time 1 hour 10 minutes (plus cooling & refrigeration time) **serves** 12

4 egg whites
1 cup (220g) caster sugar
2 tablespoons cocoa powder
200g dark eating chocolate, chopped
¾ cup (180ml) double cream
2 teaspoons cocoa powder, extra
mocha butter cream
1 tablespoon instant coffee granules
2 tablespoons boiling water
100g unsalted butter, softened
2¼ cups (360g) icing sugar

mocha butter cream Dissolve coffee granules in the boiling water in small bowl; cool 10 minutes. Beat butter in small bowl with electric mixer until pale in colour; gradually add sifted icing sugar, beating until combined. Beat in coffee mixture.

1 Preheat oven to 150°C/130°C fan-assisted. Line three oven trays with baking parchment; draw a 10cm x 25cm rectangle on each sheet of parchment.
2 Beat egg whites in medium bowl with electric mixer until soft peaks form. Gradually add sugar, beating until sugar dissolves between additions; fold in sifted cocoa.
3 Spread meringue mixture evenly over rectangles; bake about 45 minutes. Turn off oven; cool meringues in oven with door ajar.
4 Meanwhile, stir chocolate and cream in small saucepan, over low heat, until smooth, transfer to small bowl; refrigerate until firm. Beat chocolate mixture with electric mixer about 20 seconds or until just changed in colour.
5 Make mocha butter cream.
6 Place one meringue on serving plate; spread with half the chocolate mixture, then top with half the butter cream. Top with another meringue; spread with remaining chocolate mixture and butter cream. Top with last meringue layer; cover and chill 3 hours or overnight. Dust with sifted extra cocoa powder to serve.

114

chocolate ganache & raspberry cake

prep + cook time 1 hour 50 minutes **serves** 10

⅓ cup (35g) cocoa powder
⅓ cup (80ml) water
150g dark eating chocolate, melted
150g butter, melted
1⅓ cups (300g) firmly packed brown sugar
1 cup (120g) ground almonds
4 eggs, separated
200g dark eating chocolate, chopped coarsely
⅔ cup (160ml) whipping cream
300g raspberries

1 Preheat oven to 160°C/140°C fan-assisted. Grease deep 22cm-round cake tin; line base and side with baking parchment.
2 Blend sifted cocoa with the water in large bowl until smooth. Stir in melted chocolate, butter, sugar, ground almonds and egg yolks.
3 Beat egg whites in small bowl with electric mixer until soft peaks form. Fold egg whites into chocolate mixture, in two batches. Pour mixture into tin. Bake cake about 1¼ hours.
4 Stand cake in pan 15 minutes; turn, top-side up, onto wire rack to cool.
5 Stir chopped chocolate and cream in small saucepan over low heat until smooth.
6 Place raspberries on top of cake; drizzle chocolate mixture over raspberries. Stand cake at room temperature until chocolate sets.

glossary

almonds

ground also known as almond meal; nuts powdered to a coarse flour-like texture.

caramelised toffee-coated almonds available from selected supermarkets, nut stands and gourmet food and specialty confectionery stores.

baking powder a raising agent containing starch, but mostly cream of tartar and bicarbonate of soda in the proportions of 1 teaspoon cream of tartar to ½ teaspoon bicarbonate of soda. This is equal to 2 teaspoons baking powder.

bicarbonate of soda also known as baking soda.

biscuits, plain sweet a crisp sweet biscuit without icing or filling.

butter use salted or unsalted (sweet) butter; 125g is equal to one stick (4 ounces) of butter.

buttermilk originally the term given to the slightly sour liquid left after butter was churned from cream, today it is made in a similar way to yogurt. Sold alongside fresh milk products in supermarkets; despite the implication of its name, it is low in fat. Low-fat yogurt or milk can be substituted.

chocolate

chips also known as chocolate morsels; come in milk, white and dark chocolate varieties. Contain an emulsifier, so hold their shape in baking and are ideal for cake decorating.

dark eating made of cocoa liquor, cocoa butter and sugar.

milk eating most popular eating chocolate, mild and very sweet; similar in make-up to dark eating chocolate, with the difference being the addition of milk solids.

cinnamon dried inner bark of the shoots of the cinnamon tree. Available as a stick or ground.

cocoa powder also known as cocoa; dried, unsweetened, roasted then ground cocoa beans.

coconut

desiccated dried, unsweetened, finely shredded coconut.

essence produced from coconut flavouring, oil and alcohol.

flaked dried, flaked coconut flesh.

shredded strips of dried coconut.

coffee liqueur we use Kahlúa or Tia Maria, but you can use your favourite brand.

Cointreau a citrus-flavoured liqueur based on oranges. You can use your favourite brand.

cornflour also known as cornstarch; used as a thickening agent. Available as 100% maize (corn) and wheaten cornflour.

courgette also known as zucchini; small green, yellow or white vegetable belonging to the squash family.

cream cheese also known as Philadelphia, a soft cow's milk cheese. Also available as spreadable light cream cheese – a blend of cottage and cream cheeses.

cream of tartar the acid ingredient in baking powder; added to confectionery mixtures to help prevent sugar from crystallising. Keeps frostings creamy and improves volume when beating egg whites.

cream

We used fresh cream, unless otherwise stated. Also known as pure cream and pouring cream, it has no additives unlike commercially thickened cream. Minimum fat content 35%.

soured thick commercially-cultured soured cream. Minimum fat content 35%.

thick we used thick cream with 48% fat content.

whipping a cream containing a thickener. Minimum fat content 35%.

currants tiny, almost black raisins named after a grape variety that originated in Corinth, Greece.

custard powder instant mixture used to make pouring custard.

date fruit of the date palm tree, eaten fresh or dried, on their own or in prepared dishes. About 4cm to 6cm in length, oval and plump, thin-skinned, with a honey-sweet flavour and sticky texture.

dulce de leche a caramel sauce made from milk and sugar. Can be used straight from the jar for cheesecakes, slices and tarts. Has similar qualities to sweetened condensed milk, only a thicker, caramel consistency; great to use in caramel desserts.

flour

plain an all-purpose flour made from wheat.

self-raising plain flour sifted with baking powder in the proportion of 1 cup flour to 2 teaspoons baking powder.

wholemeal flours milled from the whole wheat grain (bran, germ and flour). Available in both plain and self-raising varieties.

friand a small densely-textured sponge cake, popular in Australia and New Zealand and similar to a French Financier. Traditionally baked in oval shapes, they are made with butter, ground almonds and a variety of flavourings.

ginger also known as green or root ginger; the thick gnarled root of a tropical plant.

ginger wine (green ginger wine) a beverage that is 14% alcohol by volume and has the taste of fresh ginger. You can substitute it with dry (white) vermouth, if you prefer. The character of the ginger is drawn out by infusing it in spirit for an extended period.

glacé fruit fruit such as cherries, peaches, pineapple, orange and citron cooked in heavy sugar syrup then dried.

golden syrup a by-product of refined sugarcane; pure maple syrup or honey can be substituted.

hazelnuts also known as filberts; plump, grape-sized, rich, sweet nut.

hundreds & thousands tiny sugar-syrup-coated sugar crystals that come in many bright colours. Used to decorate cakes and party foods.

jam also known as preserve or conserve; usually made from fruit.

jelly crystals a powdered mixture of gelatine, sweetener, and artificial fruit flavouring that's used to make a moulded, translucent, quivering dessert.

kirsch cherry-flavoured liqueur.

lemon butter also known as lemon cheese or lemon curd; a smooth spread, usually made from lemons, butter and eggs.

maple syrup a thin syrup distilled from the sap of maple trees found only in Canada and parts of North America. Maple-flavoured syrup is not an adequate substitute for the real thing.

marmalade a preserve, usually based on citrus fruit.

marsala a sweet, fortified wine.

mixed dried fruit a mix of sultanas, raisins, currants, mixed peel and cherries.

mixed peel candied citrus peel.

mixed spice a blend of ground spices usually consisting of cinnamon, allspice and nutmeg.

nutmeg dried nut of an evergreen tree; available in ground form or you can grate your own with a fine grater.

nuts, how to roast place shelled, peeled nuts, in a single layer, on oven tray, roast in moderate oven for 8-10 minutes. Be careful to avoid burning nuts.

pecans Native to the United States; golden-brown, buttery and rich. Good in savoury and sweet dishes; especially good in salads.

poppy seeds tiny black seeds with a pungent flavour; store in an airtight container in a cool place or freezer.

raisins dried sweet grapes.

ricotta cheese a soft, sweet, moist, white, cow's milk cheese with a low fat content (about 8.5 per cent) and a slightly grainy texture. The name roughly translates as 'cooked again' and refers to its manufacture from a whey that is itself a by-product of other cheese making.

semolina made from durum wheat; milled into either fine or coarse granules.

sugar
brown soft, finely granulated sugar retaining molasses for its characteristic colour and flavour.
caster also known as superfine or finely granulated table sugar.
demerara a rich, golden-coloured small-grained crystal sugar having a subtle molasses flavour.
icing sugar also known as confectioners' sugar or powdered sugar; granulated sugar crushed together with a small amount of added cornflour.
raw natural light-brown coloured granulated sugar with a honey-like taste.
white a coarse, granulated table sugar, also known as crystal sugar.

sultanas dried grapes, also known as golden raisins.

sweet sherry fortified wine.

tangelo an orange-coloured loose-skinned, juicy, sweetly-tart citrus fruit with few seeds. Hybrid between a grapefruit and a mandarin.

treacle thick, dark syrup not unlike molasses; a by-product of sugar refining.

vanilla
extract made by pulping chopped vanilla pods with a mixture of alcohol and water. This gives a very strong solution, and only a couple of drops are needed to flavour most dishes.
paste made from vanilla pods and contains real seeds. It is highly concentrated and 1 teaspoon replaces a whole vanilla pod without mess or fuss as you neither have to split or scrape the pod. It is found in the baking aisle of many supermarkets.
pod dried long, thin pod from a tropical golden orchid; the minuscule black seeds inside the pod are used to impart a luscious vanilla flavour in baking and desserts. A whole pod can be placed in the sugar container to make the vanilla sugar often called for in recipes.

yeast a 7g (¼ oz) sachet of dried yeast (2 teaspoons) is equal to 15g (½ oz) compressed yeast if substituting one for the other.

yogurt we used unflavoured plain yogurt unless specified.

index

conversion charts

measures

The cup and spoon measurements used in this book are metric: one measuring cup holds approximately 250ml; one metric tablespoon holds 20ml; one metric teaspoon holds 5ml.

All cup and spoon measurements are level. The most accurate way of measuring dry ingredients is to weigh them. When measuring liquids, use a clear glass or plastic jug with the metric markings.

We use large eggs with an average weight of 60g. This book contains recipes for dishes made with raw or lightly cooked eggs. These should be avoided by vulnerable people such as pregnant and nursing mothers, invalids, the elderly, babies and young children.

dry measures

METRIC	IMPERIAL
15g	½oz
30g	1oz
60g	2oz
90g	3oz
125g	4oz (¼lb)
155g	5oz
185g	6oz
220g	7oz
250g	8oz (½lb)
280g	9oz
315g	10oz
345g	11oz
375g	12oz (¾lb)
410g	13oz
440g	14oz
470g	15oz
500g	16oz (1lb)
750g	24oz (1½lb)
1kg	32oz (2lb)

liquid measures

METRIC	IMPERIAL
30ml	1 fluid oz
60ml	2 fluid oz
100ml	3 fluid oz
125ml	4 fluid oz
150ml	5 fluid oz (¼ pint/1 gill)
190ml	6 fluid oz
250ml	8 fluid oz
300ml	10 fluid oz (½ pint)
500ml	16 fluid oz
600ml	20 fluid oz (1 pint)
1000ml (1 litre)	1¾ pints

length measures

METRIC	IMPERIAL
3mm	⅛ in
6mm	¼in
1cm	½in
2cm	¾in
2.5cm	1in
5cm	2in
6cm	2½in
8cm	3in
10cm	4in
13cm	5in
15cm	6in
18cm	7in
20cm	8in
23cm	9in
25cm	10in
28cm	11in
30cm	12in (1ft)

oven temperatures

These oven temperatures are only a guide for conventional ovens. For fan-assisted ovens, check the manufacturer's manual.

	°C (CELSIUS)	°F (FAHRENHEIT)	GAS MARK
Very low	120	250	½
Low	150	275-300	1-2
Moderately low	160	325	3
Moderate	180	350-375	4-5
Moderately hot	200	400	6
Hot	220	425-450	7-8
Very hot	240	475	9

ACP Books
General manager Christine Whiston
Test kitchen food director Pamela Clark
Editorial director Susan Tomnay
Creative director Hieu Chi Nguyen
Director of sales Brian Cearnes
Marketing manager Bridget Cody
Business analyst Rebecca Varela
Operations manager David Scotto
International rights enquiries Laura Bamford
lbamford@acpuk.com

ACP Books are published by ACP Magazines a division of PBL Media Pty Limited

Group publisher, Women's lifestyle Pat Ingram
Director of sales, Women's lifestyle Lynette Phillips

Commercial manager, Women's lifestyle Seymour Cohen
Marketing director, Women's lifestyle Matthew Dominello
Public relations manager, Women's lifestyle Hannah Deveraux
Creative director, Events, Women's lifestyle Luke Bonnano
Research Director, Women's lifestyle Justin Stone
ACP Magazines, Chief Executive officer Scott Lorson
PBL Media, Chief Executive officer Ian Law

Produced by ACP Books, Sydney.
Published by ACP Books, a division of ACP Magazines Ltd, 54 Park St, Sydney; GPO Box 4088, Sydney, NSW 2001.
phone (02) 9282 8618 fax (02) 9267 9438.
acpbooks@acpmagazines.com.au
www.acpbooks.com.au
Printed and bound in China.

Australia Distributed by Network Services, phone +61 2 9282 8777 fax +61 2 9264 3278
networkweb@networkservicescompany.com.au

United Kingdom Distributed by Australian Consolidated Press (UK), phone (01604) 642 200 fax (01604) 642 300
books@acpuk.com
New Zealand Distributed by Netlink Distribution Company, phone (9) 366 9966 ask@ndc.co.nz
South Africa Distributed by PSD Promotions, phone (27 11) 392 6065/6/7 fax (27 11) 392 6079/80
orders@psdprom.co.za
Canada Distributed by Publishers Group Canada phone (800) 663 5714 fax (800) 565 3770
service@raincoast.com

A catalogue record for this book is available from the British Library.
ISBN 978-1-903777-79-4
© ACP Magazines Ltd 2010

C000096285

Contract Management: Minimal Compliance with New Safeguards for Time-and-Materials Contracts for Commercial Services and Safeguards Have Not Been Applied to GSA Schedules Program: GAO-09-579

U.S. Government Accountability Office (GAO)

June 2009

CONTRACT MANAGEMENT

Minimal Compliance with New Safeguards for Time-and-Materials Contracts for Commercial Services and Safeguards Have Not Been Applied to GSA Schedules Program

Accountability ★ Integrity ★ Reliability

GAO
Accountability · Integrity · Reliability

Highlights

Highlights of GAO-09-579, a report to congressional committees

CONTRACT MANAGEMENT

Minimal Compliance with New Safeguards for Time-and-Materials Contracts for Commercial Services and Safeguards Have Not Been Applied to GSA Schedules Program

Why GAO Did This Study

Federal agencies have used time-and-materials (T&M) contracts to purchase billions of dollars in services. These contracts are risky because the government bears the risk of cost overruns. Effective February 2007, the Federal Acquisition Regulation (FAR) was revised, pursuant to a statutory change, to allow T&M contracts to be used to acquire commercial services under FAR Part 12, which uses a streamlined procurement process. Certain safeguards were included in FAR Part 12, including a requirement that contracting officers prepare a detailed determination and findings (D&F) that no other contract type is suitable. Based on a mandate to review the use of T&M contracts for commercial services, we assessed (1) agencies' reported use of such contracts and what they acquired, (2) the degree to which agencies complied with the new safeguards, and (3) the applicability of the safeguards to General Services Administration (GSA) schedule contracts. GAO reviewed contracts and orders at DOD and civilian agencies and spoke with contracting officials.

What GAO Recommends

GAO recommends that OFPP take steps to clarify the FAR regarding labor-hour contracts and to explicitly apply the Part 12 safeguards to the GSA schedules program, and that it provide guidance to contracting officials on the Part 12 D&F. In oral comments, OFPP agreed with our recommendations. The other six agencies in our review also concurred or had no comment.

View GAO-09-579 or key components. For more information, contact John Hutton at (202) 512-4841 or huttonj@gao.gov.

What GAO Found

From February 2007 to December 2008, agencies reported using commercial item procedures under FAR Part 12 to buy a variety of services through T&M contracts; examples include emergency nursing services on Indian reservations and gunsmith services for the FBI. The reported value of these contracts was $4.4 billion—or less than 1 percent of the total federal dollars obligated for services during this period. Of the $4.4 billion, $3.1 billion had gone through GSA's schedules program. GAO identified about another $6 billion, in addition to the $3.1 billion, in T&M obligations for commercial services under GSA schedule contracts. The reliability of the data reported as T&M contracts using FAR Part 12 procedures is questionable. Of the 149 contracts GAO reviewed, 28 had been miscoded as acquiring commercial services or as T&M contracts. Another issue that indicates a potential underreporting of T&M contracts for commercial services is that contracting officials across the agencies had the mistaken impression that the fixed labor rate in T&M contracts makes these contracts fixed-price. GAO raised this issue with officials from the Office of Federal Procurement Policy (OFPP)—chair of the federal acquisition regulatory council—who agreed that clarification on what constitutes a fixed-price versus labor hour contract would be beneficial. Further, GAO found that contracting officials had different opinions of what generally constitutes a commercial service. Some viewed services intended to meet a specific government requirement as noncommercial, while others viewed similar services as commercial.

The Part 12 D&F was rarely used for the contracts GAO reviewed. The D&F must incorporate four elements, such as a description of the market research conducted. Of 82 contracts reviewed that were explicitly subject to this D&F requirement, only 5 included all the required elements, and 9 partially met the requirement. Of the remaining contracts, 33 had no D&F at all and 35 included the less stringent D&F applicable to noncommercial T&M services. GAO found a general lack of awareness of the Part 12 D&F requirement at the agencies in this review. Agencies' internal management and legal reviews generally did not detect the failure to include the D&F. OFPP officials expressed concern about the lack of compliance with the D&F requirement.

The Part 12 D&F requirement has not been applied to the GSA schedules program. GSA officials stated that the GSA Administrator has discretion about what procedures apply to the program. In a legal opinion to GAO on whether the statutory changes regarding T&M contracts for commercial services apply to the schedules program, GSA concluded that the applicability is uncertain but stated that existing regulations satisfy concerns about use of T&M under the schedules program. GAO notes that these regulations do not require the same level of detailed analysis as does the Part 12 D&F. Further, there is no indication that the statutory requirements cannot apply to items or services under the schedules program. GSA officials said they are in the process of developing a Part 12 D&F for the entire schedules program, but it is not clear how this D&F will act as a safeguard when T&M orders are used.

Contents

Figure

Abbreviations

ANPR	advanced notice of proposed rulemaking
CMS	Centers for Medicare and Medicaid Services
D&F	determination and findings
DFARS	Defense Federal Acquisition Regulation Supplement
DOD	Department of Defense
DOJ	Department of Justice
FAR	Federal Acquisition Regulation
FASA	Federal Acquisition Streamlining Act
FBI	Federal Bureau of Investigation
FPDS-NG	Federal Procurement Data System-Next Generation
GSA	General Services Administration
HHS	Department of Health and Human Services
NASA	National Aeronautics and Space Administration
OFPP	Office of Federal Procurement Policy
SARA	Services Acquisition Reform Act
T&M	time-and-materials
VA	Department of Veterans Affairs

United States Government Accountability Office
Washington, DC 20548

June 24, 2009

Congressional Committees

Time-and-materials (T&M) and labor-hour contracts are used to purchase billions of dollars in services across the federal government. Under these contracts, payments to contractors are based on the number of labor hours billed at a fixed hourly rate—which includes wages, overhead, general and administrative expenses, and profit—and the cost of materials if applicable. These contracts are considered high risk for the government because the contractor's profit is tied to the number of hours worked. Thus, the government bears the risk of cost overruns. The cost growth on T&M and labor-hour contracts can be significant; we and agency inspectors general have reported numerous instances in which the costs grew to more than double the original value—in one case a contract increased to almost 19 times the original price.[1] Although these contracts may be appropriate in certain circumstances, we reported in 2007 that contracting officers used this contract type for ease and flexibility in the face of unclear requirements or funding uncertainties and did not adequately determine, as required, that no other contract type was suitable.[2]

Until recently, the Federal Acquisition Regulation (FAR) prohibited use of any other contract type except fixed-price for the acquisition of commercial items. Under FAR procedures for acquisition of commercial items and services, government agencies can acquire goods or services via a streamlined procurement process based on the idea that market forces will help ensure good prices.[3] The question of whether or not T&M contracts could be used for commercial services had been the subject of

---

[1] See GAO, *Defense Contracting: Improved Insight and Controls Needed over DOD's Time-and-Materials Contracts*, GAO-07-273 (Washington, D.C.: June 29, 2007).

[2] In this report, we use the term "T&M" to refer to both T&M and labor-hour contracts, as labor-hour contracts differ from T&M contracts only in that the contractor does not supply materials.

[3] The FAR definition of commercial item includes commercial services, which are defined as services of a type offered and sold competitively in substantial quantities in the commercial marketplace based on established catalog or market prices. FAR § 2.101. For the purpose of this report, we are focused on the acquisition of commercial services. In addition, we use the term fixed-price to refer to both firm-fixed-price and fixed-price with economic price adjustment.

debate and an issue of some contention. Proponents believed that increased use of T&M contracts for commercial services would encourage more commercial firms to compete for government business, while others, such as the Department of Defense Inspector General, opposed expanded use of this high-risk contract type. In 2003, the Services Acquisition Reform Act[4] (SARA) explicitly provided that the FAR shall include authority for the use of T&M contracts for the procurement of commercial services. Part 12 of the FAR, "Acquisition of Commercial Items," was subsequently amended, effective February 2007, to reflect this change.

The FAR Part 12 revisions included procedural safeguards to ensure that T&M contracts for commercial services are used only when no other contract type is suitable and that cost growth is monitored due to the inherent risks to the government of this contract type.[5] Contracting officers using FAR Part 12 procedures to buy commercial services under T&M contracts are required to conduct additional, more detailed analysis than is required when buying noncommercial services using T&M contracts.[6] For example, the contracting officer must prepare a detailed justification, called a determination and findings (D&F), to explain why no other contract type is suitable for the procurement. The justification is required to contain several elements, including a discussion of market research conducted for the procurement and a description of actions planned to maximize the use of fixed-price contracts on future acquisitions for the same requirements. Additionally, the contracting officer is to include in the contract a ceiling price, which the contractor exceeds at its own risk, and any subsequent change in the ceiling price may be made only after the contracting officer determines that such a change is in the best interest of the procuring agency.

The Part 12 D&F requirement is not explicitly mentioned in FAR Subpart 8.4, which sets forth procedures pertaining to the General Services Administration's (GSA) federal supply schedules program. Under the

---

[4] Pub. L. No. 108-136, § 1436 (2003), which amended section 8002(d) of the Federal Acquisition Streamlining Act of 1994, Pub. L. No. 103-355.

[5] Our June 2007 report did not assess compliance with this requirement, as it was implemented after our review was underway.

[6] On November 24, 2008, DOD revised its acquisition regulation, the Defense Federal Acquisition Regulation Supplement (DFARS), to establish D&F requirements for all T&M contracts for noncommercial services similar to those required by section 12.207 of the FAR for T&M contracts for commercial services. DFARS § 216.601.

schedules program, GSA establishes long-term, governmentwide contracts for commercially available goods and services, under which federal agencies can issue orders. Even prior to the February 2007 changes to the FAR, GSA had schedule contracts under which agencies were issuing T&M orders for commercial services. According to GSA, it allowed this practice based on its interpretation of the Federal Acquisition Streamlining Act of 1994 (FASA), which provided that fixed-price contracts be used to the "maximum extent practicable" for acquisition of commercial items and was silent on whether T&M contracts could be used.[7]

The Conference Report for the National Defense Authorization Act for Fiscal Year 2004 directed us to report on the use of T&M contracts for commercial services across government agencies.[8] Accordingly, we (1) identified the extent to which agencies have reported using T&M contracts and GSA schedule T&M orders for commercial services and what they are acquiring using this contract type, (2) evaluated the degree to which agencies complied with the FAR Part 12 safeguards, and (3) determined the applicability of the safeguards to the GSA schedules program.

To identify the extent to which agencies have acquired commercial services under T&M contracts and orders and to determine what services they are buying, we analyzed obligations coded in the Federal Procurement Data System-Next Generation (FPDS-NG) as having used commercial item procedures, i.e., FAR Part 12 procedures.[9] We selected those agencies with the greatest reported use of this contract type during the period from October 1, 2001, to June 30, 2008. Our primary focus was on contracts outside of the GSA schedules program because the FAR Part 12 D&F requirement was explicitly applicable to those contracts. However, because the FPDS-NG data showed that a large percentage of the reported dollars and actions were through GSA schedule orders (under FAR Subpart 8.4), we also reviewed T&M orders issued under GSA schedule contracts at each agency in our review. Further, based on data

[7] Pub. L. No. 103-355, § 8002(d).

[8] Our review was directed by the conferees in the Conference Report accompanying the National Defense Authorization Act for Fiscal Year 2004. Although the Conference Report directed us to report on these issues within 1 year of enactment of the act, we initiated our review after the February 2007 FAR rule implementing the National Defense Authorization Act for Fiscal Year 2004 provision went into effect.

[9] These obligations are indicated in data element 10H in FPDS-NG, "Commercial Item Acquisition Procedures."

reported in FPDS-NG, we reviewed a limited number of T&M contracts for commercial services that had been awarded prior to the February 2007 changes to FAR Part 12 commercial procedures to better understand the circumstances of those procurements. In total, we reviewed 149 contract files. At the Department of Defense (DOD), we selected one location for each military service with high reported obligations for T&M commercial services. Our sample represents all of the T&M contracts for commercial services reported in FPDS-NG at the Departments of Justice (DOJ), Health and Human Services (HHS), and Veterans Affairs (VA), as well as the National Aeronautics and Space Administration (NASA) during the October 2001 to June 2008 time period. These 5 agencies represent 97 percent of obligations coded as T&M contracts awarded using commercial item procedures from October 2001 to June 2008.

To corroborate that the contracts in our sample were T&M and that commercial services were acquired as indicated in FPDS-NG, we reviewed the contracts and orders for commercial or T&M clauses and other contract documentation as necessary, or, when documentation was not sufficient, spoke with the contracting officer. To determine the government's use of T&M contracts for commercial services relative to its obligations for services as a whole, we analyzed FPDS-NG data from February 12, 2007 (when the new FAR rule was implemented) to December 31, 2008.

To determine the degree to which agencies' use of T&M contracts for commercial services complied with the FAR Part 12 D&F requirement, we reviewed contract files and interviewed over 100 contracting and procurement policy officials. We requested and received a legal opinion from GSA as to whether the statutory change allowing the use of T&M contracts for commercial services and the FAR D&F requirement are applicable to the GSA schedules program.[10] Appendix I contains additional details on our scope and methodology and our sample. We conducted this performance audit from September 2008 to June 2009, in accordance with generally accepted government auditing standards. Those standards require that we plan and perform the audit to obtain sufficient, appropriate evidence to provide a reasonable basis for our findings and conclusions based on our audit objectives. We believe that the evidence obtained provides a reasonable basis for our findings and conclusions based on our audit objectives.

---

[10] FASA § 8002(d) and FAR § 12.207.

Background

Federal agencies can choose from among several different contract types, including T&M contracts, to acquire products and services. This choice is the principal means that agencies have for allocating cost risk between the government and the contractor. The government's basis for payments, contractor's obligations, and the party assuming more risk for cost overruns changes depends upon the type of contract used—fixed-price, T&M, or cost-reimbursement.

Table 1: Contract Types

Fixed-price	T&M	Cost-reimbursement
Government pays a fixed price and is guaranteed an end item or service whether actual total cost of product or service falls short of or exceeds the contract price. May also pay an award or incentive fee related to performance.	**Government** pays fixed per-hour labor rates that include wages, overhead, general and administrative costs, and profit; government may reimburse contractor for other direct costs, such as travel and materials costs. Government is not guaranteed a completed end item or service within the ceiling price.	**Government** pays contractor's allowable costs, which do not include profit. Also pays a fee, which may be related to performance. Government is not guaranteed a completed end item or service within the estimated cost.
Contractor provides an acceptable deliverable at the time, place, and price specified in the contract.	**Contractor** makes good faith effort to meet government's needs within the ceiling price.	**Contractor** makes good faith effort to meet government's needs within the estimated cost.
Who assumes risk of cost overrun? Contractor.	**Who assumes risk of cost overrun?** Government.	**Who assumes risk of cost overrun?** Government.

Sources: FAR, Defense Federal Acquisition Regulation Supplement, DOD Contract Pricing Preference Guide (data); GAO (presentation and analysis).

T&M contracts constitute a high risk to the government.[11] The contractor provides its best efforts to accomplish the objectives of the contract up to the maximum number of hours authorized under the contract. Each hour of work authorizes the contractor to charge the government an established labor rate which includes profit. These contracts are considered high risk for the government because the contractor's profit is tied to the number of hours worked. Thus, the government bears the risk of cost overruns. Therefore the FAR provides that appropriate government monitoring of contractor performance is required to give reasonable assurance that efficient methods and effective cost controls are being used. Further, because of the risks involved, the FAR directs that T&M contracts may only be used when it is not possible at the time of award to estimate accurately the extent or duration of the work or to anticipate costs with

---

[11] The FAR provides that a time-and-materials contract provides no positive profit incentive to the contractor for cost control or labor efficiency. T&M contracts exhibit some characteristics of fixed-price contracts in that T&M contracts contain fixed hourly labor rates and a ceiling price which the contractor exceeds at its own risk. FAR § 16.601.

any reasonable degree of confidence.[12] For many years, federal regulations have required contracting officers to justify in writing that no other contract type (such as fixed-price) is suitable before using a T&M contract.[13]

Commercial services comprise services for support of commercial items and services of a type offered and sold competitively in substantial quantities in the commercial marketplace based on established catalog or market prices.[14] During the 1990s, Congress enacted a number of laws to increase the government's use of commercial practices to make government buying more efficient. The benefits of using commercial practices were seen as creating greater access to commercial markets (products and service types) with increased competition, better prices, and new market entrants and/or technologies. Commercial acquisition practices also present several advantages to contractors when doing business with the government, such as generally not being required to submit cost or pricing data. While the acquisition procedures in FAR Part 12 for purchasing commercial services allow for a streamlined process, prices are accepted based on competition and availability in the marketplace rather than the government's review of a contractor's cost and pricing data. Improperly classifying an acquisition as commercial can leave the government vulnerable to accepting prices that may not have been established by the marketplace.[15]

FASA authorized the use of fixed-price contracts for the acquisition of commercial items, but it did not explicitly authorize the use of T&M

---

[12] FAR § 16.601(c).

[13] FAR § 16.601(d).

[14] Commercial items include items that are of a type customarily used by the general public or nongovernmental entities for purposes other than governmental purposes and have been sold, leased, or licensed to the general public or have been offered for sale, lease or license to the general public. 41 U.S.C.§ 403(12); FAR § 2.101, definition of commercial item.

[15] Contracting officers may not request cost or pricing data if they determine that prices have been subject to adequate price competition, prices are set by law or regulation, or when a commercial item is acquired. FAR § 15.403-1(b). The government is permitted to obtain pricing information from sources other than the offering contractor to support a determination of price reasonableness. If this information proves inadequate, the government can require the offering contractor to provide additional information, known as information other than cost or pricing data, although the government must, to the maximum extent practicable, limit the scope of the request to include only information in a form regularly maintained by the offering contractor. FAR § 15.403-3.

contracts for such acquisitions. [16] SARA specifically authorized the use of T&M contracts for the acquisition of commercial services with certain safeguards to ensure proper use of these contracts. [17] The implementing regulations included additional requirements as safeguards under FAR Part 12. [18]

Table 2 summarizes the FAR safeguards when using T&M contracts under FAR Part 12 acquisition procedures for commercial items; under FAR Part 16, acquisition procedures for noncommercial services; and under FAR Subpart 8.4, GSA schedule contracts.

---

[16] Pub. L. No. 103-355, § 8002(d).

[17] Section 1432 of SARA, which is Title XIV of the National Defense Authorization Act for Fiscal Year 2004, Pub. L. No. 108-136, (2003), amended section 8002(d) of FASA.

[18] FAR § 12.207.

Table 2: Summary of Relevant FAR Provisions Pertaining to T&M Contracts and to Orders Under the GSA Schedule Program.

	Requirements for T&M contracts for commercial services. FAR Section 12.207(b)	Requirements for T&M contracts for noncommercial services. FAR Section 16.601(d)	Requirements when ordering off the GSA schedule. FAR Section 8.405-2(e)
Justification for using T&M	The contracting officer must execute a D&F for the contract that no other contract type is suitable. At a minimum, the D&F shall— (i) Include a description of the market research conducted; (ii) Establish that it is not possible at the time of placing the contract or order to accurately estimate the extent or duration of the work or to anticipate costs with any reasonable degree of certainty; (iii) Establish that the requirement has been structured to maximize the use of firm-fixed-price or fixed-price with economic price adjustment contracts on future acquisitions for the same or similar requirements; and (iv) Describe actions planned to maximize the use of firm-fixed-price or fixed-price with economic price adjustment contracts on future acquisitions for the same requirements. The D&F shall be signed by the contracting officer prior to the execution of the base period or any option periods of the contracts and approved by the head of the contracting activity prior to the execution of the base period when the base period plus any option periods exceeds three years.	The contracting officer must prepare a D&F that no other contract type is suitable. The D&F shall be signed by the contracting officer prior to the execution of the base period or any option periods of the contracts and approved by the head of the contracting activity prior to the execution of the base period when the base period plus any option periods exceeds three years.	The ordering activity shall document the rationale for using other than a firm-fixed-price order.
Ceiling Prices	The contracting officer must include a ceiling price in the contract or order that the contractor exceeds at its own risk and authorize any subsequent change in the ceiling price only upon a determination, documented in the contract file, that it is in the best interest of the procuring agency to change the ceiling price.	The contract must include a ceiling price that the contractor exceeds at its own risk. The contracting officer shall document the contract file to justify the reasons for and amount of any subsequent change in the ceiling price.	No requirement specified.

Source: FAR.

Note: It is important to note that, as of November 24, 2008, T&M contracts for noncommercial services awarded by DOD require similar procedures, including the more detailed D&F described in FAR Part 12, as that required for T&M contracts using acquisition procedures for commercial items and services. DFARS § 216.601. This requirement went into effect after the time frame of our contract sample for this review. It has not been applied to civilian agencies with respect to T&M contracts for noncommercial services.

The FAR Part 12 revisions also added safeguards for agencies using T&M pricing on indefinite-delivery contracts for commercial services.[19] Specifically, indefinite-delivery contracts for commercial services awarded using Part 12 procedures may allow for the use of fixed-price or T&M orders, and contracting officers are required to execute the Part 12 D&F for each order placed on a T&M basis. If the contract only allows for the issuance of orders on a T&M basis, the Part 12 D&F is required to be executed to support the basic contract and also explain why using an alternative fixed-price structure is not practicable. The D&F for this type of contract is required to be approved one level above the contracting officer. By contrast, the section of FAR Part 16 pertaining to T&M services does not explicitly address the D&F requirement for indefinite-delivery contracts.[20]

Concerns by DOD and Congress over the increased use of T&M contracts have sparked some actions to curb DOD's use of T&M in general and for the acquisition of commercial services in particular. In June 2007, we reported that DOD's use of T&M contracts had steadily increased and that contracting officials frequently failed to ensure that this contract type was used only when no other contract type was suitable.[21] Little effort had been made to convert follow-on work to a less risky contract type when historical pricing data existed, despite guidance to do so. Based on our recommendations for improved oversight, DOD's Defense Procurement and Acquisition Policy office, in March 2008, began requiring military departments and defense agencies to establish procedures for analyzing whether T&M contracts and orders under indefinite-delivery contracts are used when other contract types are suitable. Each department or agency was to provide an assessment of the appropriate use of T&M contracts for any contracting activity that obligated more than 10 percent of its total fiscal year 2007 obligations for services using T&M contracts or orders. The assessment was to include actions that will be taken to reduce the use of T&M contracts whenever possible.

Further, the Acquisition Improvement and Accountability Act of 2007 required DOD to revise its acquisition regulation to require contracting officers to determine in writing that the offerer has submitted sufficient

---

[19] FAR §12.207(c).

[20] FAR §16.601.

[21] GAO-07-273.

information to evaluate price reasonableness for commercial services that are not offered and sold competitively in substantial quantities in the commercial marketplace but are "of a type" offered and sold competitively in substantial quantities in the commercial marketplace. The act also specifies that DOD's revised regulation shall ensure that the procedures applicable to T&M contracts for commercial services may be used only for the following:

- services procured for support of a commercial item;
- emergency repair services;
- any other commercial services only to the extent that the head of the agency approves a determination in writing by the contracting officer that
  - the services to be acquired are commercial services;
  - the offeror has submitted sufficient information to evaluate the price reasonableness of the services, if they are not offered and sold competitively in substantial quantities in the commercial marketplace;
  - such services are commonly sold to the general public through use of T&M or labor-hour contracts; and
  - the use of a T&M or labor-hour contract type is in the best interest of the government. [22]

We did not assess DOD's compliance with these provisions because they have not yet been implemented. [23]

---

[22] 41 U.S.C. § 403 (12).

[23] See section 805 of Title VIII of the National Defense Authorization Act for Fiscal Year 2008. Pub. L. No. 110-181. As of May 29, 2009, the DFARS case that will implement this provision had not been issued. The National Defense Authorization Act for Fiscal Year 2009, enacted October. 14, 2008, directed that the FAR be modified within 180 days of enactment to include a similar provision, which would be applied to all government agencies. Pub. L. 110-417 § 868 (2008). As of May 29, 2009, the FAR had not been revised to include the provisions.

Federal Agencies Have Reported Limited Use of T&M Contracts for Commercial Services but Reliability of Data Is in Doubt

Federal agencies have reported relatively limited use of T&M contracts and GSA schedule T&M orders to purchase commercial services, based on those obligations coded in FPDS-NG as using T&M contracts and orders under commercial item procedures. From February 12, 2007, when the FAR change that allowed T&M acquisitions for commercial services was implemented, to December 31, 2008, $4.4 billion—less than 1 percent of total federal obligations for services—was reported.

Figure 1 presents information on the total reported obligations for services (i.e., commercial and noncommercial) compared to obligations coded as (1) having acquired commercial services, (2) as T&M contracts for services, and (3) as T&M contracts for commercial services from February 12, 2007, to December 31, 2008.

Figure 1: Total Reported Obligations for Services Compared to Obligations Coded as (1) Having Acquired Commercial Services, (2) as T&M Contracts for Services, and (3) as T&M Contracts for Commercial Services From February 12, 2007 to December 31, 2008

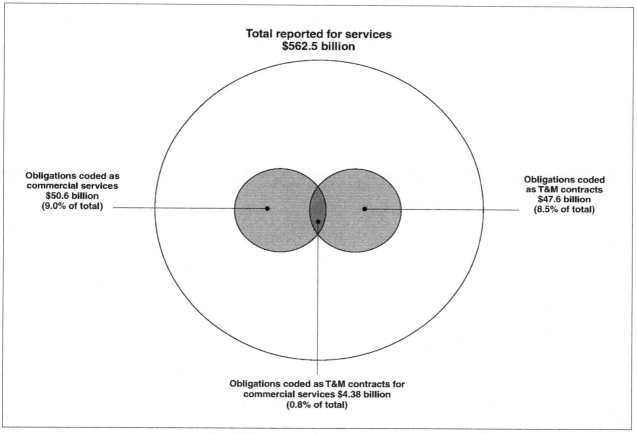

Total reported for services
$562.5 billion

Obligations coded as
commercial services
$50.6 billion
(9.0% of total)

Obligations coded
as T&M contracts
$47.6 billion
(8.5% of total)

Obligations coded as T&M contracts for
commercial services $4.38 billion
(0.8% of total)

Source: FPDS-NG for data; GAO for presentation.

Note: T&M dollars include labor-hour contracts and orders.

The vast majority of the $4.4 billion in obligations coded as T&M for commercial services were for services actually acquired under GSA schedule contracts ($3.1 billion). The FPDS-NG user manual defines commercial item procedures as those that use FAR Part 12 acquisition procedures, but our analysis of FPDS-NG data showed that these orders had been issued through FAR Subpart 8.4, pertaining to GSA schedule contracts, and thus had been miscoded based on the definition in the user

GAO-09-579 T&M Contracts for Commercial Services

manual.[24] Although our overall focus was on nonschedule T&M orders for commercial services, we identified additional obligations under T&M orders placed on GSA schedule contracts. From February 2007 to December 2008, approximately $6 billion of the $47.6 billion in obligations coded as T&M contracts were through the GSA schedule program, in addition to the $3.1 billion that had been miscoded as having used FAR Part 12. Thus, the full picture of the government's use of T&M for commercial services for this time period was approximately $10.4 billion—about 90 percent of which was under GSA schedule contracts.

Agencies reported purchasing a variety of commercial services using T&M contracts and orders during this time period. The top 10 types of commercial services reported as purchased using T&M contracts were as shown in table 3.

Table 3: Top 10 Commercial Services Coded as Using T&M Contracts and Orders to Acquire Commercial Items from February 12, 2007, to December 31, 2008

Type of commercial services	Dollars obligated	Percent of total dollars obligated under T&M contracts and orders for commercial services
Other Automatic Data Processing & Telecommunications Services	$686,044,403	15.7
Engineering and Technical Services	647,682,748	14.8
Other Professional Services	478,541,816	10.9
Program Management/Support Services	357,981,397	8.2
Automated Information System Services	225,187,839	5.1
Management Services/Contract and Procurement Support	201,641,198	4.6
Logistics Supports Services	189,831,359	4.3
Other Management Support Services	186,479,109	4.3
Automatic Data Processing Systems Analysis Services	182,481,817	4.2
Automatic Data Processing Systems Development Services	$120,849,955	2.8

Source: FPDS-NG for data; GAO for presentation.

---

[24] We brought this issue to the attention of officials at the Office of Federal Procurement Policy and GSA, who said they would look into the matter.

GAO-09-579 T&M Contracts for Commercial Services

Our sample of 149 contracts and orders provides additional details on the variety of commercial services procured under T&M contracts. For example:

- The Army purchased patent legal services for inventions resulting from biomedical, chemical, and other research.
- The Indian Health Service, within HHS, entered into a contract for emergency nursing services and inpatient nursing services for a healthcare center.
- The Navy contracted for repair services for a Navy vessel undergoing overhaul at the Norfolk Naval Shipyard.
- The VA purchased project management services for its MyHealtheVet Web site, which provides access to health information, tools, and services.
- The Federal Bureau of Investigation (FBI) purchased certified gunsmith services to repair and perform preventative maintenance on firearms.
- NASA entered into a contract for translation, interpretation, visa processing, and logistical support services.

Errors, Misunderstandings, and Differing Opinions Cast Doubt on Reliability of Reported Data

Maintaining accurate data is an essential component of good oversight and helps lead to informed decisions. In our sample of T&M contracts for commercial services, we found that the quality of the data reported in FPDS-NG was compromised in several ways.

First, 28 of the 149 contracts and orders in our sample from October 1, 2001, to June 30, 2008, were incorrectly coded in FPDS-NG. Our review of the contract files revealed that 19 were coded as having acquired commercial services when they did not, and 10 were coded as T&M contracts when they were fixed-price, as shown in table 4.[25]

---

[25] To confirm that the contracts in our sample were correctly coded as having acquired commercial services or as T&M, we reviewed the contracts and documentation in the contract files. For example, we looked for relevant FAR clauses (FAR 52.212-4—Contract Terms and Conditions- Commercial Items) in the contract to confirm that commercial services were acquired. Where the documentation was not clear, we spoke with contracting officers.

Table 4: Contracts and Orders from our Sample Incorrectly Coded in FPDS-NG as Having Acquired Commercial Services or as T&M

Agency	Miscoding Type	
	Incorrectly coded as having acquired commercial services	Incorrectly coded as T&M
Air Force	9	0
Army	0	0
Navy	0	6
DOJ	4	1
HHS	4	1
NASA	1	0
VA	1	2
Total[a]	19	10

Source: GAO file reviews.

Note: This table does not address the overall coding errors, discussed above, where GSA schedule orders had been coded as using FAR Part 12 procedures.

Twelve of the 28 contracts or orders were awarded prior to the February 2007 FAR change pertaining to the use of T&M contracts for commercial services.

[a]One contract at DOJ was incorrectly coded as both T&M and as having acquired commercial services.

Several of the contracting officers we interviewed attributed these miscodings to errors made during input of data into the federal procurement data system. For example, the Air Force had planned to establish indefinite-delivery/indefinite-quantity contracts for advisory and assistance services using FAR Part 12 acquisition procedures for commercial services. However, because cost-reimbursement orders were contemplated under the contracts—which the FAR prohibits for commercial services—the Air Force decided not to award the contracts using FAR Part 12 acquisition procedures. Agency officials stated that the contracts were then mistakenly coded as having used acquisition of commercial item procedures.

In addition, we found that T&M contracts for commercial services may be underreported based on a misunderstanding about contract type among contracting officials in most of the government agencies in our review. Some contracting officers had the incorrect belief that the fixed labor rate component of T&M contracts renders them fixed-price. [26] In fact, some contracts in our sample were referred to in the contract file as "firm fixed price labor hour," a contract type that does not exist. Despite the fact that labor rates are fixed under T&M contracts, the overall ceiling price is not a firm, fixed price because the contractor will be paid based on the number of hours worked (up to the ceiling price). Some contracting officers acknowledged having coded other similar contracts outside of those in our sample as fixed-price, thus potentially understating the use, and correlated risk to the government, of T&M contracts. Following are some examples that highlight contracting officials' confusion about fixed-price versus labor-hour contracts (even though these contracts in our sample had been correctly coded as labor-hour).

- Contracting officers at HHS's Indian Health Services stated that although a few of their contracts for medical professionals had been coded as labor-hour, these contracts were typical of the contracts they usually code as fixed-price. One contracting officer explained that if the hours are reasonably well known in advance—"shift labor," for example—then the estimated hours written into the contract are considered fixed-price. However, another contracting officer explained that Indian Health Services pays contractors for actual hours worked, regardless of the estimate written into the contract.

- A contracting officer at HHS's Program Support Center told us that a contract in our sample, for maintenance and repair services, had mistakenly been entered as a labor-hour contract in FPDS-NG. He believed it should have been coded as fixed-price because the dollars obligated reflected a fixed hourly rate multiplied by the hours worked, but later conceded that the contract was actually a labor-hour contract.

- An FBI contracting officer maintained that a labor-hour contract in our sample, for gunsmith services, should have been coded as fixed-price because the labor rate was fixed. The contract purchases the services of one person to repair and maintain firearms for FBI training teams. Although the contract requires these services during "normal business hours" 5 days a week, it also allows the contractor to bill for preapproved overtime when necessary and includes a maximum number of hours to be billed on the contract.

---

[26] A fixed-price contract provides for a firm price or, in appropriate cases, an adjustable price. FAR § 16.201.

When we raised this confusion about contract type with officials from the Office of Federal Procurement Policy (OFPP), they agreed that clarification to the contracting community on what constitutes a fixed price versus a labor hour contract would be beneficial.[27]

We also spoke with contracting officers about how they generally define a service as commercial and found that individuals had different opinions about whether or not certain services are commercial, which may be contributing to issues with data reliability in FPDS-NG.[28] Many contracting officers defined a commercial service as being readily available in the commercial marketplace. However, several officials told us that in certain cases, a service could reasonably be considered either commercial or noncommercial. For example, a DOD official stated that a contract for aircraft repair services could be considered either a commercial or noncommercial purchase depending on the contracting officer's interpretation. On the other hand, Air Force officials we spoke with view aircraft maintenance—even on military aircraft—as predominantly commercial since aircraft mechanics are broadly available commercially. Some contracting officers stated they would consider services that require specific knowledge of government requirements to be noncommercial. For example, a DOJ procurement policy official told us that although a contracting officer used FAR Part 12 commercial acquisition procedures to award a contract for technical services, including the installation of modules for DOJ's financial management system (one of the T&M contracts in our sample), he did not consider the service to be commercial because it was specific to DOJ's needs. He cited a contract for trash pick-up as an example of a commercial contract. In another example, a Navy contracting officer explained that although the majority of her purchases are for commercial items or services, if a purchase is completely exclusive to the Navy—such as for equipment used on submarines or Navy ships—she would consider it noncommercial.

---

[27] The OFPP Administrator serves as chair of the Federal Acquisition Regulatory Council (FAR Council). The FAR Council—whose members include the DOD Director of Defense Procurement and Acquisition Policy, NASA's Associate Administrator for Procurement, and the GSA Chief Acquisition Officer—oversees development and maintenance of the FAR.

[28] Our discussions with contracting officers on this matter were of a general nature. For specific procurements, market research is an essential element for the acquisition of commercial items and is used to establish the foundation for the agency description of need, the solicitation, and resulting contract. FAR § 12.202.

In addition, although all services available on the GSA schedule are described as commercial in the FAR, we found cases where agencies ordering these services did not consider them to be commercial.[29] GSA officials confirmed that they consider everything under the schedules program to be commercial, even if items or services are slightly modified to meet specific requirements. However, they acknowledged that if significant modifications are made, the items ordered may be out of scope of the underlying GSA contract. The following are some examples from our review where agency officials used the GSA schedules program but considered the procurement to be noncommercial.

- At one Air Force location, contracting officers told us that they did not consider any of their seven GSA orders in our sample, such as an order for program management and technical support for the Air Force's telecommunications monitoring and assessment program, to be commercial. They only discovered that these orders were being automatically coded in FPDS-NG as having used commercial procedures when we identified them in our sample for review.

- NASA had purchased environmental management and safety support services under a GSA schedule contract, but, according to NASA contracting officers, the actual services ordered were so technical and specialized that they did not consider them to be commercial services. They had used the GSA schedule primarily to identify qualified commercial vendors who could perform this specialized work.

- The Centers for Medicare and Medicaid Services (CMS) at HHS issued an order under a GSA schedule contract for the design and build of a knowledge management system for CMS's Center for Beneficiary Services. According to the contracting officer, because the system was custom-designed for CMS, it is not commercial.

FAR Safeguards for T&M Contracts for Commercial Services Rarely Used

Under FAR Part 12, T&M contracts or orders may be used to acquire commercial services if the contracting officer executes a D&F which sets forth sufficient facts and rationale to justify that no other contract type is suitable. At a minimum, the D&F must:

1. include a description of the market research conducted;

---

[29] FAR Section 8.402(a).

2. establish that it is not possible at the time of placing the contract or order to accurately estimate the extent or duration of the work or to anticipate costs with any reasonable degree of certainty;
3. establish that the requirement has been structured to maximize the use of fixed-price on future acquisitions for the same or similar requirements; and
4. describe actions planned to maximize the use of fixed-price contracts on future acquisitions for the same requirements.

Of the 149 contracts and orders in our sample, 82 were subject to this D&F requirement.[30] Of these 82 contracts and orders, only 5 had a FAR Part 12 D&F that addressed each required element. No D&F had been prepared for many of the contracts and orders. Further, for almost half of the contracts and orders, contracting officials had improperly used the less rigorous Part 16 D&F instead of the Part 12 D&F for commercial services. We found a general lack of awareness of the Part 12 D&F requirement at the agencies in our review. Many contracting officials, including some policy officials, across the agencies in our review were unfamiliar with this Part 12 safeguard. We raised this issue with officials from OFPP, who were concerned at the general lack of compliance with this key safeguard pertaining to T&M contracts for commercial services.

Table 5 sets forth the breakdown of D&Fs for the 82 contracts and orders in our sample that were subject to the Part 12 D&F.

---

[30] These 82 contracts and orders were confirmed as (1) T&M contracts or orders for commercial services (2) having been awarded after the FAR revisions to Part 12 took effect on February 12, 2007, and (3) not having been awarded through GSA schedule contracts.

Table 5: Number and Type of D&Fs for Non-GSA Contracts and Orders in Our Sample Subject to the FAR Part 12 D&F Requirement

Agency	Non-GSA contracts and orders				
	Complete Part 12 D&F	Partial Part 12 D&F	Part 16 D&F	No D&F	Total
Air Force	2	1	5	0	8
Army	0	2	18	8	28
Navy	2	2	8	4	16
DOJ	0	2	3	2	7
HHS	1	2	0	14	17
NASA	0	0	1	0	1
VA	0	0	0	5	5
Total	**5**	**9**	**35**	**33**	**82**

Source: GAO analysis of data from agency contract files.

Note: We determined that a D&F was complete if it made reference to FAR Section 12.207 and at least mentioned all of the four required elements of the D&F. For example, if a D&F stated the outcomes of the market research conducted but did not describe the research conducted, we still gave credit for having addressed the requirement in FAR Section 12.207(b)(1) to describe the market research conducted. A partial Part 12 D&F included some but not all of the four required elements.

Sixteen of the contracts and orders in our Army sample had the same Part 16 D&F that was used to award a multiple award contract for patent legal services.

In some cases, contracting officers had incorrectly concluded that a D&F was not necessary. For example, two contracting officers at the Navy told us that they did not complete a D&F because they did not believe contracts below the simplified acquisition threshold required a D&F—which is inconsistent with the FAR. [31] In another instance, an Air Force contracting officer who had included Part 12 D&Fs in two contracts in our sample executed only a Part 16 D&F for a third contract because he believed that a Part 12 D&F was not required for a simplified acquisition.

The nine D&Fs in our sample that had some but not all of the discrete elements required by FAR Part 12 typically omitted a description of the market research conducted or actions planned to maximize use of fixed-price contracts for future acquisitions for the same or similar services. For

---

[31] There is no indication in the FAR that FAR Section 12.207 does not apply to contracts below the simplified acquisition threshold, which is generally $100,000. FAR Section 12.207 does not, however, apply to purchases below the micropurchase threshold, which is generally $3,000. See FAR Section 2.101 definition of the simplified acquisition and micropurchase threshold.

GAO-09-579 T&M Contracts for Commercial Services

example, one D&F for a DOJ contract for consulting services for the National Prison Rape Elimination Commission, awarded on a sole-source basis, included information on the services needed but did not describe the market research conducted. The D&F states that neither the scope of work nor the contractor's level of effort can be determined with a degree of accuracy necessary to develop a reliable cost estimate on which to base a fixed-price award. It further states that the work entails professional and other administrative services for which no reliable specifications exist, and the precise method of accomplishment cannot be established in advance. However, the D&F does not describe actions planned to maximize the use of fixed-price contracts on future acquisitions for the same requirements.

The five FAR Part 12 D&Fs we found that addressed all the required elements included the rationale for a T&M contract and discussed how future requirements could potentially shift to a fixed-price contract. For example, in preparing a D&F for a Navy contract for the overhaul and repair of naval vessels, contracting officials not only described the market research, but thoroughly documented the market survey performed, including a description of applicable services provided by potential bidders in the marketplace. They also described how they would employ fixed pricing for stable labor expenses and monitor the volatility of other labor categories to determine if the services could be purchased on a fixed-price basis in the future. In another example, at HHS, a contracting officer completed a Part 12 D&F for a contract for less than 6 months of network administrative support services. The D&F stated that the market research had identified an 8(a) company to provide the services.[32] It also explained that the requirement had been structured to maximize fixed pricing by limiting the period of performance and that there was no anticipated need for this service to continue in the future. In yet another example, at the Air Force, the contracting officer prepared a complete Part 12 D&F for a contract for intelligence support services that addressed all of the required elements. The D&F explained that a small business was identified as the best option for the procurement and described the outcome of the market research conducted. Further, the D&F stated that information obtained from the procurement would be used to develop

---

[32] The 8(a) program is one of the federal government's primary means for developing small businesses owned by socially and economically disadvantaged individuals. Firms approved as 8(a) participants can receive business development assistance from the Small Business Administration.

fixed pricing for future procurements, which would be better defined and more concise.

In addition to a more detailed D&F, the FAR also requires the contracting officer to document that each change to the ceiling price of a T&M contract for commercial services is in the best interest of the procuring agency. In general, the contracts in our sample that were subject to the FAR Part 12 requirements did not have increases in the ceiling price. However, in the instances where an increase did occur, contracting officers did not always follow the FAR requirement. A contract at HHS for financial services management more than doubled in value over the original "estimated not-to-exceed" cost. No written justification was provided for why this increase was in the best interest of the procuring agency. The contracting officer stated that the not-to-exceed amount on the contract was only an estimate and had not identified a separate ceiling price—which is required by the FAR Part 12. On the other hand, some contracts with ceiling price increases did include a description of why the increase was necessary.[33] For example, we reviewed three orders at the Army for patent legal services that documented why ceiling price increases were necessary—which was essentially due to a change in the acquisition strategy for obtaining these services. After establishing a multiple award contract with 23 vendors, contractors were asked to submit proposals to complete ongoing work that, according to contracting officials, was previously purchased on government credit cards. In one case, a task order increased from approximately $100,000 to $500,000 because the contractor had initially misunderstood the request for proposals and submitted a proposal for only a limited scope of work; it subsequently revised its proposal to address all of the Army's stated requirements. In another example at the U.S. Marshals Service, the ceiling price on a contract for aircraft maintenance services increased from $250,000 to $400,000 through three successive modifications, and all the modifications included a detailed description of the need for additional funds.

---

[33] FAR Section 12.207 (b)(ii) provides that the contracting officer authorize any subsequent change in the ceiling price only upon a determination, documented in the contract file, that it is in the best interest of the procuring agency to change the ceiling price. In the examples presented here, the contracting officer did not always include the statement that this change was in the best interest of the procuring agency in the documentation, but nevertheless did include information on the rationale for the ceiling price change.

Agency Training and Contract Review Processes Did Not Include FAR Part 12 Safeguards

Clear guidance and training are needed to successfully introduce and implement changes to regulations. The DOD offices we visited were the only locations in our review that provided general training seminars or guidance on the changes to FAR Part 12 permitting the use of T&M contracts for commercial services, but none provided written guidance or training on the more detailed D&F requirement. Navy contracting officials recognized this omission during our visit and subsequently provided additional training to their contracting officials.[34] Army officials told us that they had discussed the new D&F requirement in a meeting with contracting officers but had not issued any written guidance. None of the civilian agencies in our review had provided formal guidance or training to their contracting officers on the safeguards.

Officials who were aware of the Part 12 safeguards frequently found out through their own initiative. For example, in our sample of 17 HHS contracts subject to the FAR Part 12 D&F requirement, 2 contained partial D&Fs and 1, issued by the Program Support Center, contained all of the D&F elements. The contracting officer responsible for the complete D&F indicated that he became aware of the D&F requirement through his own FAR research and had not received guidance from headquarters. The other 2 partial Part 12 D&Fs were issued by another HHS component, the Food and Drug Administration. The head of contracting who signed these D&Fs said that she had also learned of the Part 12 D&F requirement by researching the FAR. At DOJ, officials at the Office of Justice Programs explained that they became aware of the FAR Part 12 D&F requirement through a paid subscription for updates to a contract checklist from an outside vendor. When awarding a contract for consulting services, a contracting officer from that office prepared a Part 12 D&F in the file, but it did not address all of the required elements. Several contracting officials at different agencies noted that their contracting staff is very overworked or inexperienced, which may have contributed to the general lack of awareness of the new D&F requirement.

Internal controls, such as contract reviews, administered by informed agency personnel can also help ensure that policies and processes are translated into practice. In some cases, the contracts in our sample had been reviewed by staff, including legal officials, who did not detect that the required Part 12 D&Fs were missing. For example, while six of the

---

[34] In addition, Navy headquarters issued a memo on March 31, 2009, reminding contracting officials that the D&F is required for T&M contracts for commercial services.

eight contracts at the Air Force were reviewed by attorneys or contract management officials, five contract files still contained the incorrect Part 16 D&F rather than the Part 12 D&F for commercial acquisitions. At the Navy, one attorney reviewing a contract file identified the need to include the Part 12 D&F, but another attorney reviewing a different Navy contract failed to do so. In another example at NASA, an attorney and associate division chief had reviewed the contract and did not identify that the Part 12 D&F was missing, but the associate division chief did inquire as to whether part of the work could be fixed-price. In other cases, contract reviews either failed to ensure that any D&F was included in the contract file or there was no evidence that reviews of the acquisition approach had occurred. Four of the five VA contracts we reviewed were subject to internal reviews by VA technical and legal staff based on factors such as value and contract type, yet none contained a D&F of any type. At the Army location we visited, there was no indication that the contracts' acquisition approach had been reviewed, and most of the contracts in our sample contained the Part 16 D&F or had no D&F at all. However, this Army contracting activity updated its internal contract review checklist in December 2008, after our visit, to include a reference to the Part 12 D&F requirement.

Our review of contract files and interviews with agency officials further revealed that awareness of the new D&F requirement even varied among the staff of a single contracting office. For example, three T&M contracts for commercial services were issued during a 6-month period by U.S. Marshals Service contracting officials for aircraft maintenance and pilot services in Puerto Rico. One contract file contained a partial Part 12 D&F, one contained a Part 16 D&F, which is less rigorous, and the third had no D&F.

FAR Part 12 Safeguards Have Not Been Applied to GSA Schedules Program

The vast majority of reported obligations for commercial services acquired through T&M contracts went through GSA's schedules program from February 2007 to December 2008, but the FAR Part 12 D&F requirement has not been applied to the use of schedule contracts. The February 2007 revisions to FAR Part 12 did not specifically address the applicability of the D&F provisions to GSA schedule contracts or orders issued under them.[35] Further, the section of the FAR that governs ordering procedures for GSA schedules contracts does not refer to the Part 12 D&F requirement to either make it explicitly applicable or inapplicable as it does with other FAR provisions.[36] GSA has not incorporated the D&F requirement in its own acquisition manual, for use by its contracting officers, and has not instructed ordering agencies to comply with the Part 12 D&F requirement when issuing T&M orders under its schedule contracts. For example, the Part 12 D&F is not discussed in GSA's ordering guidance for schedule contracts or in the frequently asked questions on the schedules program Web site. Accordingly, there is uncertainty in the contracting community about the extent to which the Part 12 D&F is required for schedule orders. Our file review revealed that only 2 of the 19 GSA orders we reviewed that were awarded after the February 2007 FAR changes contained the Part 12 D&F. Eleven of the orders contained the less rigorous FAR Part 16 version which would be properly used in conjunction with the purchase of noncommercial services using T&M contracts, and 6 had no D&F, as shown in table 6.

---

[35] 71 Fed. Reg. 74,667 (Dec. 12, 2006). We note that the September 20, 2004, advance notice of proposed rulemaking (ANPR), which solicited comments that could be used to assist in implementing section 1432 of the National Defense Authorization Act for Fiscal Year 2004 stated that "This ANPR is not intended to affect the special ordering procedures issued by the GSA pursuant to FAR 8.402.... [Schedules program] policies regarding the placement of orders on a T&M and [labor hour] basis will be conformed to the FAR when FAR coverage is finalized." 69 Fed. Reg. 56,316 (Sept. 20, 2004).

[36] See Subpart 8.4.

Table 6: Number and Type of D&Fs for GSA Orders in our Sample Awarded After the FAR Part 12 D&F Requirement Became Effective.

Agency	GSA schedule orders				
	Complete Part 12 D&F	Partial Part 12 D&F	Part 16 D&F	No D&F	Total
Air Force	0	0	0	0	0
Army	0	0	4	1	5
Navy	0	0	4	1	5
DOJ	1	0	0	0	1
HHS	0	0	0	0	0
NASA	0	0	0	0	0
VA	1	0	3	4	8
Total	2	0	11	6	19

Source: GAO analysis of data from agency contract files.

Note: FAR Subpart 8.4 does not specifically require a D&F. However, GSA ordering procedures require the ordering agency to make a determination that it is not possible at the time of placing the order to estimate accurately the extent or duration of the work or to anticipate costs with any reasonable degree of confidence.

Further, the FAR Part 12 requirement to document ceiling price changes on T&M contracts is not included in FAR Subpart 8.4, which pertains to schedule purchases. We found a few GSA orders at the VA location we visited that had ceiling price increases with no documentation on why the increase was in the best interest of the VA. For example, one order for information technology support services increased from $3.5 million to almost $4.8 million with minimal explanation as to why this increase occurred.

GSA policy officials told us that the statutory authority that created the schedules program is unique and allows the administrator the flexibility to decide what procedures to apply to the schedules program.[37] They noted, however, that they were planning to issue a procurement information notice in the spring of 2009 to put in place a Part 12 D&F for the entire GSA schedules program. It is not clear how this D&F will address the specific elements required by Part 12 of the FAR, or how it will act as a safeguard to ensure that each agency using GSA's schedule contracts has made the necessary determination that no other contract type is suitable.

---

[37] 40 U.S.C § 501.

On March 6, 2009, we requested a legal opinion from GSA on the applicability of FASA section 8002(d), as amended by section 1432 of SARA, and the implementing FAR section 12.207(b) D&F requirement to the GSA schedules program. In its April, 15, 2009, response, GSA stated that the statutory language of FASA is not explicit and is unclear regarding applicability of the FASA provisions to the GSA schedules program, and therefore concluded that applicability is uncertain with regard to T&M commercial services contracts and orders under the program. In this regard, GSA recognized congressional concerns expressed regarding the use of T&M contracts for commercial services, which in some cases have led to inefficient and costly procurements. Specifically, GSA recognized the concern of the Senate Armed Services Committee that T&M commercial services contracts "are potentially subject to abuse because . . . it [is] very difficult to ensure that prices are fair and reasonable." GSA stated, however, that it "has exercised the agency's authority over the Schedules program to create safeguards so as to mitigate the issues presented by T&M commercial services contracts" and that existing provisions in the GSA Acquisition Regulation (GSAR) and FAR Subpart 8.4 "satisfy any concerns about the use of T&M orders in the Schedules program."

It is not apparent to us that the regulations cited by GSA provide the government with risk mitigation equivalent to that provided by the Part 12 D&F requirement that T&M contracts will only be used when no other contract type is suitable. For example, GSA points to the FAR Section 8.4 requirement for the ordering activity to document the rationale for using other than a firm-fixed price order for services.[38] This documentation requirement is minimal, requiring only the "rationale" for using other than a firm-fixed price order rather than the more detailed rationale required in FAR Part 12 to demonstrate that there is no other suitable contract type. GSA also points to two existing price reasonableness requirements as safeguards: (1) the GSAR requirement that before a schedule contract is awarded, the GSA contracting officer must determine that the prices offered are fair and reasonable[39] and (2) the FAR requirement that the ordering activity contracting officer must consider the level and mix of labor proposed and determine that the total price of the schedule order is

---

[38] FAR § 8.405-2.

[39] GSAR § 538.270.

reasonable.[40] Again, these provisions do not address the more detailed rationale required in FAR Part 12.

We see no reason why the concerns which led Congress to require the Part 12 safeguards for the use of T&M contracts would be any less compelling in those instances in which an agency proposes to use a GSA schedule to obtain commercial services on a T&M basis. GSA did not provide any rationale why T&M contracts and orders for commercial services should be treated differently under the GSA schedules program, or be subject to fewer safeguards than those purchased outside of the GSA schedules program where the more heightened FAR section 12.207 requirements would be required. Further, we note that in section 8002(d) of FASA, as amended, there is no indication that the D&F requirement cannot apply to the purchase of any commercial item or service to include items or services available for purchase under the GSA schedules program.

Conclusion

The FAR Part 12 D&F requirement for the use of T&M contracts to acquire commercial services helps to ensure that this contract type is used only when no other contract type is suitable and to instill discipline in the determination of contract type with a view toward managing the risk to the government. The general lack of awareness of this requirement among contracting officers across all agencies in our review—more than 2 years after its implementation—coupled with the failure of management to detect the lack of compliance with this key safeguard suggests that further actions are necessary. In addition, miscoding of labor-hour contracts as fixed-price, when based on a misunderstanding about this contract type, potentially understates the risk to the government. Further, the fact that the safeguards put in place by Congress are not applied to GSA schedule contracts or orders raises concerns that the safeguards are not being used for the vast majority of T&M contracts for commercial services. When these safeguards are not used, the government may be assuming more risk than necessary.

---

[40] FAR § 8.405-2(d).

Recommendations for Executive Action

To help ensure that the risks associated with T&M contracts are understood and that safeguards are followed and to ensure consistency in the use of T&M contracts regardless of which part of the FAR authorizes their use, we recommend that the Administrator of the Office of Federal Procurement Policy take the following three actions:

- Take steps to:

    - amend FAR Subpart 16.6 (T&M, Labor-Hour and Letter Contracts) and FAR Subpart 16.2 (Fixed-Price Contracts) to make it clear that contracts with a fixed hourly rate and an estimated ceiling price are T&M or labor-hour contracts, not fixed-price-type contracts and

    - amend FAR Subpart 8.4 (pertaining to the GSA schedules program) to explicitly require the same safeguards for commercial T&M services—i.e., the FAR Part 12 D&F and the justification for changes to the ceiling price—that are required in FAR section 12.207.

- Provide guidance to contracting officials on the requirements in FAR section 12.207 for the detailed D&F for T&M or labor-hour contracts for commercial services and encourage agencies to provide training regarding the D&F requirement.

Agency Comments and Our Evaluation

We requested comments on a draft of this report from OFPP, NASA, HHS, GSA, DOD, VA, and DOJ. In oral comments on a draft of this report, OFPP's Acting Administrator concurred with our recommendations. In written comments, included in appendix II, NASA stated that the report provides a balanced view of the issues. HHS also provided written comments. Although our recommendations were directed at OFPP, HHS stated that it agrees with them and outlined several steps it is taking to reinforce the need for its acquisition community to comply with requirements for T&M and other contract types. HHS's comments are included in appendix III. In comments provided via e-mail, DOD's Director, Defense Procurement and Acquisition Policy, concurred with our findings related to DOD contracts. The Director stated that DOD fully supports the objectives of promoting awareness and compliance with existing requirements related to the safeguards employed to ensure that T&M contracts are used only when justified.

GSA, DOJ, and VA provided no comments.

We are sending copies of this report to interested congressional committees; the Secretaries of Defense, Justice, Veterans Affairs, and Health and Human Services; the Administrators of the General Services Administration, Office of Federal Procurement Policy, and NASA. In addition, this report will also be available at no charge on GAO's Web site at http://www.gao.gov.

If you or your staff have any questions about this report or need additional information, please contact me at (202) 512-4841 or huttonj@gao.gov. Contact points for our Offices of Congressional Relations and Public Affairs may be found on the last page of this report. Staff acknowledgements are provided in appendix IV.

John P Hutton

John Hutton, Director
Acquisition and Sourcing Management

List of Committees

The Honorable Carl Levin
Chairman
The Honorable John McCain
Ranking Member
Committee on Armed Services
United States Senate

The Honorable Joseph I. Lieberman
Chairman
The Honorable Susan M. Collins
Ranking Member
Committee on Homeland Security and Governmental Affairs
United States Senate

The Honorable Ike Skelton
Chairman
The Honorable Howard P. McKeon
Ranking Member
Committee on Armed Services
House of Representatives

The Honorable Edolphus Towns
Chairman
The Honorable Darrell Issa
Ranking Member
Committee on Oversight and Government Reform
House of Representatives

Appendix I: Scope and Methodology

The objectives of this review were to assess (1) the extent to which agencies have reported using time-and-materials (T&M) contracts and General Services Administration (GSA) schedule T&M orders for commercial services and what they are acquiring using this contract type, (2) the degree to which agencies complied with the FAR Part 12 safeguards and (3) the applicability of these safeguards to the GSA schedule program. To address these objectives, we identified through the Federal Procurement Data System-Next Generation (FPDS-NG) all reported T&M contracts and orders—including GSA schedule orders—that were coded as using commercial item acquisition procedures from October 1, 2001, to June 30, 2008. We then selected five federal departments to review—based primarily on their high-dollar obligations and high numbers of contract actions—which represent 97 percent of total obligations coded as T&M contracts awarded using commercial item procedures for this time period:

- Department of Defense (DOD)
- Department of Health and Human Services (HHS)
- Department of Justice (DOJ)
- National Aeronautics and Space Administration (NASA)
- Department of Veterans Affairs (VA)

While the focus of our engagement was non-GSA contracts awarded after the February 2007 changes to the FAR, we also reviewed some GSA orders and contracts awarded by selected defense and civilian agencies prior to the FAR changes to get a better understanding of the circumstances of those procurements—such as whether the contracts were miscoded. We corroborated contract file information by interviewing over 100 contracting and policy officials at all of the selected agencies.

At DOD, we selected Air Force, Army, and Navy locations that had high reported obligations for commercial services using T&M contracts, coupled with the geographic location of the contracting activities. At each DOD location, we conducted a preliminary review of the contracts through the department's electronic database system to corroborate FPDS-NG information. We conducted file reviews and interviewed contracting officials at the following locations:

| Army | • U.S. Army Medical Research Acquisition Activity, Fort Detrick; Frederick, Maryland |

| Air Force | • Air Force Intelligence, Surveillance, and Reconnaissance Agency, Lackland Air Force Base; San Antonio, Texas
• Air Combat Command Acquisition Management and Integration Center, Langley Air Force Base, Virginia (Contracts at this location were awarded prior to the FAR change) |

| Navy | • Fleet Industrial Supply Center, Norfolk; Norfolk, Virginia; Philadelphia, Pennsylvania; Portsmouth, New Hampshire; Millington, Tennessee; and Great Lakes, Illinois. |

At the Army's Medical Research Acquisition Activity, we randomly selected 20 non-GSA schedule contracts awarded after the February 2007 FAR Part 12 change, 5 non-GSA contracts awarded prior to the FAR change, and 5 GSA schedule orders issued after the FAR change. Ten of the 20 non-GSA contracts were indefinite-delivery contracts and 2 were blanket purchase agreements. For these, we reviewed 13 T&M orders under the indefinite-delivery contracts and 3 orders that had been placed under 1 of the blanket purchase agreements. At the Navy, we reviewed all of the non-GSA schedule contracts awarded during our selected time period of October 1, 2001, to June 30, 2008, which included 20 contracts awarded after the FAR change and 5 awarded prior to the FAR change.[1] We also reviewed 5 randomly selected GSA schedule orders that were awarded after the FAR change. At Lackland Air Force Base, we reviewed all non-GSA schedule contracts reported as T&M using commercial items acquisition procedures, including 1 awarded prior to the FAR change. We reviewed all 7 GSA schedule orders awarded after the FAR change that were reported as using T&M contracts for commercial services. At Langley Air Force Base, which had the largest obligations reported as T&M contracts for commercial services prior to the enactment of the Services Acquisition Reform Act in November 2003, we selected and reviewed 2 non-GSA T&M orders awarded prior to November 2003 that had been

---

[1] We eliminated three Navy contracts that had been coded as non-GSA schedule contracts awarded by the Norfolk location from our review for different reasons: one turned out to be a blanket purchase agreement under a GSA schedule contract; one had been awarded by a different Navy location according to DOD's electronic contract database system; and finally, contracting officers at the Norfolk Navy Shipyard could not locate the third contract file.

recently modified to better understand the circumstances of these contracts. These 2 orders turned out to have been miscoded in FPDS-NG as having used commercial items acquisition procedures.

For the civilian agencies included in our scope, we reviewed all of the T&M contracts for commercial services reported in FPDS-NG during the October 2001 to June 2008 time period. We conducted file reviews and interviewed contracting officials at the following civilian agency components:

Department of Justice

- Bureau of Alcohol, Tobacco, Firearms, and Explosives; Washington, D.C.
- Drug Enforcement Agency; Arlington, Virginia
- Federal Bureau of Investigation; Washington, D.C.
- Justice Management Division; Washington, D.C.
- Office of Justice Programs; Washington D.C.
- U.S. Marshals Service; Washington, D.C. and Oklahoma City, Oklahoma

Health and Human Services

- Centers for Disease Control and Prevention; Atlanta, Georgia
- Food and Drug Administration; Rockville, Maryland
- Health Resources and Services Administration; Rockville, Maryland
- Indian Health Service; Oklahoma City, Oklahoma; Phoenix, Arizona, and Window Rock, Arizona
- National Institutes of Health; Bethesda, Maryland and Research Triangle Park, North Carolina
- Program Support Center; Rockville, Maryland; Kansas City, Missouri; and Perry Point, Maryland
- Substance Abuse and Mental Health Services Administration; Rockville, Maryland
- Centers for Medicare and Medicaid Services; Baltimore, Maryland

NASA

- John H. Glenn Research Center; Cleveland, Ohio
- Goddard Space Flight Center; Greenbelt, Maryland

Veterans Affairs

- Cleveland Business Center; Cleveland, Ohio
- Acquisition Management Section; Austin, Texas

Table 7 contains details about the distribution of our contract sample across the agencies in our review.

Table 7: GAO Sample of T&M Contracts and Orders for Commercial Services Awarded Prior to and After the February 2007 FAR Change

Agency	Non-GSA contracts and orders		GSA schedule orders		Total
	Pre-FAR change	Post-FAR change	Pre-FAR change	Post-FAR change	
Air Force	3	8	0	7	18
Army	5	28	0	5	38
Navy	4	20	0	5	29
Justice	5	7	0	1	13
Health and Human Services	2	20	4	0	26
NASA	0	1	1	0	2
Veterans Affairs	1	5	7	10	23
	Total non-GSA contracts and orders	109	Total GSA schedule orders	40	
Total contracts and orders in sample					149

Source: GAO file reviews.

Note: Our sample of contracts and orders was selected from FPDS-NG data from October 1, 2001, to June 30, 2008. "Pre-FAR change" means that the contract or order was awarded prior to the changes to FAR Part 12 effective on February 12, 2007; "Post-FAR change" means the contract or order was awarded after the FAR change effective date.

To identify the extent to which agencies have reported using T&M contracts and GSA schedule orders for commercial services, we used FPDS-NG data to determine the obligations reported as T&M awarded using FAR Part 12 commercial items acquisitions procedures between February 12, 2007, when the FAR change authorizing T&M contracts for commercial services went into effect, and December 31, 2008. We compared this figure to total reported federal obligations for services, obligations coded as having acquired commercial services, and obligations coded as T&M contracts and orders during the same time period in order to demonstrate the relative magnitude of T&M contracts for commercial services. We discovered that many GSA schedule orders for T&M services had been miscoded as having used FAR Part 12 procedures (when they had actually used procedures under FAR Subpart 8.4) and brought this issue to the attention of the Office of Federal Procurement Policy officials. To determine the full picture of T&M obligations for commercial services, we identified GSA schedule T&M orders that had not been coded as having used commercial item procedures. We also used FPDS-NG data to assess what proportion of the total reported T&M contracts for commercial services was purchased through the GSA schedules program.

To test the reliability of FPDS-NG data, we used information from the contract file and discussions with contracting officials. We confirmed that a contract was used to acquire commercial services by reviewing the contract for relevant commercial clauses (52.212-4—Contract Terms and Conditions—Commercial Items) and other contract file documentation— such as the acquisition plan or the standard contract form for commercial item acquisitions (SF 1449)—that indicated that commercial services were purchased. In some cases, in which the evidence in the files was not sufficient to make this determination, we confirmed that commercial services were acquired by speaking with the contracting officer. To confirm that a contract was T&M, we reviewed relevant contract documentation such as contract line item notations (CLIN) and invoices, spoke with contracting officers, and applied FAR descriptions of T&M or labor-hour contracts. To identify the types of services agencies are acquiring using T&M contracts for commercial services, we used FPDS-NG data to identify the top 10 commercial services purchased under T&M contracts from February 12, 2007, to December 31, 2008. We also analyzed the statements of work from selected contracts in our sample to provide more detailed examples of the types of services agencies are acquiring using these contracts.

When we discovered that some contracting officers had mistakenly interpreted the fixed labor rate component of T&M contracts to mean that these contracts are fixed-price type contracts, we decided to review a nonrepresentative sample of contracts labeled as fixed-price in FPDS-NG that were coded for the same types of services as the T&M contracts for commercial services identified in our sample. Using DOD's electronic database, we conducted a preliminary review of 60 DOD contracts that had been coded as fixed-price contracts and selected 16 that possibly could have been T&M, based primarily on our interpretation of language in the contract that suggested that the contract was not fixed-price. To confirm whether these contracts were T&M, we spoke with contracting officials and requested additional contract documentation for 10 contracts at Lackland Air Force Base and 6 managed by the Fleet and Industrial Supply Center at Norfolk Naval Base. Of these 16 contracts, 3 were confirmed to be incorrectly coded as fixed-price in FPDS-NG due to data entry errors, and should have been coded as T&M contracts.

To determine the degree to which agencies' use of FAR Part 12 to acquire T&M services complies with the safeguards as incorporated in the FAR, we reviewed the contract files for our sample contracts. Specifically, we assessed: 1) whether the files contained a determination and findings (D&F) stating that no other contract type is suitable; 2) if applicable, the extent to which the D&F included FAR Part 12 or Part 16 requirements for T&M contracts; and 3) whether ceiling price increases included written documentation from the contracting officer that they were in the best interest of the procuring agency. We determined that a D&F met all the criteria if it made reference to FAR Section 12.207 and at least mentioned all of the required elements. For example, if a D&F stated the outcomes of the market research conducted but did not describe the research conducted, we still gave credit for having addressed the requirement in FAR Section 12.207 to describe the market research conducted. A partial Part 12 D&F included some but not all of the four required elements. We also reviewed federal and agency-specific acquisition guidance and regulations.

To determine the applicability of these safeguards to the GSA schedules program, we reviewed GSA's ordering guidance to agencies and to its own contracting officers and interviewed GSA policy and legal officials. We also sent a letter on March 6, 2009, to GSA's General Counsel seeking an opinion on the applicability of Section 8002(d) of FASA, as amended, and FAR Section 12.207 to the GSA schedules contracts. We received a response on April 15, 2009. Finally, we reviewed relevant past GAO and Inspectors General reports on T&M contracts and commercial contracts for context.

We conducted this performance audit from September 2008 to June 2009, in accordance with generally accepted government auditing standards. Those standards require that we plan and perform the audit to obtain sufficient, appropriate evidence to provide a reasonable basis for our findings and conclusions based on our audit objectives. We believe that the evidence obtained provides a reasonable basis for our findings and conclusions based on our audit objectives.

Appendix II: Comments from NASA

National Aeronautics and
Space Administration

Headquarters
Washington, DC 20546-0001

June 11, 2009

Reply to Attn of: Contract Management Division

Mr. John P. Hutton
Director, Acquisition and Sourcing Management
United States Government Accountability Office
Washington, DC 20548

Dear Mr. Hutton:

Thank you for the opportunity to review draft report, "CONTRACT MANAGEMENT: Minimal Compliance with New Safeguards for Time-and-Materials Contracts for Commercial Services and Safeguards Have Not Been Applied to GSA Schedules Program," (GAO-09-579).

We found the report to be complete, concise, and accurate. In our opinion, it provides a balanced view of the issues related to the additional safeguards required to offset the potential risks associated with using time-and-material contracts to purchase commercial services. We do not have any technical comments to the draft report.

Again, thank you for the opportunity to provide comments on the draft report and for your continued interest in improving Government contract management.

Sincerely,

William P. McNally
Assistant Administrator for
Procurement

Appendix III: Comments from the Department of Health and Human Services

DEPARTMENT OF HEALTH & HUMAN SERVICES   OFFICE OF THE SECRETARY

Assistant Secretary for Legislation
Washington, DC 20201

JUN 5 2009

John P. Hutton
Director
Acquisition and Sourcing Management
U.S. Government Accountability Office
441 G Street NW
Washington, DC 20548

Dear Mr. Hutton:

Enclosed are comments on the U.S. Government Accountability Office's (GAO) report entitled:
Contract Management: Minimal Compliance with New Safeguards for Time-and-Materials
Contracts for Commercial Services and Safeguards Have Not Been Applied to GSA Schedules
Program"(GAO-09-579).

The Department appreciates the opportunity to review this report before its publication.

Sincerely,

Barbara Pisaro Clark

Barbara Pisaro Clark
Acting Assistant Secretary for Legislation

Attachment

GENERAL COMMENTS OF THE DEPARTMENT OF U.S. HEALTH AND HUMAN SERVICES (HHS) ON THE GOVERNMENT ACCOUNTABILITY OFFICE'S (GAO) DRAFT REPORT ENTITLED, "CONTRACT MANAGEMENT: MINIMAL COMPLIANCE WITH NEW SAFEGUARDS FOR TIME-AND-MATERIALS CONTRACTS FOR COMMERCIAL SERVICES AND SAFEGUARDS HAVE NOT BEEN APPLIED TO GSA SCHEDULES PROGRAM" (GAO-09-579)

HHS agrees with GAO's recommendations to the Administrator of the Office of Federal Procurement Policy. We will reinforce the need for our acquisition community to comply with requirements for T&M and other contract types. This will be accomplished through: (a) conducting additional training; (b) discussing GAO's findings and sharing successful practices at our quarterly Executive Committee for Acquisition meetings; (c) incorporating Commercial Acquisition and FAR Part 12 D&F requirements in our Procurement Management Review protocols; and (d) verifying applicable FPDS coding.

Further, HHS issued mandatory, standardized contract file checklists to its acquisition community in May 2009. These checklists are intended to: (a) facilitate the consistent and logical placement of required supporting documentation in contract files; (b) expedite the review of acquisition files and the conduct of procurement management reviews; (c) serve as a learning tool for contracting staff; and (d) foster consistent implementation of acquisition regulations, policies, and procedures. The checklists encompass all relevant Federal and HHS acquisition guidance, including guidance pertaining to the requirements identified in GAO's draft report (e.g., FAR Part 12 D&F).

Appendix IV: GAO Contact and Staff Acknowledgements

GAO Contact	John Hutton, (202) 512-4841 or huttonj@gao.gov
Acknowledgements	In addition to the individual named above, Michele Mackin, Assistant Director; Nicholas Alexander; Keya Chateauneuf; and Tatiana Winger made key contributions to this report. Marie Ahearn, Arthur James, Jr., Julia Kennon, and Kenneth Patton also made contributions.

Lightning Source UK Ltd.
Milton Keynes UK
UKOW04f0648240417
299766UK00010B/453/P

So You Want To Learn To Improvise?

A step-by-step guide to creative piano playing

Andrew Higgins

Editorial Proof: Leonie McCaughren

Alfred

Produced by
Alfred Music Publishing (UK) Ltd
Burnt Mill, Elizabeth Way, Harlow
Essex, CM20 2HX
alfredUK.com

ISBN-10: 1-4706-1170-8
ISBN-13: 978-1-4706-1170-5

ABOUT THE AUTHOR - Andrew Higgins

Andrew Higgins was born in 1960 in England. Following a traditional musical education in Manchester he spent fifteen formative years touring the world as a session musician and music producer in the 'not so swinging eighties'. At the end of this sojourn into popular culture he took time out to complete his music studies: first studying Piano at the London College of Music, before graduating from the University of Surrey specialising in Composition and Performance with Musicology.

During the 1990's he decided to devote more time to composition and to piano teaching as well as the teaching of music history, theory and composition. Several of his piano pupils have since gone on to study at specialised music schools or at University level with one now a concert pianist in his own right. He also continued to accompany for ballet schools, singers, and to give solo recitals in the UK.

Andrew joined Alfred Music in 1996, which coincided with his discovery of the pedagogical insights of the late Dr Amanda Vick-Lethco in the now classic Alfred's Basic Piano Library. Her all-encompassing holistic approach focussing on the 'pianist as musician', inspired him to develop Dr Lethco's ideas still further by incorporating improvising and memorising techniques into ABPL's teaching philosophy. So much so, that when Dr Lethco attended one of his seminars, she confessed to having no idea that her books could be used in such a creative way!

Andrew now works extensively with Alfred Music in the UK and Europe promoting their ideals of musicianship through Alfred's Basic Piano Library and Premier Piano Course with workshops and lectures, meeting with teachers, performers and their pupils, to discuss piano teaching techniques. Many teachers have remarked on the freedom and flexibility in his approach to music, and, while Andrew considers improvisation and composition an intrinsic aspect of making music in the 21st century, this is always underpinned by a clear emphasis on sound technique and musicality.

This progressive approach can be heard in his own music, which takes advantage of contemporary and modernist styles (bi-tonality, ostinato, modal harmony) whilst reflecting on the forms and disciplines of earlier composers. The Three Celtic Legends published by Alfred Music are evocative tone pictures for the piano reflecting English coastal landscapes.

So You Want To Learn To Improvise?

The art of improvisation is no different from any other artistic discipline - it is, as is often said, 95% perspiration and 5% inspiration. Unfortunately the quickest way to reach the inspiration is through the sweat of hard work. In short, improvisers are as much made as born. There is no doubt that people have a predilection that leads them to play freely with musical elements as soon as they acquire them, and there are others who have all the technical mastery in the world, but to whom 'messing around at the piano' simply never occurs. I was quite clearly in the former category much to my teacher's chagrin. As soon as I learnt my first arpeggio I was up and down the keyboard trying this and that. It seemed natural to me to take the concepts I was learning and experiment with them, and, in doing this, I stumbled across a whole range of sounds and shapes that were appealing and interesting.

As my technical skill increased then so did the nature of my experimentation. Fortunately, I had the most wonderful Bechstein piano with extraordinary resonances, so I could conjure the sounds of the harp or banjo as well as the deeper darker 'orchestral textures' for Brahms and Debussy. For improvisation, the piano was a great friend offering a range of sounds that would fascinate and delight at any time. In the end, I probably spent an equal amount of my time improvising or 'extemporising' as I did practising, and, in a sense, despite my teacher's protestations, I was 'practising', practising improvisation.

So for this book the intention is to map the journey made in those first days when the instrument was new to me. Not to accept the limitations of knowledge as a barrier to improvising, but as a starting point so that skills are acquired at every step of the learning process. All too often in modern piano playing improvising is seen as a skill that is 'instinctive', one that you either have or you don't, or alternatively one whose acquisition can only be achieved when a certain level of skill is reached. By then it is often too late! It is, in fact, just like sight-reading or scale playing or piece learning, a series of acquired skills that develop over time sufficiently, in this case, to 'free the mind' from the constraints of notation. In other words it requires steady and patient practise, and an immense intuitive knowledge of harmonic movement, melodic construction, and structural awareness. That improvisers do this at will does not mean it is effortless, it simply means the effort has accumulated over many hours and now the rewards are being garnered.

It often dismays me when I see practitioners, even brilliant ones, talking about improvising, explaining how they just make it up from nothing – they clearly don't. They always start somewhere with something, and I have tried to offer starting points for improvising throughout the book. All points where I myself stepped off the notation trail and decided to explore the new possibilities the notes suggested to me.

One more thing to bear in mind – in encouraging improvising I would earnestly entreat all students not to overlook the acquisition of technical skill. The stronger your technique, the more possibilities will become available to you. You will notice as we proceed that there are many pages of apparently 'innocuous' exercises; these should be practised until 'effortless' in the true sense of the word so that the construction of ideas 'on-the-spot' that is the object of this book becomes the focus of the later exercises, not the stumbling around trying to 'remember' what chord comes next. What comes next is inspiration, the elusive 5% that makes all the rest worthwhile. Good Luck.

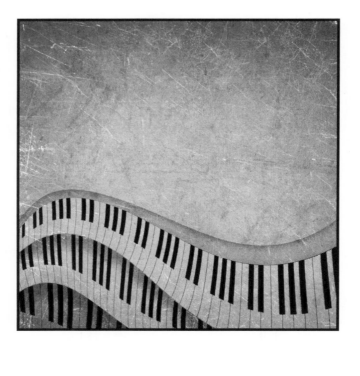

CHAPTER ONE: BEGINNINGS

FIVE-FINGER IMPROVISATIONS BLACK NOTES

One must start somewhere, and, ideally, as soon as possible. So, once the student has sufficient hand co-ordination to play individual fingers and to hold a fifth, you can commence. This exercise can be done without notation, but I include it here for your teacher who can advise and help if required.

Simply place your left hand on the black note pattern fifth finger on the F♯ and thumb on the C♯ either as a block chord or rock between in a gentle but steady even rhythm. Practise this until it is comfortable.

Now, with the right hand, play the two notes C♯ and D♯ near the C above middle C. Create a sentence using these two notes – use words if you need to, so there is a sense of phrase: *'how are you today?'* play it with the same rhythm you would speak, perhaps with a little exaggeration: so you might say: *How Are Yoouu To Day?*

Then choose the three black notes either lower or higher than the C♯ and D♯: answer your question using these three notes: *'I am feeeeling very well my friend'*

This is simply 'call and response'. It will allow you to build little phrases (tunes) over the simple left hand accompaniment. Perhaps choose a partner, or your teacher, and enjoy the musical conversations you can have creating phrases without words: so using the sound of the tones themselves. Play gently and softly to begin.

Now we can add a further element to the left hand. This time rock as follows: F♯ C♯ F♯ D♯, and repeat: so moving your thumb out every other time to play the black note above C♯. This gives us a gentle 'ostinato', a useful repetitive device we will hear a lot more of before this book is over. Practise this until it is nice and fluent: slow and gentle.

Add a new call and response RH and practise until fluent.

Now we can use all five fingers of the right-hand across both patterns of black notes: C♯ D♯ F♯ G♯ A♯ - this is the 'Pentatonic' Scale.

A five note scale regarded by many as the basic building block of melody and harmony. Many fine melodies are built on this five note scale. Now build your phrases (sentences) from all five notes, using the by now familiar call and response technique.

...and finally for the right-hand, we can now move the hand to any of the five black note positions anywhere on the keyboard above middle C – simply move your hand up to the next position and experiment in the same way. Don't forget you can also go back to the 23 and 234 finger positions we started with too – all of this is possible.

...and finally for the left-hand we can transpose our LH ostinato to a new black note position and then alternate between the two positions.

This is music-making using only a limited number of elements, but with just these we can create a huge variety of musical effects, especially if we experiment with dynamics (loud and soft) and mood (gentle and bold). Even for me, after many years, doing this simple and restricted exercise remains a pleasure. Teasing out melodies and moods with just two chords and five notes is a real challenge at any level of proficiency.

I hope you enjoyed your first experiments in improvising.

FIVE-FINGER IMPROVISATIONS WHITE NOTES

Here is a typical early piece from *Alfred's Premier Piano Course Level 1B*:

The Library

- Try inverting the melody given: you will be surprised how different it can sound (make up new words if it helps).

The Library (Improvisation 1)

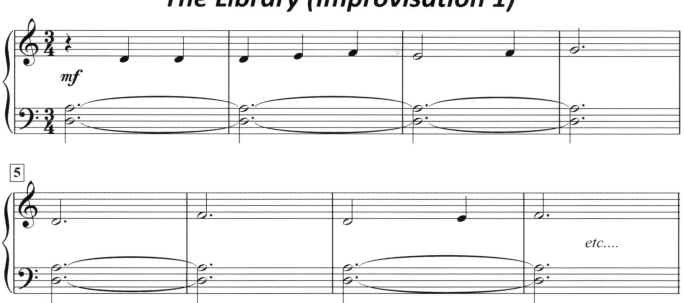

- Play the five finger pattern in the right-hand freely. (Be careful to advise the students on the variety available to them; from up and down, to side-to-side, and repeated notes. Also, 'leaps' from 1 to 4 or 5, or 'skips' from 1 to 3, 2 to 4, and 3 to 5; AND most importantly – vice-versa 'inversions').

The Library (Improvisation 2)

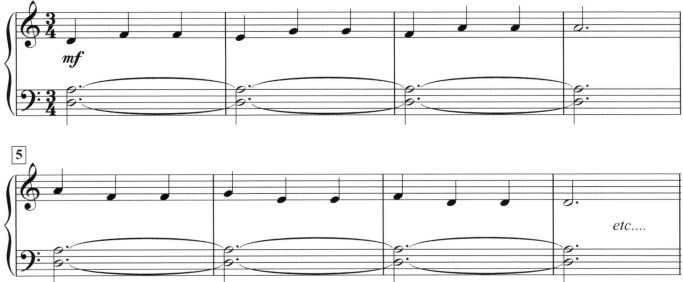

The work should be unencumbered by structures and phrasing, however a few words on the nature of breathing, or an exhortation to 'imagine you are playing a flute', or creating an 'echo' might, quite unconsciously, give 'shape' to the melodic material.

Here is a slightly later piece from the same book: *Alfred's Premier Piano Course Level 1B:*

My Yo-Yo

- Repeat the chords, a little faster, a little slower…and when the student can remember where his/her hands are, removing the score, might, at this stage, be advantageous.

My Yo-Yo (Improvisation 2)

- An advanced student, or quick learner, may also be able to turn the LH drone into a 5 -1 oscillating ostinato, (like the black notes exercise) creating a rhythmic impetus to accompany the right hand – or you might provide this as a duet partner, or a variation of the given LH - the extra sound promotes active listening and can inspire unusual results.

- Now compare the two examples. See if the student notices the subtle differences between the mood and colour for each 'position'. Remember, it may well be obvious to us, but to a student this is a fascinating discovery and an opportunity to understand simple differences of position at the piano should not be overlooked. After all, the same notes and patterns are being played, but by simply starting in a different position a whole new effect is produced – a first hint of 'magic'.

Here the student has learnt about:

- Ostinato
- Pedal/Drones
- Inversions
- Positions on the keyboard
- But most importantly, that the score is only a starting point!

TONIC & DOMINANT

Using just the normal five finger position we can count the fingers from 1 to 5. The two most important notes are the Tonic – which is the starting note (1) – and the Dominant – which is the last of the pattern (5). They are called Tonic and Dominant and the relationship between these two notes is very important for understanding harmony. Play them up and down and you can hear there is a sense of departure and arrival.

C Five-Finger Pattern

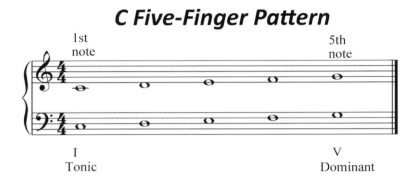

Tonic and Dominant

Cornelius Gurlitt (1820-1901)
Adapted from Op.117, No. 5

EXTENSIONS

Knowing just these two chords can open a world of possibilities: here is the first part of a piece called Rockets from *Alfred's Basic Piano Course 1A:*

Rockets

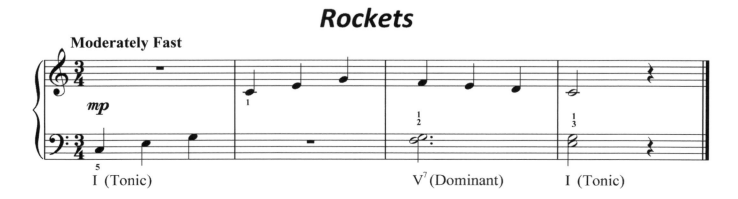

With just these two chords and some inversions of the melodic material, we can create 24 bars of music covering the whole keyboard, and well within the grasp of the first year student.

Here is the same piece after some extended use of these basic materials – 'improvised through extension'.

Rockets Extended

The same two chords, Tonic & Dominant, appear in all keys – and the same 'extensions' can be applied in every case. Here is the Harp Song from *Alfred's Basic Piano Course 1B:* by now the student is working in G position.

Harp Song

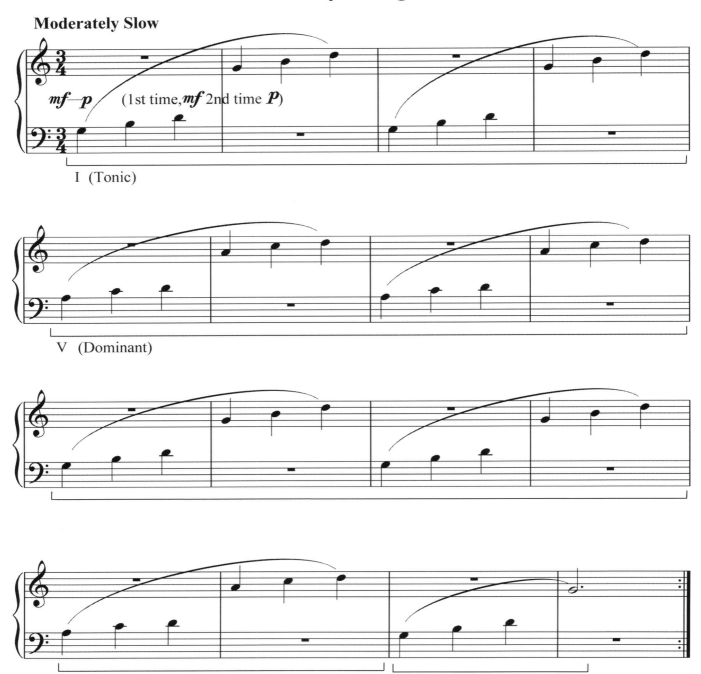

VERY IMPORTANT!
Also Play Harp Song in the following ways:
1. Play the 3rd and 4th bar of each line one octave higher than written.
2. Play the 1st and 2nd bar of each line one octave lower than written.
3. Any combination of the two above ways.

In the above example, to the author's advice on alternate versions of Harp Song...we can add more...

Now we apply the same techniques we used in Rockets, to 'extend' the piece...start with a descending inversion of the pattern and then in the third line play ascending. Notice how using the pedal creates a rich and full sound across the whole keyboard* using just two chords – Tonic and Dominant.

Harp Song (Revisited)

Moderately Slow

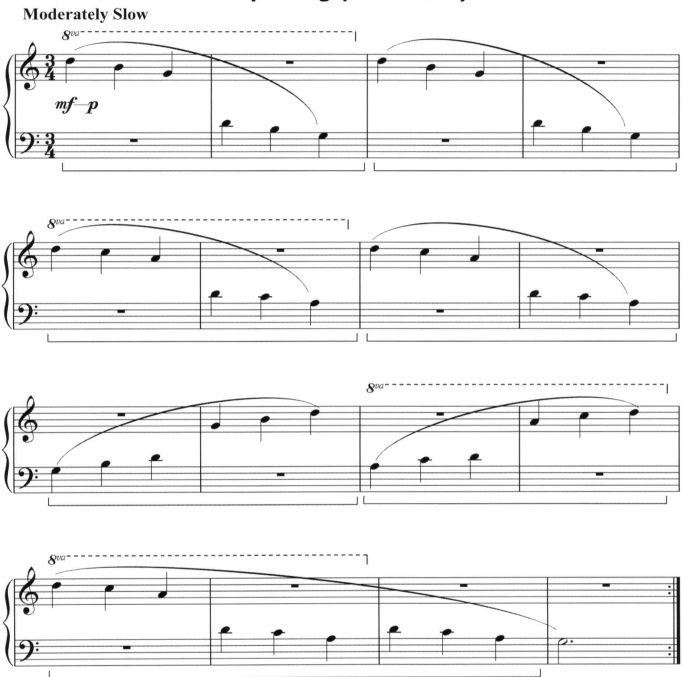

** The student will be delighted to be playing the 'whole' range of the keyboard after such a short learning time; also parents will feel that the new piano they just bought is getting full use!

CHAPTER TWO: THE TRIAD VOCABULARY

TRIADS

A Triad is a three note chord built on the 'Root' of the chord with an added third and then fifth. Like this:

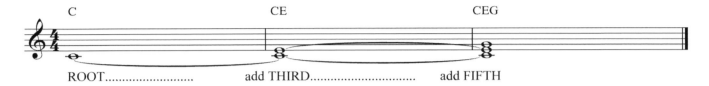

Here is a scale, with a Triad Chord (a three-note chord in thirds) for each note: we call this the **'Triad Vocabulary'**. Memorising this is a key component of understanding how chords are spelt and described (A chord, B chord etc....) as they remain unchanged throughout all the music theory we will learn.

Here it is....

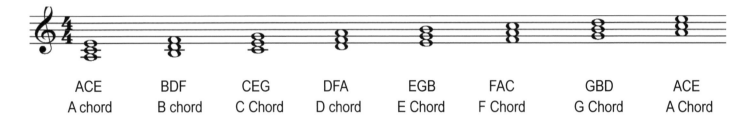

Say it and play it several times a day and soon enough you will have it fixed in your memory.

Here are several ways you might practise this exercise...

EX. 1

EX. 2

EX. 3

| A C E | B D F | C E G | D F A | E G B | F A C | G B D | A C E |

THE MAJOR SCALE

A key building block in the understanding of how music works is the major scale. Derived from the 'Ionian' mode, (white notes C to C on the keyboard) it contains a selection of intervals that create a clear hierarchy of notes and chords that reinforce the Tonic-Dominant relationship most effectively. This is one of the reasons why this 'church mode' of the renaissance period held a higher status than the other modes during the ensuing development of 'art' music, becoming the pre-eminent tonality for the baroque and classical composer.

So, how does it do this?

Firstly: the two halves are made up of the same intervallic relationships: these four-note patterns have become known as 'tetrachords', 'tetra' from the Greek for four.

Here is the major scale of C.

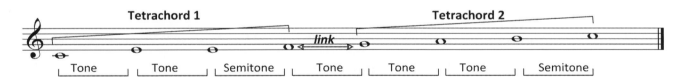

- Notice that the intervals between C-D, D-E, are 'whole tone' and then E-F is a 'semi-tone'.
- Then that the notes G-A, A-B, are 'whole-tone' and then B-C a 'semitone'.

Two identical tetra-chords make up the major scale linked by a tone F-G.

Secondly: the two 'semi-tone' intervals are an augmented fourth apart: F-B (or diminished fifth in inversion B-F): this 'discord' (known as the 'devil's interval') demands resolution outwards to its semi-tonal partners – F to E and B to C. Like this:

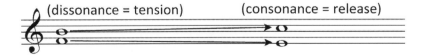

Thirdly: the start of the next scale on the clockwise circle of fifths always commences with the second tetrachord of its predecessor:

So C major can become G major by the simple addition of a tetra-chord that includes an F♯ like this.

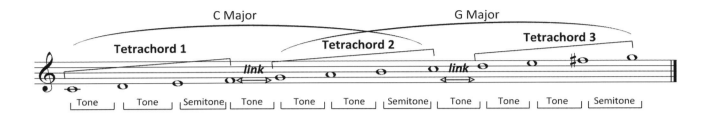

Fourth: the reverse is true – the starting tetra-chord of C major is the final tetra-chord in the key anti-clockwise on the circle of fifths, F. Like this:

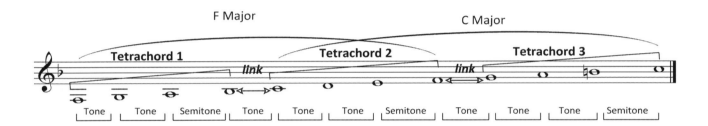

So the structure of the scale itself is representative of the harmony it underpins offering a sense of 'predictability' from which composers were able to suggest moods and set up expectations for the listener. The art of the tonal composer is to either fulfil or deny those expectations in a variety of ways we will discover as we progress.

Additionally, moving smoothly from one tonal region to another allows a composer to 'structure' music harmonically. This was the key principle for the composers of instrumental music in the baroque and classical period especially, but also beyond, through romanticism to the present day. Music without an external structure (story, lyrics, dance for instance) needed a narrative of its own to be intelligible, and harmony or 'tonality' gave it that narrative.

TRIAD VOCABULARY in C MAJOR

Once we have established the notes that make up a scale we can look at how melody (the scale) fits with harmony (the chords).

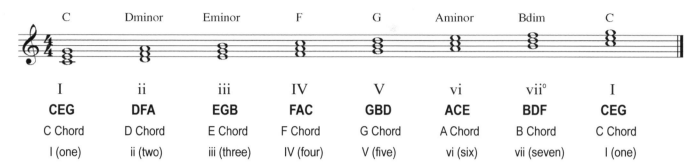

C	Dminor	Eminor	F	G	Aminor	Bdim	C
I	ii	iii	IV	V	vi	vii°	I
CEG	**DFA**	**EGB**	**FAC**	**GBD**	**ACE**	**BDF**	**CEG**
C Chord	D Chord	E Chord	F Chord	G Chord	A Chord	B Chord	C Chord
I (one)	ii (two)	iii (three)	IV (four)	V (five)	vi (six)	vii (seven)	I (one)

Play through this triad vocabulary in C in all the ways you did the earlier triad vocabulary: Say it and Play it!

Here are some new examples to help....

Triad Vocabulary In C

PRIMARY TRIADS & THE DOMINANT 7th

PRIMARY TRIADS

Students should notice that the two chords with the same 'quality' (major/minor/diminished) as the key chord CEG are FAC and GBD. They are all major chords. That is why they are called the 'Primary Triads' – they also are known as chords 1, 4, 5 because of their degree on the scale, and often written as Roman numerals: I - IV - V upper case = major: a major triad consists of a major third interval (C-E) followed by a minor third (E-G).

The other chords will be: 2, 3, 6 or, in Roman form, ii, iii, vi, – lower case = minor: a minor triad consists of a minor third interval (A-C) and a major third (C-E).

Chord vii is a diminished chord – we can ignore this chord for now, but, for the record, a diminished chord is made from two minor third intervals (B-D) (D-F).

Now we have learnt that the most important chords at this stage are the <u>Primary</u> Triads as they are unified, sharing the same 'qualities' in their natural state (major or minor), as the key chord. Now we can look at the Dominant Seventh chord.

DOMINANT 7th

As we know the dominant is the triad built on the fifth (V) degree of the scale. And we also know that triads are built from a root note, added 3rd, added 5th – so the Dominant chord in C is GBD. However, if we 'add' a seventh, we count up seven notes from the root of the chord G (GABCDE = F) and we create a Dominant chord with a seventh, which we call either a Dominant seventh, or a five-seven chord, (V7), or , in C major, G7.

It is a lot of names I know, but different styles of music tend to one or the other so it is as well to be familiar with them all.

Primary Triads & Dominant 7th

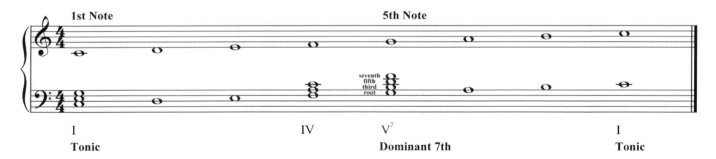

The emotional power of this chord lies in the interval between the 3rd (B) and the seventh (F). It is a fifth, but not a perfect fifth like C-G or G-D. Play it and you will hear it is 'discordant' – it is known as a 'tri-tone' or diminished fifth. As we know, in medieval times it was considered the 'devil's chord' and demanded instant resolution!

So play your B-F interval, and resolve each note in a contrary fashion – the F descends to the E; the B ascends to the C – this creates a major 3rd C-E which is the root and 3rd of the Tonic C chord.

If we add the 'Root' of the chord, in this case, G for chord V and C for chord I, we get this:

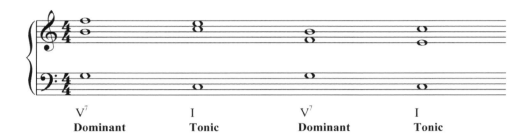

| V^7 | I | V^7 | I |
| Dominant | Tonic | Dominant | Tonic |

It sounds like an ending doesn't it? It is called a *'Perfect Cadence'*. This tension and release, or discord to concord, is at the heart of tonal music and to understand this is critical in developing expressive playing.

CHORD PROGRESSIONS

When we change from one chord to another, we call this a chord progression; chord sequence, or; 'chord change'. Again, several names for several styles, but they are all useful to know.

If we played all the chords in root position alone, as we did in the triad vocabulary exercise, we would be leaping across the keyboard from one chord to the next. So to prevent this, we 'rearrange' the notes of the chord in a different order. This is called an 'inversion'. It allows the hand to move from chord to chord with minimum effort to create a smoother sound.

The chords retain their name: C chord for example, even if the notes are in a different order: E in the left hand and GC in the right, for example. That is why knowing the Triad vocabulary is so useful, a C chord CEG is always that, wherever the notes are played.

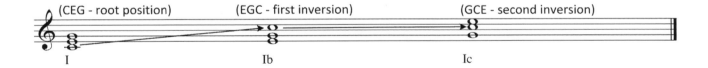

In the example above they are all C chords, because they all include CEG, but the notes appear in different 'inversions'. Below I have used inversions of chords IV and V7 so you can see how this works in practise. Play the C chord and then either of the IV and V7 options – which one requires the least physical effort and sounds the smoothest?

Chord Progressions

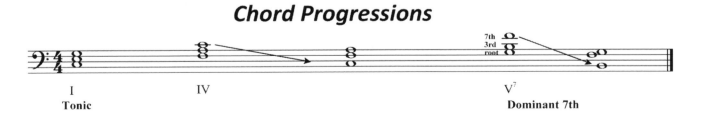

| I | IV | | V^7 |
| Tonic | | | Dominant 7th |

 Imagine you are in a choir and had to sing all the notes based on just root position chords – your voice would tire very quickly and it would sound 'unmusical' to the audience. That is why we call this selection of 'inversions' for chords, 'voicing': that is choosing which note follows in each part to create a smooth harmonious sound. Like this:

I	IV	V⁷
Tonic	**Subdominant**	**Dominant 7th**

Practise playing the two exercises below so your hands become familiar with the shapes and patterns of the chords – this should also be done in G major. Using the information above work out what the primary triads are for G major, and transpose the exercise accordingly.

Now here is the triad vocabulary using inversions starting on A:

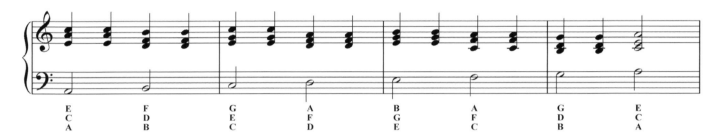

E C A	F D B	G E C	A F D	B G E	A F C	G D B	E C A

.......and now on C:

Notice how the right hand stays closer together instead of just rising up with the left.

Notice that the 'quality' (major, minor, diminished) is retained even when we invert the chords.

Notice the names of the chords above. Where just the capital letter is written: C for example, that means C major – it is assumed where nothing but the letter is indicated, that it is major.

Other chords are indicated with their letter and a description of their quality: like E minor (sometimes shortened to Emin or Em) or, Bdim.

Try playing the triad vocabularies in A and C using inversions – start with a different one than I have so you don't simply copy what I have done here. Then play them in the various styles (arpeggios, through the hands, waltz time etc...) we used when playing in root position.

Chord Progressions

Play RH one octave higher....

Chord Progressions

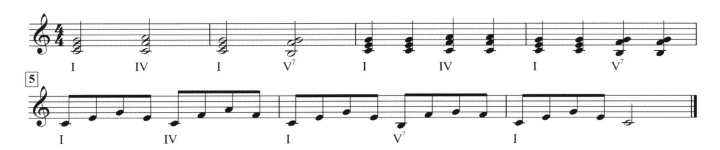

12-BAR BLUES PROGRESSION

Often, when talking about popular styles of music, the words 'three chord songs' are mentioned. It is these three primary chords on the first, fourth, and fifth degree of the scales they are referring to. They are very important in all music, but in popular music they have a special prominence because the roots of many popular styles lie with the 'blues', where these chords have particular resonance.

The blues is a style particularly associated with American music from the early part of the twentieth century, but it has left its mark on all forms of music ever since it first came to prominence in the 1900s. Its power lies in a simple progression of chords over 12 bars that lend themselves to endless variation and re-interpretation; and, of course, the chord progression uses but three chords. Chord I, IV and V7.

So, as a useful way to practise our chord progression I, IV and V7, we can learn the blues progression at the same time. It is written on the next page for LH and one octave higher using the RH so both your hands becomes familiar with these chord shapes.

The outline of the progressions is this:

Bar 1	Bar 2	Bar 3	Bar 4	Bar 5	Bar 6
C	C	C	C	F	F
Bar 7	Bar 8	Bar 9	Bar 10	Bar 11	Bar 12
C	C	G	F	C	C

...and it sounds like this:

12-Bar Blues Progression

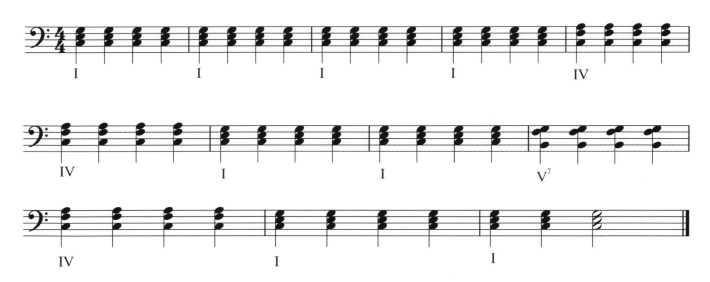

Play the additional root notes (one per bar) in the left hand once you have mastered the chords in the right hand. Notice, I have added a seventh to the G chord (GBDF the F) – more about this next chapter, for now just enjoy the sound and familiarise yourself with this progression. Use different inversions for the right hand chords when you have built sufficient confidence.

12 Bar Blues Progression (RH)

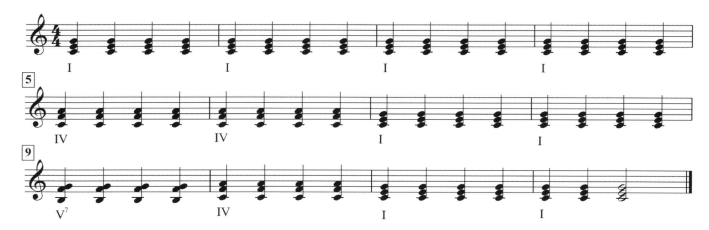

CHAPTER THREE – INVERSIONS

INVERSIONS REVISITED

FIRST INVERSION

A root position triad is inverted when we move the root to the top.

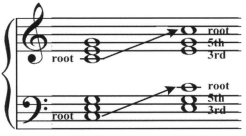

The letter names remain the same, as does the description (like C chord, A chord etc...) – but the root is at the top and the 3rd at the bottom.

The interval between the top two notes is a 4th with the root as the top note.

CEG becomes **EGC**

Play the following hands separately at first...

SECOND INVERSION

A first inversion triad is inverted when we move the 3rd to the top.

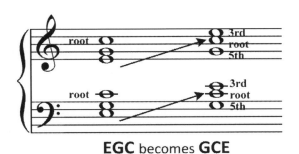

The letter names remain the same, as does the description (like C chord, A chord etc...) – but the 3rd is at the top and the 5th at the bottom.

The interval between the bottom two notes is a 4th with the root as the top note of the 4th.

EGC becomes **GCE**

Second Inversion Triads

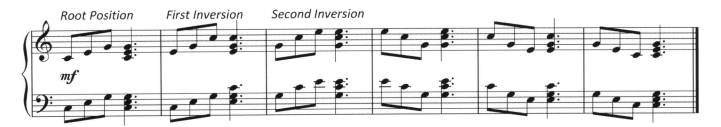

Now transpose to: G major, F major, D major.

STUDIES IN INVERSIONS ON PRIMARY TRIADS

Here is a short selection of quick studies using inversions in smooth 'voicings'. Practise these as written to begin, and then expand – I have offered some starting bars for you to continue...over time you should be able to memorise the inversions which will free you from the notation so you can explore the chords for yourself. You should do this exercise until you can achieve this state of freedom.

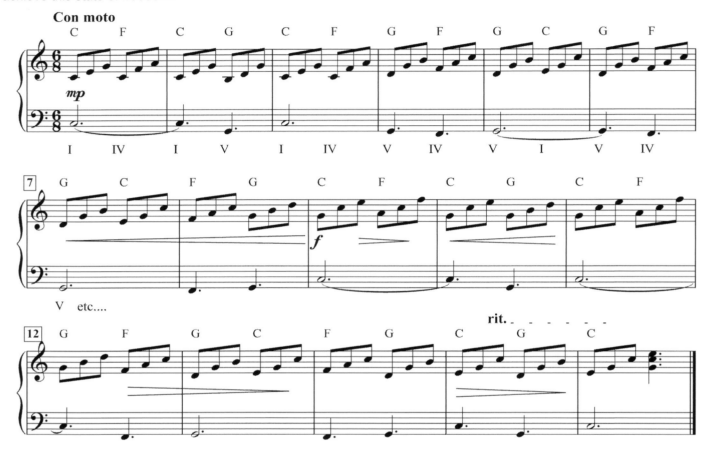

Do the above as: blocked chords, waltz time, a la Marcia, arpeggios...transpose this study to other keys you know or experiment with your own study.

For the LH, I offer only the basic chords – it is up to you to provide an accompaniment – it could be in 6-8 as above, or 4-4 like a march, or Alberti bass, or 3-4 waltz time, you decide, or, better still, try all of them!

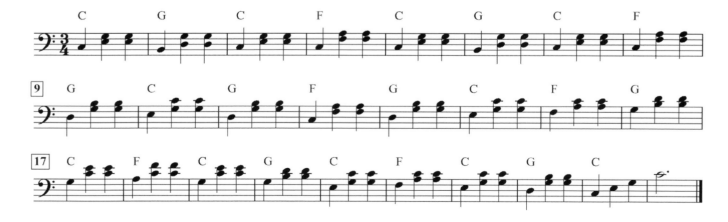

Transpose this to G, F major – use the chord numbers or names as a reference...and then play 'through' the hands.

SECOND INVERSION IMPROVISATION

Here is a piece called: Space Shuttle Blues from *Alfred's Basic Piano Library Level 4*:
It is blues piece that follows the 12-bar pattern, but with a twist. It has a shortened dominant bar. Learn the piece first and then we will do some improvisation exercises based on its main features.

Space Shuttle Blues

Play the LH alone first, naming the root of each triad.
Every LH chord is a 2nd inversion triad, so the root is always the MIDDLE note!

*   **Play the pairs of eighth notes a bit unevenly, long-short.**

** **Notice that the time-signature changes for one measure (bar) only.**

IMPROVISING ON SPACE SHUTTLE BLUES

1.   Take the left hand figure from Bar 2 and play it as an 'ostinato'…a repeated figure…until fluent…

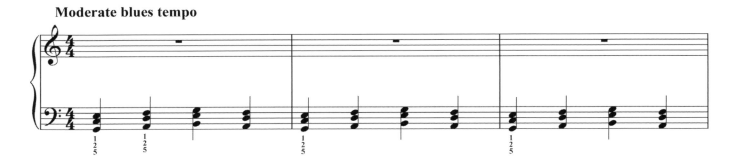

2.   Now look at the RH melody notes….practise this like a scale; as follows...

3.   Play them in any order, freely, above the ostinato. Remember to come up for air from time to time (breathe) like this….

4.   Now keep the LH going, but extend the RH notes into any octave above middle C…remember to breathe… and to use only the notes from the original melody…like this…

USING INVERSIONS CREATIVELY

Using the broken chord exercise that every Grade 1 student must learn and the examples above, we now have inversions under our fingers. But this 'physical' experience must be married to the knowledge of how they work in theory. Start with harmonising a scale, pay special attention to the voicing.

Also, for this exercise we will use the G7 chord we learnt in Chapter 1. GBDF is the full chord, but, the best 'voicing' in this case is GBF. Here is an example:

HARMONISING THE C MAJOR SCALE WITH PRIMARY TRIADS

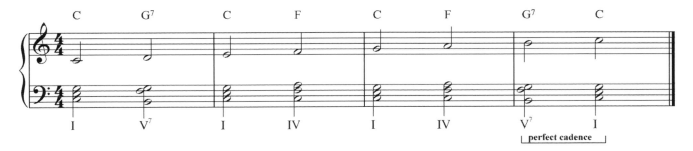

Now turn the LH into an 'Alberti bass' – be as patient as necessary, this is right and left brain co-operation. This should be done ascending and descending:

Now do the same exercise in G…
1. Play the scale and work out your primary triads
2. Work out which primary chord fits with each note
3. Decide on a smooth voicing using inversions
4. Play your blocked chords under your scale
5. Now play an Alberti bass using the chords
6. Now change the direction of the scale

LEFT-HAND SCALE

…and now the RH using a descending bass scale…

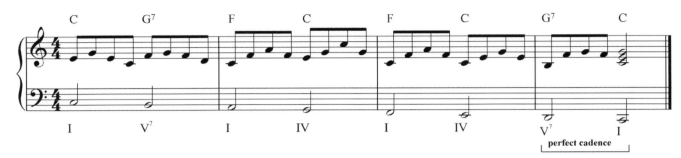

…and an ascending bass scale…

Do the same exercise in G and each key as you discover it… follow the steps outlined above, and reverse the hands.

CADENCES IN THREE POSITIONS

RIGHT-HAND

Here we use root LH notes, with inversions in the right hand: practise daily, also in G and D, and all subsequent new keys as they are learnt.

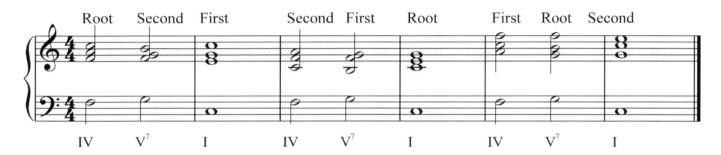

The above can be embellished to make it more 'pianistic' using all the familiar devices deployed when learning chords: here are a few options:

It is also possible to 'mix' inversions as appropriate: so using the above 'stylings' we can add more variety thus:

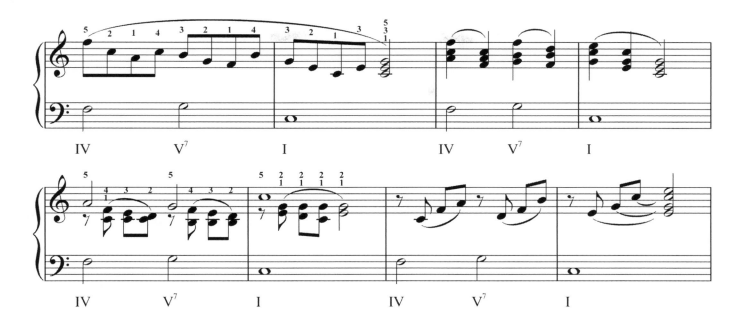

In the example above we see:

1. Extended arpeggio through first; second and root positions.
2. Two RH position chords.
3. Inner voice passing notes under second; first and first positions.
4. Graceful ascending arpeggios in second; second and first positions.

Now make up your own cadences developing these ideas. Try to be musical always, add crescendos, play loud, soft, in 3-4 or 6-8, a la waltz, a la Marcia, an octave higher etc...

LEFT HAND

Notice that we used only root positions in the LH so we could focus on the RH inversions. Now it is time to consider the Left hand.

On the previous page I have used 'Alberti' bass figurations exclusively, now you need to expand this with other techniques; here are two for starters:

I hope these exercises demonstrate just how much choice there is available to you with these three primary chords. The musical aspects (expression, dynamics, rubato) really do come from the player, and best practise suggests that if the simplest of exercises can be made to sound musical – those above for example – musical playing will become part of our natural approach to the instrument and therefore, 'effortless'. Of course, all the effort has been expended in the practise and that is why, throughout this book you will be urged to practise and experiment always, and in every key!

At the end of this chapter you have learnt about inversions, ostinato and riffs, harmonising scales, Alberti's bass, and a little bit more about the blues!

CHAPTER FOUR – TRIAD HIERARCHIES

Now you have learnt the basic Triad Vocabulary, we can start to transpose it to the specific keys we will be using. The first is the white key, C Major. Don't forget to say the triad notes when you play each chord; at least until it is second nature.

TRIAD VOCABULARY in C MAJOR REVISITED

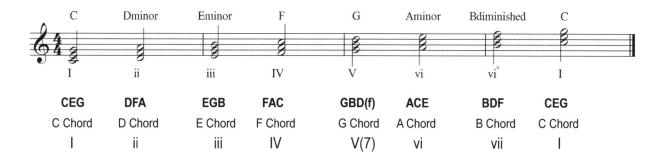

Play through this in all the ways you did the triad vocabulary in part 2, like this:

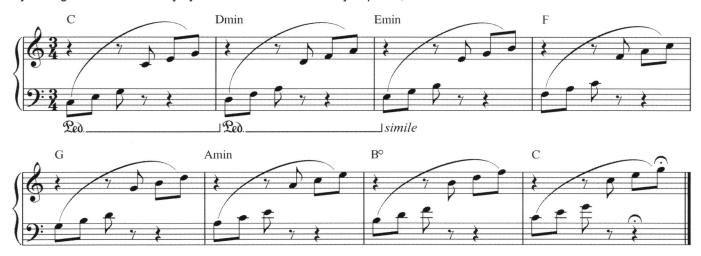

...or this...using inversions too:

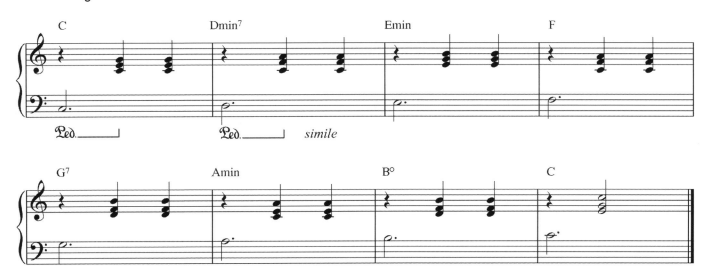

I have indicated the chords above the stave. You will notice a little short-hand happening with the spelling. To remind you, the rules are simple enough. A major chord requires nothing more than the letter; for example: C is assumed to be C Major. A minor chord is abbreviated to Amin or to Am – use varies but both are valid. The circle after the B signifies 'diminished' although some use Bdim – again, both are valid.

Students now know that the two chords with the same 'quality' (major) as the key chord CEG are FAC and GBD, are called the 'Primary Triads' – they also are known as chords 1, 4, 5 because of their degree on the scale. And often written as Roman numerals: I - IV - V upper case = major. The other chords will be ii, iii, vi, vii – lower case = minor. A useful way to think about this is as a pyramid...a Hierarchy.

TRIAD HIERACHIES

Remember, we start with the Primary Triads; well each primary chord has a relative minor. That is a key that shares the same key signature but starts on a different key note based on the sixth degree of its relatives ascending major scale, so has a different 'pattern' or 'mode' of notes.

For example in the key of C, the notes are CDEFGABC ascending – the sixth is A, so its relative minor is A minor.

In G, the scales ascends GABCDEF#G – the sixth degree is E, so E minor is the relative minor of G.

Look at this Triad Hierarchy in C Major*:

A minor is the relative of C Major

D minor to F Major   E minor to G Major

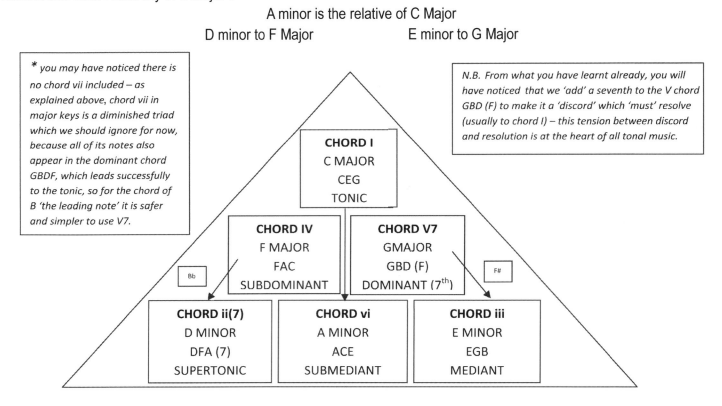

The arrows indicate the relative minors, and you can see, in each case, some of the same notes are present in both chords (CEG/ACE or FAC/DFA or GBD/EGB)

- The chords to the left (F major and D minor) both have a B♭ in the key signature.
- The chords to the Right (G Major and E minor) both have an F# in the key signature.
- The chords down the middle have neither sharp nor flat – they are C major and A minor.

SECONDARY CHORDS

These chords add an entirely new dimension to your improvising and consequently a whole new layer of expression; if you think about it, to add a minor chord to a major key melody even sounds quite interesting doesn't it? It is worth looking at the key of C triads again; here is the Triad Vocabulary in C with a little more detail...

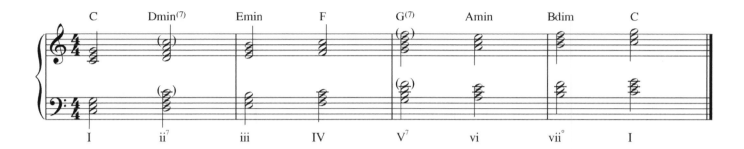

The Triad Vocabulary above suggests that each note of the C major scale could be harmonised with a different chord. However, as we know, to do it in this 'simplistic' triadic way wouldn't be very musical so from these chords we select chords and inversions that flow smoothly from one to another to create 'progressions' (one chord progressing to another) and support the melody. We call this 'voicing'.

RELATIVE SUBSTITUTES

So, when and where do we use these 'secondary' chords (that bottom layer of the Hierarchy) – well the most obvious way is as a 'substitute' for a Primary chord. And the first, but by no means only, substitute is the 'relative minor'.

So where we might have used an F chord FAC in a progression, we can safely 'substitute' D minor DFA because it shares two of its properties FA moreover if we add a seventh DFA(C), they are completely compatible. This is a secondary seventh about which we will learn more in the next chapter.

     Similarly for G (GBD) use E (EGB) minor (GB being the common tones)
     Similarly for C (CEG) use A (ACE) minor (CE being the common tones)

Also, remember that typically the chord before the end is V7 (GBDF in C major) as that leads most successfully to the tonic chord I (CEG). Following these simple rules we can create progressions of chords that lead away from, then back to, the tonic. Using the idea of substitutes we can 're-harmonise' the C major scale as follows...

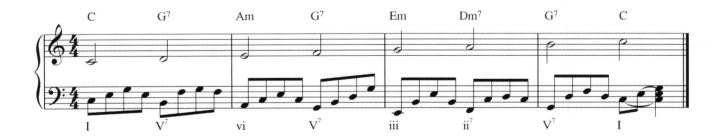

NOW TRY THE ABOVE USING THE DESCENDING SCALE IN C MAJOR:

1. Look at the notes in the scale.
2. Decide which chords, and which inversions, work well with the notes.
3. Select the chords and perhaps write them under the notes in short hand (Am, G7 for example).
4. Play through slowly. Use block chords at first, then try Alberti, Waltz time, arpeggios, repeating chords.
5. Do it again but change your chords and/or inversions this time.
6. Continue with this until you can do it without referring to your notation.

NOW REPEAT IN THE KEYS OF G, D, AND F.

Create a Triad Hierarchy for each key and follow the steps above in each case…

I've started G major for you…just fill in the missing parts….

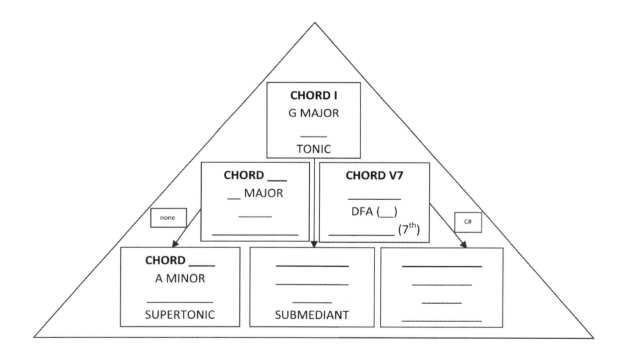

TIME TO BE CREATIVE!

Now we have a practical grasp of harmonic theory we can begin to discover which combinations of chords work especially well together. Take the Hierarchy and simply play round the chords in various different directions. Remember to use inversions and, to begin with, use the root of each chord as the LH bass note: play as arpeggios, as repeated chords, as waltz-time or 'a la can-can'.

Don't forget you can play the same chord more than once if you wish, and try to think in terms of four and eight bar phrases to begin with (one chord per bar).

Here are some examples to start you off:

CLOCKWISE IN C

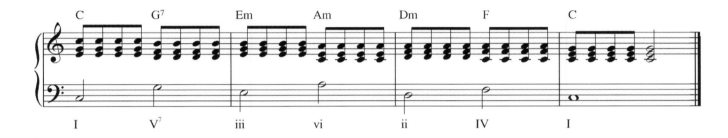

ANTI-CLOCKWISE IN G

Here are some staves to help: try to do everything in shorthand, and use pencil so you can do several attempts:

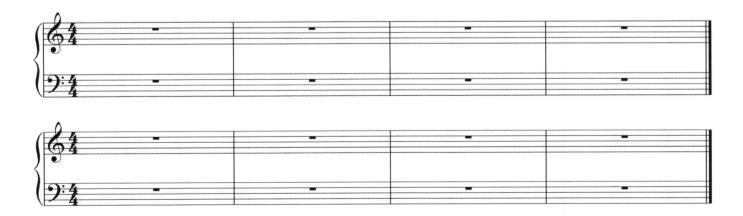

MAJOR KEY CHORD PROGRESSIONS

Over time, particular chord progressions become fundamental to a style: the 12-bar blues pattern we discovered in Chapter 3 for instance: composers return to them because they have a wide scope of expressive possibilities: here are two of the most common using the Triad Hierarchy:

Practise this daily….as block chords to begin, then as arpeggios, waltzes, etc…

'DOO-WOP'　　　　C　　　　　　Amin　　　　　Dmin7　　　　G7　　Repeat…
　　　　　　　　　　　I　　　　　　　vi　　　　　　ii7　　　　　V7

…you should be able to do this without the help of music, just playing through the shapes and inversions of the chords using the techniques like arpeggiating and waltzing. Here are two examples to start you off:

Now try this longer chord progression…

'PACHELBEL'　　　　C　　G7　　Amin　Emin　F　　　C　　　F (Dmin7)　　G7　　　Repeat…
　　　　　　　　　　　I　　V7　　vi　　iii　　IV　　I　　　IV (ii7)　　　V7

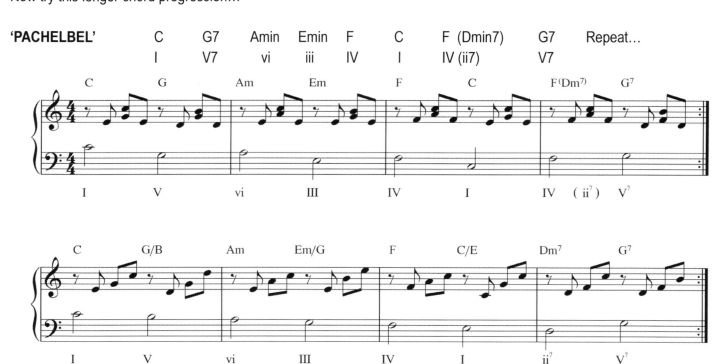

...in the first case I use the root notes as the LH bass notes, but in the second I use a stepwise descending bass derived from inversions of the chords...so even using the same chord progression I can create a different texture... Notice how it is spelt above the stave: the chord name followed by the bass note i.e. G/B = G chord with a B bass....you try it...and then transpose both exercises to the keys of G, D, and F.

LEAD SHEETS

Now you are familiar with the names and numbers of the chords, we can consider Lead Sheets.

A Lead Sheet is a basic outline of a piece of music – it includes: melody, chords, and lyrics where necessary. It is shorthand for musicians, who then combine to 'create' their own parts to make up the ensemble sound. It is easier for the writer, because he can just jot down the essential details and then allow the musicians to do the rest. Small Combo Jazz and Popular musicians use this model almost exclusively...

Here is an example of Silent Night as a lead sheet:

Using the basic outline above, and its chord indications, we can begin to work out an accompaniment suitable for the solo line. First we just 'comp' our way through the chords like this....

A WORD ON COMPING

This method of just playing through the chords in a basic rhythm is often called 'comping' - it is a term derived from 'accompaniment' and refers to an accompaniment that is really only a very broad outline of the harmony rather than an elaborate identifiable part. It is like 'strumming along'. Sometimes it is all that is required, sometimes it is rather too simple, but it is an ideal way of becoming familiar with the shapes and patterns of the chords before we start to add the elaborations.

Notice the 'harmonic rhythm' – the rate of chord change - hitherto we have allowed one chord per bar, except for the 12-bar blues which has its own harmonic rhythm, but harmony is very flexible and we can see from Silent Night that the chords change in four, two, and one bar sections...the harmonic changes work to support the melodic material, and knowing when and where to change the chords is part of the skills required for a good accompanist. Here is Silent Night 'comped'....sing along...

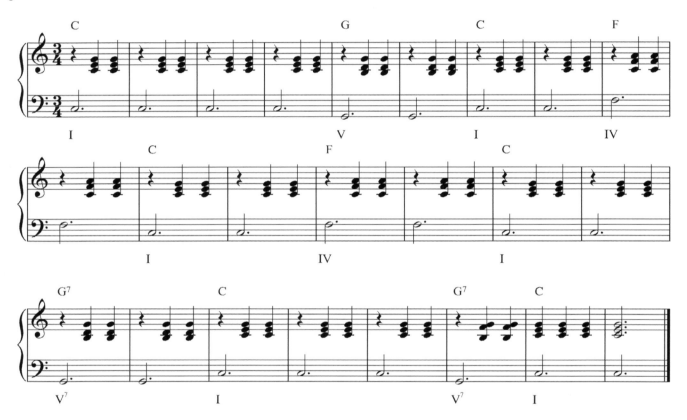

...next we look at the key pitches of the melody line...this gives us a clue as to the inversions we might use.

Remember that especially when accompanying a singer your accompaniment will be used not just to outline the harmony, but also to provide the essential pitches for the singer(s) to remain confident of their tuning. We can also add some inversions by amending the bass notes a little, so the bass has some 'movement' of its own to complement the melody:

Like this....

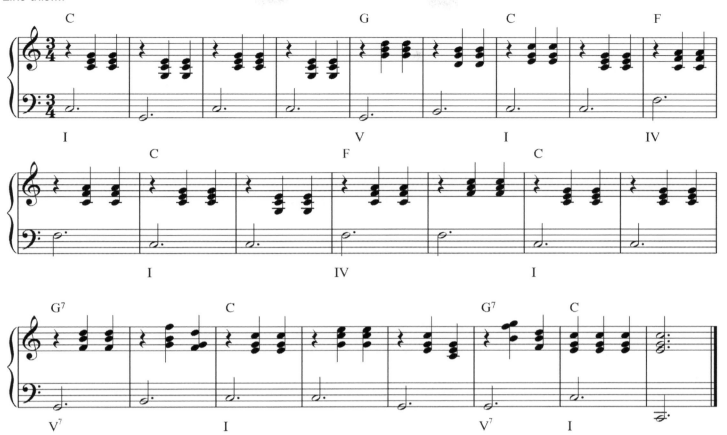

...it is still a little rough and ready, but decent enough to sing too.

Now we can look at the mood and the style and begin to work on the accompaniment a little, just adding some more interesting detail, and perhaps a pattern that gives it rhythm and fluency. We don't want too much, because, after all, we are accompanying, not soloing.

We need to listen to the vocal melody in our heads or, even better, sing it out loud.

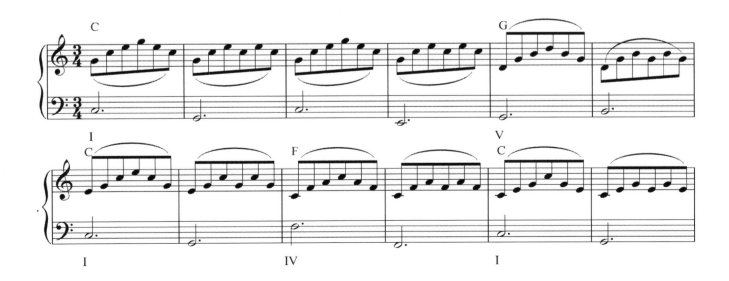

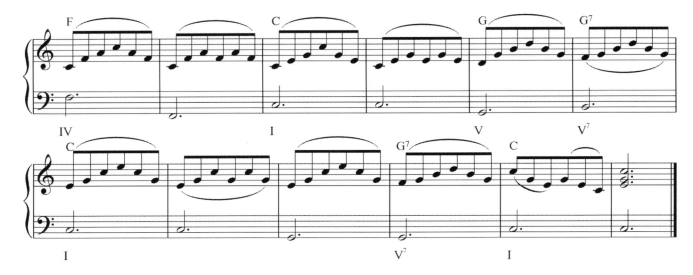

...so now we have an accompaniment that works, we can look to 'add' some substitute chords using our triad hierarchy. Have a look at the chords above and see if you can substitute them successfully with their relative minors...this may take a little experimentation at the instrument, but take your time and play around, making sure what you change still underpins the melody. Most of all, enjoy this process of exploration.

Below is a version I have done, but I recommend you do your own experimenting first, then compare!

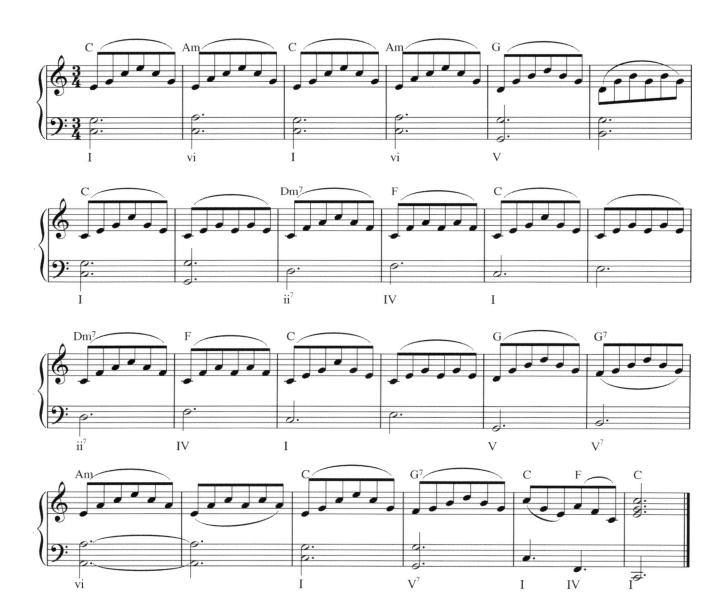

So how did you get on? I hope you were happy with your harmonisation. You may have agreed or disagreed with my choices, but that is fine, it is what music is about.

As a final exercise, I would use my left hand as an Alberti bass accompaniment and play the melody in the right hand. This melody and accompaniment texture is vital when you have a singer or instrumentalist who is not sure of their own melody – by playing along with them you are helping them learn – but also, if ever you are asked to play some Christmas tunes as a preamble to an assembly or a dinner, you can easily accompany your singing right hand with your accompanying left – here, I've started you off....

Now find more Christmas Carols or other songs of your choice and create more accompaniments!

CHAPTER FIVE – SEVENTHS

SEVENTHS

A seventh may be formed when adding a note that is a seventh above the root of a root position triad:

They can look like this....   or like this....

7th chord in spaces   **7th chord on lines**

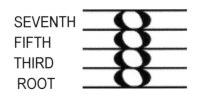

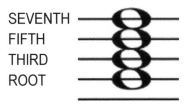

THE COMPLETE SEVENTH CHORD VOCABULARY

Here is the Seventh Triad Vocabulary and below is the 'symbol' we would give to the chords based on their qualities in C major: using this vocabulary you can play seventh chords in any key just by using the 'key' signature, but remember when we 'change the key' this changes the quality of the chords too! Play them on the piano...you can use both hands by taking the bottom two notes in the LH and the top two notes in the RH if it is easier...then play them using the key signature of D or G or F major...can you hear how the 'quality' of some chords changes...?

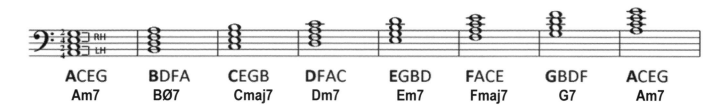

ACEG	BDFA	CEGB	DFAC	EGBD	FACE	GBDF	ACEG
Am7	BØ7	Cmaj7	Dm7	Em7	Fmaj7	G7	Am7

MEMORISING THE SEVENTH CHORD VOCABULARY

As with the triad vocabulary, the best way to secure your memory is to play and say the vocabulary in many different ways, daily. Here are some examples for you to start with, and then think of some for yourself. Blocked Chords:

A C E G B D F A   C E G B D F A C   E G B D F A C E   G B D F A C E G

...Arpeggios through the hands...

A C E G   B D F A   C E G B   D F A C

Ped. _____ simile...

5

E G B D   F A C E   G B D F   A C E G

Now we apply inversions....

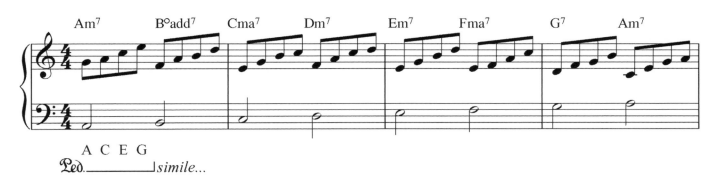

A C E G

Ped. _____ simile...

Try sevenths with the Doo-Wop – it sounds quite jazzy:

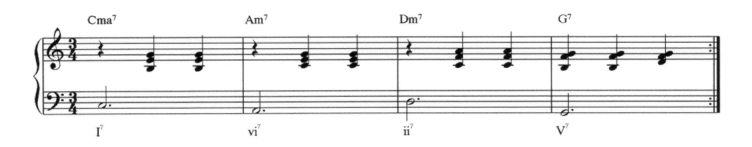

And with the Pachelbel – again it sounds a little jazzy:

Remember to do all of this in every key you know!

SCALES WITH SEVENTHS

Using just two seventh chords it is possible to practise scales in both hands: it is a good way to practise sevenths and scales at the same time!

In C major chord Cmaj7 (Imaj7)= CEGB; dmin7 (ii7) = DFAC; within these two chords all the notes of the C scale (CDEFGAB) are included, so add a simple chord accompaniment and play your scales.

It sounds quite 'jazzy', doesn't it? Apply the same two chords in G major and you can practise your RH scales in this same jazzy style...don't forget the F♯ in the key signature!

For the LH, try a 'walking bass' for your scales and use the right hand to add some 'swinging' chords – again it sounds neat.

Transpose to G, D and F. Remember to include any sharps and flats suggested by the key signature.

PASSING NOTES & NON-HARMONIC TONES

The point of the exercise is to demonstrate that not all melody notes, (in this case notes of the scale) all of the time, need to be harmonised by a chord. Sometimes the notes in the melody (or bass line) can pass between the 'harmony' notes – we call these 'passing notes' for obvious reasons, but also we refer to them as 'non-harmonic tones' – that is, notes that do not belong to the prevailing chord.

Here is the start of the C scale with the non-harmonic tones indicated. See how they pass between the 'harmonic' notes (the notes of the chord): this tension between the melody and underpinning harmony is another expressive device we can use in our music making.

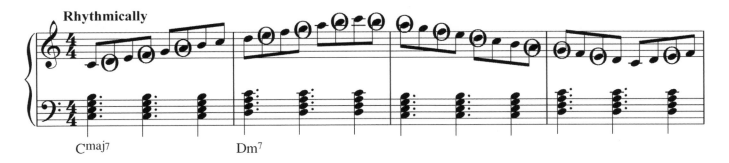

It is reasonable to say, that providing you remain within key, and as long as the structural points (cadences, ends of phrases) are harmonically clear, melodies can literally dance over the top of the harmony quite freely, especially quick moving melodies where the chord/melody 'collision' isn't prolonged and it resolves to a harmony note. Improvisers call this *'making a wrong note right!'*

VOICING SEVENTH CHORDS

You may have noticed that playing ALL the notes of a seventh chord create a 'dense' sound – especially when played below middle C. In the right hand it is less obvious, but we want the melodies to sing, so having too much sound in close proximity is not necessary. To maintain the impact of the harmony, but create spaciousness for the melodies to 'breathe' we introduce the phenomena called 'voicing'.

We have met this before when deciding which inversion of triad would pass most effectively to another. Where this differs slightly is that we now remove the inessential notes of the seventh chord to create space. It may be voiced in another part, like the melody, or is simply omitted as it is not essential for defining the harmony. Of course we can't remove the root as that spells the chord (although we will later!); nor the seventh as that is the point; the third defines the quality (major or minor) but the fifth of a seventh chord for example doesn't really affect the overall impression, so could be omitted with little impact.

...sevenths without fifths....

...additionally, if the melody contains the third, or notes that revolve around the third, where this is the case, we can happily omit it from the seventh chord to create seventh chord where the 'quality' is left ambiguous (is it major or minor...?) and this useful expressive device is often used in jazz and popular music.

...sevenths without thirds....

EXERCISE:

Swingin' Sevenths from *Alfred's Basic Piano Library Level 4* is a useful piece for demonstrating both voicing and passing notes or non-harmonic tones.

1. Put a circle round the 'non-harmonic' notes in Swingin' Sevenths. There are 5 in the first 8 bars...did you get them – and do they pass between harmonic notes?

2. Now look at the LH chords and identify which have had the fifth or the third omitted?

Swingin' Seventhss

Now we have mastered Swingin' Sevenths, we can use the LH chords and the RH positions to 'improvise' a version of our own Swingin' Sevenths, here are the opening bars re-imagined...

Swingin' Sevenths Re-Imagined

Moderately Slow with a "Swing Feeling"

Notice how I varied the voicing in the LH in bars 1, 3, 5: where the melody changed its focus from third to fifth, I reflected this in the accompaniment. It is not essential to do this, but it keeps the chords complete.

Melodically, I simply turned the tune upside down and varied the starting pitch but for the most part kept the same rhythm. This could be expanded much more, but at this stage it is useful to take small steps until confidence facilitates giant leaps... one must climb trees before mountains. Try Swingin' Sevenths for yourself, adding new melodic material to the chords given, and selecting the appropriate voicing.

Now try the scale exercise again, but with varying voicing for the chords: here are two examples...

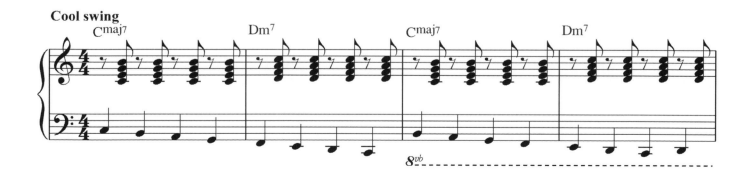

A WORD ABOUT SEVENTHS

Look at this seventh vocabulary in C Major:

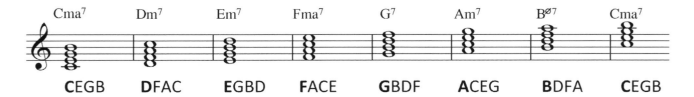

Cma⁷	Dm⁷	Em⁷	Fma⁷	G⁷	Am⁷	Bø⁷	Cma⁷
CEGB	DFAC	EGBD	FACE	GBDF	ACEG	BDFA	CEGB

When we add a minor seventh to a chord we 'heighten' the dominant impulse. That is to say we add a discord which needs resolution; this propels the music forward harmonically. The most powerful of the sevenths is the aptly named Dominant which comprises a major triad with a minor third. Play them through and listen carefully to their qualities: can you hear that there is only one 'dominant' seventh in the vocabulary above – one per key?

There are three minor sevenths (ii7, iii7, vi7): two major sevenths (Ima7, IVma7) and a diminished chord with a seventh BDFA. Minor sevenths are weaker: they hold the seventh discord, but not the devil's interval or impulse of 'the leading note'; the major seventh is discordant, but more decorative. The diminished chord is powerfully expressive, and occasionally used as a substitute for Chord V7, but does not contain the strong rooted structure of a Perfect fifth, so the chord upon which it might resolve is 'variable' – that is to say it could be a chord other than the tonic. V7, like gravity, pulls inexorably toward the tonic.

Look at the hierarchy of scale degrees for the major key: some of these are familiar, but what is interesting is where the notes within the V7 chord reside:

Tone-----------Tone------Semi-tone-----Tone-----------Tone---------Tone------Semi-tone

Tonic   Supertonic   Mediant   Subdominant   Dominant   Submediant   Leading Note   Tonic

1.   D between C and E   2. F falling to E

3.   B rising to C   4. G (and F) mid-way between the high and Low Tonic C

Also, two of the notes from the G7 chord fall or rise a semitone to the defining notes of the tonic chord.

This leaves the dominant as the only 'primary' dominant seventh per key – so in reality it is not the quality of the 'tonic' that defines a key, but its dominant – the rooted perfect fifth (G-D) interposed by a diminished 5th interval of the V7 chord notes 3 and 7 (B – F) must resolve outwardly (C – E) to establish tonality. This creates the cadence we saw in Chapter One. And later on, we shall see it is the power of the dominant chord that propels you around the circle of fifths.

I often use the analogy of chess to describe the role of the dominant in music: in chess we protect the king at all costs (the Tonic), but it is in fact the queen (the dominant) that wields the most power!

THE INTERRUPTED CADENCE

Using the power of the dominant we can set up expectations and either satisfy or deny them. Music has the power to sound predictable, as if everything is moving along quite nicely, and then suddenly the direction changes and we have to rediscover the path again. Such is the nature of the interrupted cadence.

The interruption can effectively be to any other chord than the expected tonic, but the most common are: relative minor (V7 – vi) and the subdominant (V7 – IV). Here is a wonderful example of the former from Chopin and also a lovely use of the augmented sixth chord in its Italian version as the second interruption - try playing an E minor chord in the first case, then a perfect cadence in the second – can you hear how much 'drama' has been lost by simply ending the piece in a conventional way?

Chopin Prelude in E minor (ending)

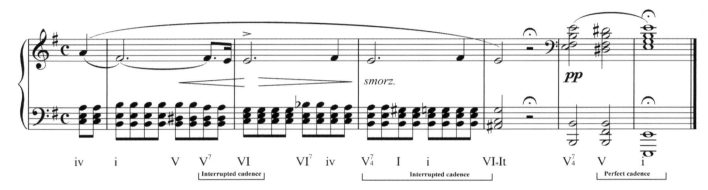

Additionally we can use the interrupted cadence to extend a progression making it a more complex musical statement than say a straight four chords: take the two slightly different interpretations of the cadence mentioned above using the Doo-Wop progression:

Interrupted Cadence to the Relative Minor:

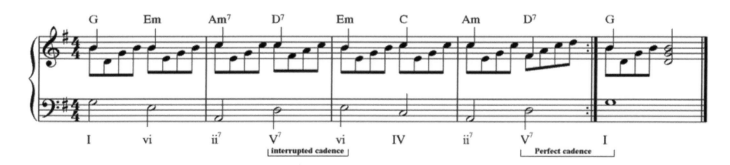

Interrupted Cadence to the Subdominant:

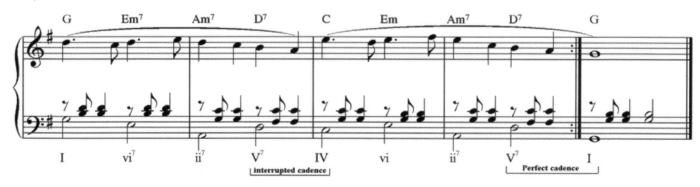

CHAPTER SIX – THE BLUES

ABOUT THE BLUES

Now we understand the primary triads in C, G and F, and have played them so often, we can begin to add variations. The blues is a form of music developed in the USA, and its three most typical characteristics are:

- **The flattened seventh chord**
- **The 12-bar pattern**
- **The blues scale**

1. The flattened seventh: simply put, each chord is a dominant seventh. So where previously we have used a dominant seventh chord only, now we make every chord sound like a dominant seventh.

2. The 12-bar pattern is a chord progression that is uniquely suited to this music and holds the same place as binary form might for a baroque composer or sonata form for a classical composer. It seems to be the most suitable structure into which to pour the musical ideas.

Here is the pattern in C with the seventh chords:

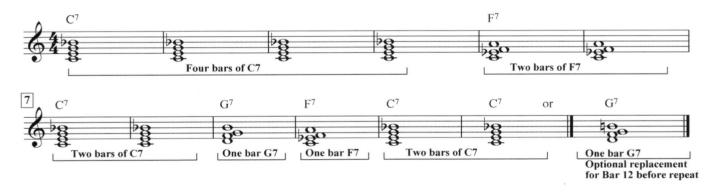

This pattern should be practised and memorised. Did you recognise it? You played it in Chapter One only on that occasion it was in G, and also when playing Space Shuttle Blues in Chapter Two. If you go anywhere in the world and meet a group of musicians who all say 'let's play a blues in C' you will be able to join in using this pattern.

Now practise this chord sequence using a comping technique learnt from previous exercises – use the chord names (C, F, G) as the bass notes and use inversions. Let me start you off....

Notice in bar 2-3: I used slashes rather than write out the individual notes – this is a shorthand way of saying play the chord again – jazz/pop musicians use this technique frequently.

Notice in Bar 4: I used a 'repeat previous bar' sign, this is also a shorthand technique, and used by classical musicians too – it simply means repeat the previous bar. If you are repeating the previous two bars you add a slash, %. and place it on the barline between the two bars.

We will discover other useful 'shorthand' techniques as we progress.

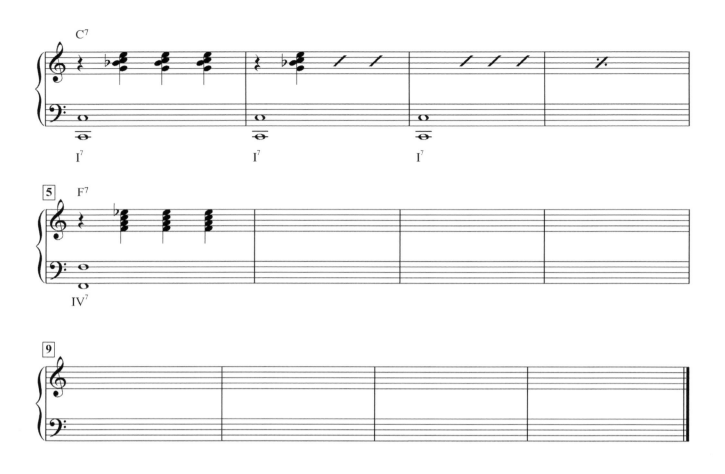

3. Now for the blues scale: here it is in C…

Did you notice the E♭? this would ordinarily make a minor triad in C (C-E♭-G), but the chord is definitely major (C-E-G)! This is the distinct 'bittersweet' quality of the blues: it is at once major and minor. That's why we don't say 'Blues in C major', we just say 'Blues in C' it is perfectly ok to play E natural, and many do for variety, but less authentically 'bluesy'!

Practise this scale daily using whichever fingering you feel most comfortable with. Play in every octave of the piano, so you can hear its possibilities. Then practise the three note patterns either side of the F♯ - did you notice how one is C7 the other F7 – that is why this single scale works so well over the whole chord progression.

4. An optional aspect of the blues is the 'Walking Bass' line. This is a bass line that 'walks' up and down the notes of the chord giving the music both rhythm and harmony, like a baroque continuo. Here are the basslines for the three chords in C.

EXERCISE:

Put a circle round the 'harmony' notes, and a cross through the 'non-harmonic tones'. Practise this in the 12-bar sequence with your left hand daily!

5. The 'walking bass' works especially well with the 'comping' technique, especially if you add a little swing – here is the first bar to start you off – see if you can get throught the whole 12-bar sequence doing this – it sounds great, just like that old Elvis Presley song All Shook Up.

Practising the blues is great fun, but needs patience. Also, there are three elements here.

The blues scale

The seventh chords

The walking bass-line

...it would be impossible to practise them all at once, so the best strategy is to do two at any one time. Simply transfer the chords to the left hand while the right hand practises the scale. Like this:

*don't worry about changing scale when you change chord, as we noticed before, astonishingly the scale still works; that is the 'magic' of the blues!

6.   Now transpose all of the above to G, D and F, and practise some more… here, I started you off in G with the chords and some clues; play with a little swing so the rhythm 'grooves'…

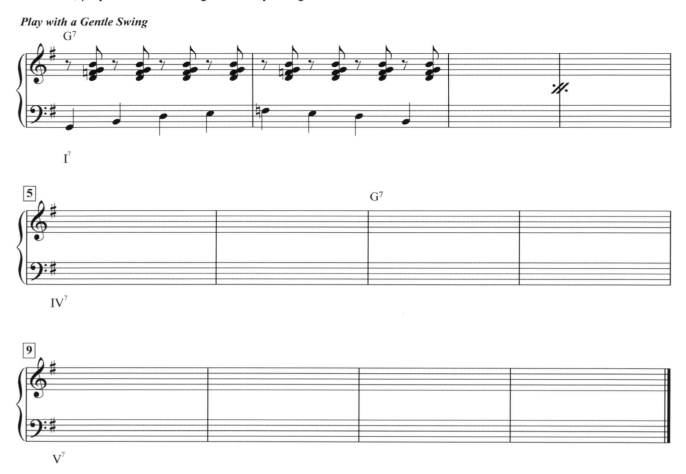

…and F with the scale…but fewer clues…

Now you need to play in D without any help from me....write down the chords if you want, and even notate the blues scale and the walking bass, so you can practise separately – just a quick memo like this:

Blues Scale in D

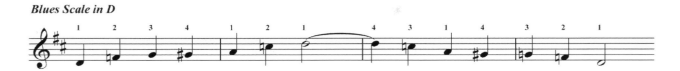

Blues Seventh Chords in D

Walking Bass in D

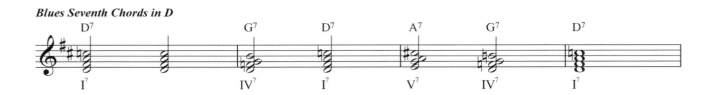

Don't forget to try the chords in all inversions, and practise the walking bass in each LH position.

The Blues scale should be practised as a scale, and then using selected 'riffs' – that is little patterns that sound neat repeated; like this one...

...or this...

Now you should be able to put them together as we did the C, G and F

Play with a Gentle Swing

7.   Remember to change the inversions of the seventh chords so that you get a different sound. Try to imagine a bass player, or even better, ask a friend or your teacher to play the bassline while you play the chords and improvise a melody… below is an example of what I mean…and, you might swap over, so that everyone gets a chance to improvise and practise all the elements of the blues. Do this in every key you know!

THREE HAND BLUES

Here is the basic outline in C (again I include the major third as optional) – try it with a friend or your teacher. *....(I've included the major third in the blues scale as an option – it is permissible though unorthodox, and again depends on taste)

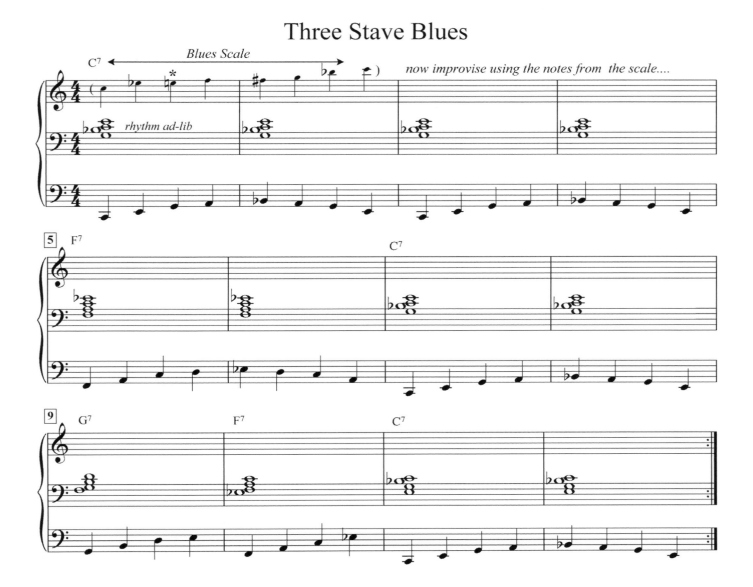

Three Stave Blues

Of course there is so much more to the blues than what we have covered in this chapter, it is a lifetime of study really, and we will be revisiting the style further down the line for sure, but I have always found this starting approach effective and enjoyable. Typical of the blues, but also music in general, combinations of the simplest elements can produce striking results. This means that after only a few weeks of good practise a musician can exercise their creativity and make enjoyable music that will impress their friends.

CHAPTER SEVEN – AN EXCURSION IN MINOR KEYS

MINOR SCALES

Let's explore minor scales in a little more detail: first the D minor (relative of F major) scale triad vocabulary;

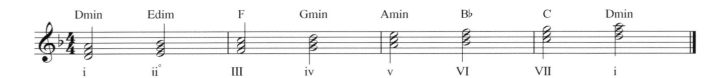

Can you hear that the major triads are now <u>not</u> the primary chords, but occur of the third, sixth and seventh degrees of the scale? The same chords as in F Major (the relative major) are present, just in a different order, so when devising a 'progression' the same rules can apply. However, there is an additional one. Chord v (A minor in this case) can be temporarily turned into a major chord V (raising the seventh note – the leading note C♯) so it, along with the seventh (A C♯ E G), creates the 'dominant' impulse V7 necessary for the effective resolution to the tonic. Here is the graphic illustration:

TRIAD HIERARCHY in D Minor*

CHORD ii(7)
Edim
EGBb(D)
SUPERTONIC

CHORD i
D MINOR
DFA
TONIC

CHORD iv
G MINOR
GBbD
SUBDOMINANT

CHORD v(7)
A MAJ/MIN
AC(#)E (G)
DOMINANT (7th)

CHORD VI
Bb MAJOR
BbDF
SUBMEDIANT

CHORD III
F MAJOR
FAC
MEDIANT

CHORD VIIC
MAJOR
CEG
LEADING NOTE

The chords to the left (B♭ major and G minor) both have a B♭ and E♭ in their key signature.

The chords to the right (C Major and A minor) both have no sharps/flats in the key signature.

The Chords down the middle have one flat B♭ – they are F major and D minor.

You may have noticed there is no chord ii(7) included in the hierarchy – in D minor EGB♭(D) it is a diminished triad but unlike in the major keys, because of the expressive nature of minor keys, we can use it as we would in the major keys, as a substitute for chord iv (ii7 - V7 - i) and, because we have chord VII, a major chord, available too, we have an extra chord to work with in the minor keys.

MINOR KEY INVERSIONS IN PRACTICE

Having concentrated on major keys until now, we will need to revise some of those exercises we applied to major keys for the minor keys so we have the shapes and patterns under our fingers. The principle is the same, but the sound is quite different. Also, there is an accidental, 'the raised seventh' discussed with the Hierarchy so it will serve us well to hear these in action: here is a delightfully simple piece by Ludwig Shytte which will serve as a useful starting point:

CHORD BLOCKING: a useful way to start this exercise is to simply play the chords as blocks in each hand. It consolidates the hand shape and also indicates the best fingering.

DEFINE INVERSIONS: as you play through the exercise say aloud the inversion: Root; First; Second.

DEFINE CHORDS: as you play, name the chords: C chord, A minor, etc....

Waterfall

Ludwig Shytte
(1848-1909)

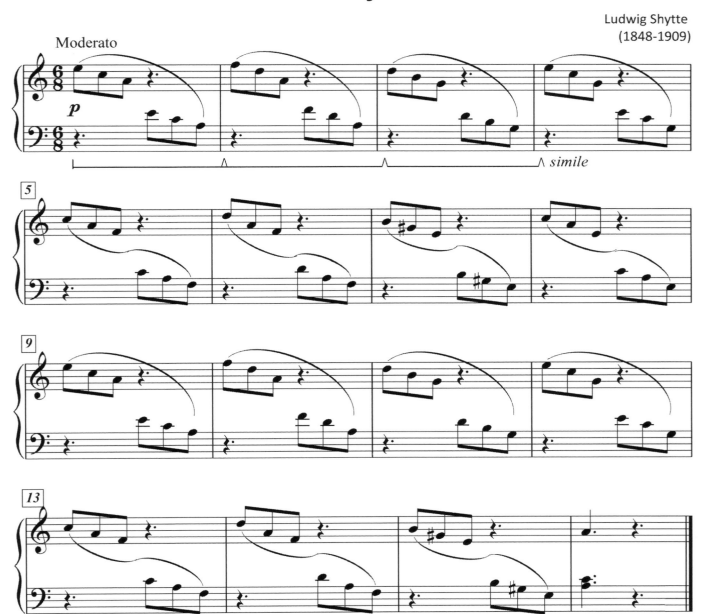

IMPROVISING ON WATERFALLS

Using the chord progression, and Ludwig Schytte's model, we can 'expand' the ideas presented to develop our fluency and control...here are some starting points for your improvising....continue these through the whole piece, and then think of some new ones...

1.   Reverse the arpeggios...

2.   Contrary arpeggios....

3.   Two octave rapid hand-over-hand arpeggios...

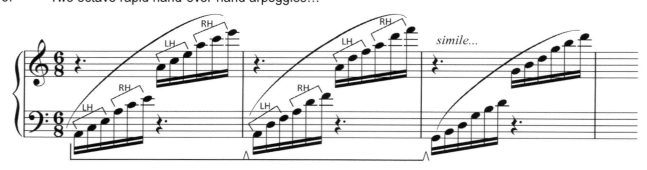

4.   Waltz time...

HARMONISING THE MINOR SCALE

Here is the D minor scale harmonised in 3/4, play it with and without the sharps, and you may hear what I mean about the dominant impulse, especially at the end. To play without the sharps sounds 'medieval' or 'modal', and that is because the 'natural' minor scale is in fact the 'Aeolian' mode – we create the artificial 'harmonic' and 'melodic' minor scales specifically to retain the impulse of the dominant/tonic relationship.

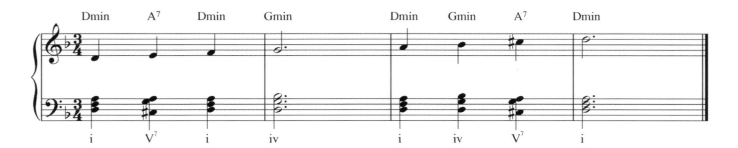

SUBSTITUTIONS IN THE MINOR KEY

The great thing about relatives is that you can slip in and out of their houses and know you will be always welcome. It is the same with music. Relative major and minor keys can effortlessly slip in and out of one another. Here is D minor harmonised again, but notice how many more major chords there are this time, and how it seems to be in F major in the middle with C7 as a dominant:

Now do the above in the keys of Amin, Emin and B minor working out your own chord progression. Here are some empty staves to help – remember to use shorthand only!

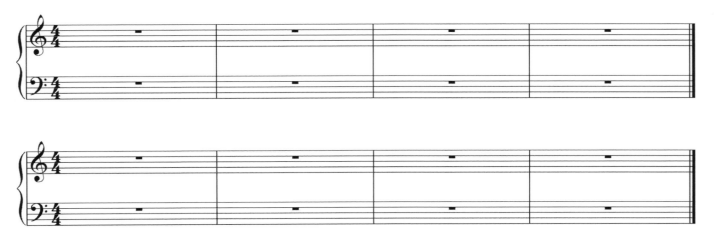

TRANSPOSING DOO-WOP and PACHELBEL TO THE MINOR KEY

Remember the 'Doo-Wop' chord progression we practised in the major key – here it is again:

'DOO-WOP'	C	Amin	Dmin7	G7	Repeat…
	I	vi	ii7	V7	

Play it through – referring back to Chapter 4.

So what would it sound like 'transposed' to the minor key?

	Amin	F	Bdim7	E7	back to Amin….
	i	VI	iiØ7	V7	

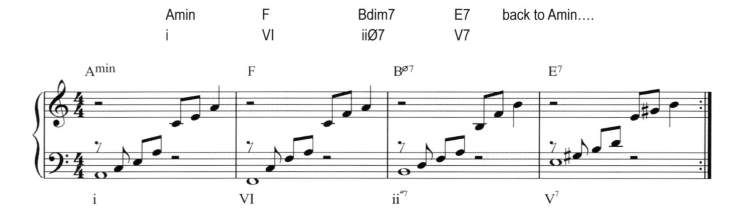

Now try it in D minor….remember the raised 7th!

…and here is the other 'classic' chord progression: the 'Pachelbel'…

'PACHELBEL'	C	G7	Amin	Emin	F	C	Dmin7	G7	Repeat…
	I	V7	vi	iii	IV	I	ii7	V7	

…and the **PACHELBEL MINOR**

	Am	E7	F	C	Dm	Am	Bdim	E7	back to Amin….
	i	V7	VI	III	iv	i	iiØ7	V7	

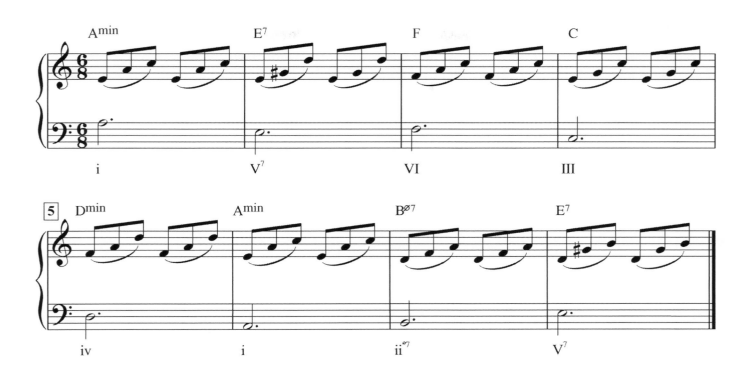

Doesn't it sound exotic? Especially the B diminished with seventh (iio7) – you can make this a minor seventh chord by changing the F♮ to a ♯ if you wish, especially if it rises to the G♯, try it, I think it sounds less exotic, but it is a matter of choice in the end.

Now your turn in D minor

Now transpose these progressions into B minor and E minor. Use the chord numbers and the triad hierarchy to establish the chords - write them down shorthand if you wish in a rough style like this….

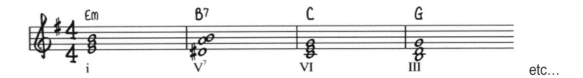

etc…

66

GROUND BASS

Try this…

Am	Em/G*	F	C/E*	Dm	Am/C*	Bdim (orBm)	E7	Repeat
I	IV	VI	III	iv	I	iio7	V7	

*g bass   *e bass *c bass

*N.B. *Remember when a chord symbol is written thus: G/D - it means a G chord with a D bass.*

Here it is as a lead sheet:

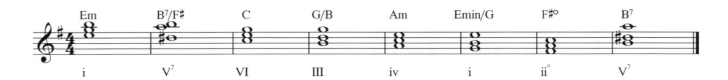

…and as a notated chord progression:

…and now you try it in E minor:

Remember to vary the texture and rhythm once you have the chords under your fingers. Here are some ideas:

1. Arpeggios through the hand
2. Waltz time
3. Polka
4. Alberti bass – play the chord in the LH using the descending bass note as the lowest note
5. As above and add a melody in the RH
6. Transpose to D minor and B minor

SOME OBSERVATIONS

- We are using the stepwise descending bassline trick again – isn't it neat?

- In early music, this was often called a 'ground bass'.

- Notice how all these progressions seem to take up 4, 8 or 16 bars. This is useful because they are natural devices by which you can structure your music. So you don't forget where you are and also it has a natural sense of phrase and the audience doesn't just hear an endless succession of chords, but a coherently organised piece. It also derives from dances, where regular patterns were essential.

- The structure also allows you to shape your melodies; using the cadence points to bring the melody back in line with the harmony: in other words 'resolving' the tension.

CLASSIC MINOR KEY PROGRESSIONS

Just like the major keys, minor keys have progressions that work especially well, and we find them recurring in various guises throughout music history.

Here are two to start with:

…a very simple minor key progression is the 'Spanish':

'SPANISH'   Amin   G   F   E7 Repeat

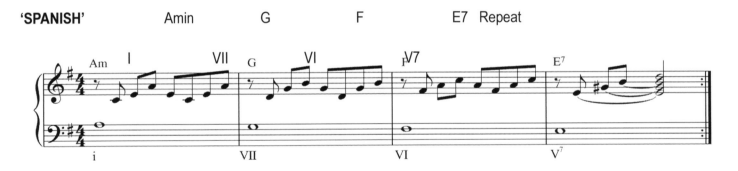

…and a lovely baroque classic used by many composers including: A. Scarlatti, Corelli, and more recently, Rachmaninov:

'LA FOLIA'

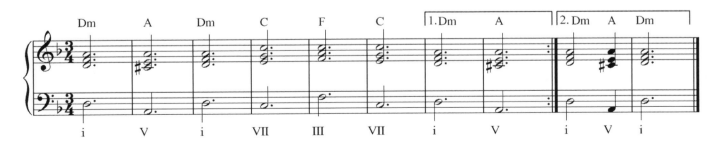

Notice how the first section ends in the dominant – we call that an 'imperfect cadence' – it is not an ending, but a pause. Now transpose both of the above to E minor and B minor. Write it down in shorthand or use the chord numbers as a guide. Then play through the chords in all the ways we have previously.

'ADELITA'

We will finish this section on minor keys with some improvisation on the A section of *Adelita* by Tarrega – here it is notated.

Adelita (excerpt)

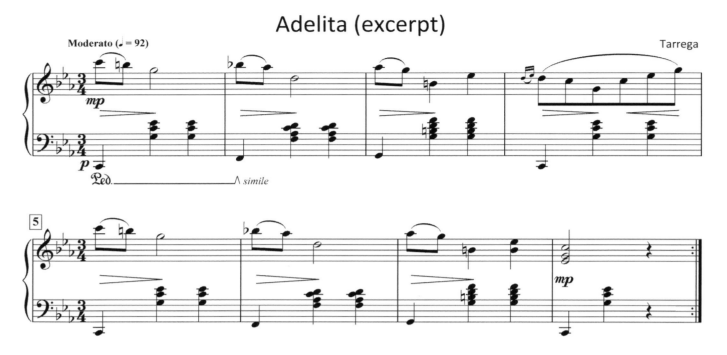

Here are the steps we can follow:

1. Learn to play the section then analyse the chord progression: jot it down if you need to…

2. Play through the chords as arpeggios; through the hands; right hand over LH bass; LH as Alberti bass (RH play melody or chords or new melody…)

3. Look at the melody and play it upside down; or backwards; or add passing notes.

4. Now you should have the structure of the music in your memory and understand the melodic pattern (C harmonic minor) and be able to play freely with all of the elements above to create your own version of Adelita. Don't worry if you take a few wrong turns, your ears will start to guide you.

5. Try playing the piece as written but remove the accidentals (C major) – isn't it transformed? It now has a different kind of beauty!

6. Now play it as written – this will also sound much better – as if you yourself composed it!

Once you have absorbed all the information about Adelita, you can really play with the elements to create quite different music. Here is an example - Adelita as a Calypso – I have taken the outline of the descending melody, used the harmonic outline and given the left hand a presto walking bass. Then I include a section where I change the order of the chords and create a 'castanet' figure in the right hand, before returning to the first section to create an ABA structure. It doesn't sound much like Tarrega's Adelita now, but it is clearly derived from it.

You are now halfway through the book, and if you stuck with it and practised thoroughly, you will have a range of expressive devices under your fingers: a good understanding of chords, keys and transpositions: not to mention a repertoire of great chord progressions to 'play around' with. You should now be confident enough to sit at the piano and play some music 'without the dots' but with structure and expression. In the second half of the course we will look more closely at existing pieces of music and explore how we can use them as a basis for 'exploration' and improvisation. We will also see how many times what we have already learnt appears in very famous pieces of music.

CHAPTER EIGHT – GETTING TO KNOW THE CIRCLE

THE CIRCLE OF FIFTHS

To understand harmony is to understand music and the task is clear and unequivocal:

Triad Vocabulary; Triad Hierarchy; Inversions; Secondary Chords; Substitutions; Chord Progressions; ii – V – I chord progression; Minor Keys; Mixing Major and Minor...are the starting points.

Below is the Circle of Fifths – the real Magic Circle – did you notice how each segment of 3 is a Triad Hierarchy? Getting to know the circle will be the starting point for the next chapter in the journey to creative piano playing.

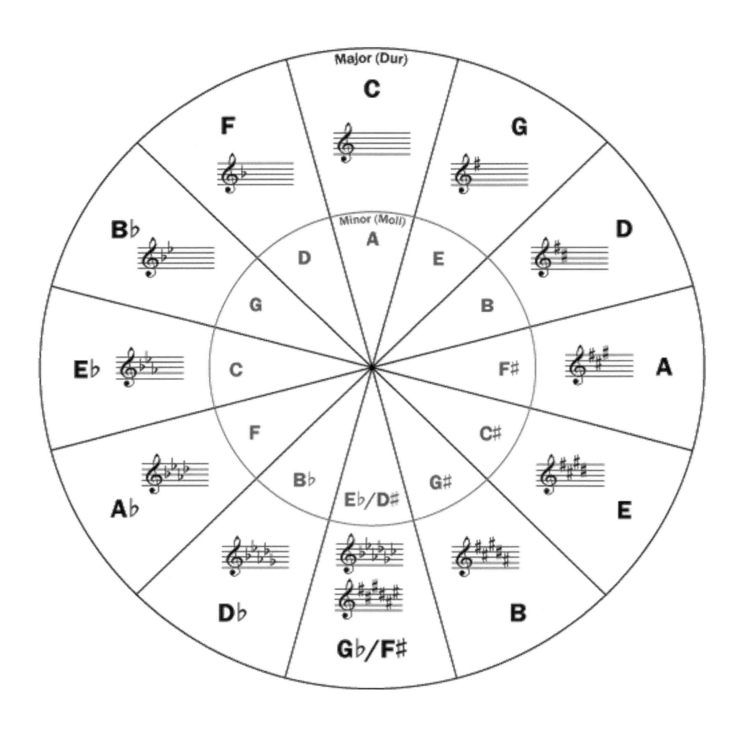

ANTI-CLOCKWISE: A CIRCLE OF FOURTHS

This is much the easier of the processes to grasp, as it requires only the addition of one new accidental, which creates a dominant 7th chord to be resolved in the 'new' key. Learn this after you have mastered Bach's Prelude in C (from where investigation of the circle can easily arise) and impose the pattern derived from Bach's original, but definitely NO score, although the chart above is permissible. I also suggest you 'talk' your way round the circle in a SatNav/GPS voice; C major, add dominant seventh B♭, resolve to F Major; F Major add dominant seventh E♭ resolve to B♭ major; and so on...

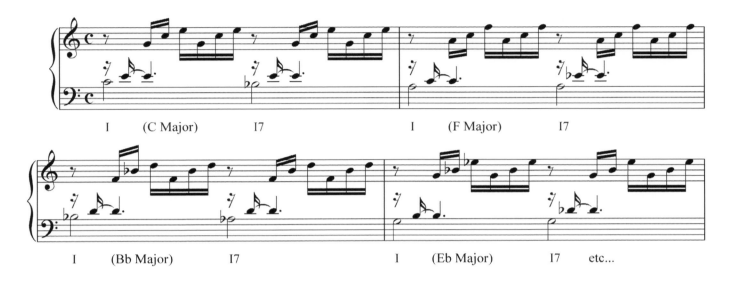

This process also consolidates the principle of 'inversions' and, in my experience, the learning pianist who completes this journey, arriving back at the home key of C major, has done something quite remarkable usually revealing this in a visible show of wonderment at their achievement. Thus the 'science' and the 'magic' of music becomes something of interest and we are on the way to making a musician.

After this step, we can vary the texture and inversions of the exercise; perhaps add waltz tempo with blocked chords; or an Alberti bass with a right-hand melody. These new journeys then become starting points for explorations of tonal relationships and piano styles which can be referred to in the context of the more advanced repertoire they are about to encounter.

The model above of further exploration through varying textures and techniques applies to all of the following exercises round the circle. It is vitally important for the improviser to understand the relationships in the circle from a practical perspective. Many students can 'work it out' for their theory exams, but playing them literally whilst talking through the theory will impress them on the mind so that they will be easily replicated when necessary; facilitate transposition; enable analysis and reading of music to an incomparable degree. But most of all, the student will have a full command of the keyboard for experimentation and improvisation thereby widening the possibilities for creativity.

IMPORTANT
Do not be tempted to short cut these exercises – even if they are difficult, return to them periodically using target driven practise sessions. For example: take just one quarter at a time and become fluent. Then the following week select another quarter, and then merge these two. Then take the third and so on...eventually you will be able to complete the circle in one journey and the satisfaction will be worth the hard work, but also, you will have cemented a practical understanding of a theoretical concept in your mind – truly a remarkable achievement!

CLOCKWISE: THE CIRCLE OF FIFTHS

This is a more difficult exercise, but can be approached in a similar way. Usually I allow a gap of a few months (perhaps a graded exam) between these two stages, unless the pianist is particularly enthusiastic (or brilliant!). Concomitant with this process is the opportunity to teach the ii-V-I turnaround so familiar to jazz in all keys! This 'gateway' to a popular music style allows the student to see that ALL tonal music(s) obeys the same fundamental laws and that their differences are often more concerned with style, technique, extension, modality and context.

In the example below, again using Bach's template, I move the pianist through the chord sequence: I-vi-II7-V however, using the supertonic major II7 as a Dominant Seventh (secondary dominant) we add the extra accidental required to propel us round the circle. The vi then becomes chord ii in the target key and the II7 becomes V7.

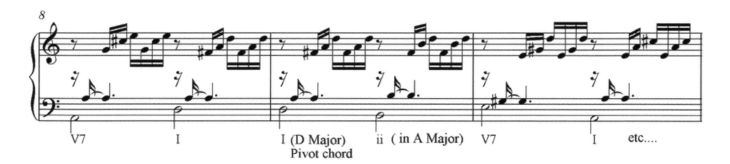

Once again the pianist should try to achieve this without written music, so they 'feel' their way around the keyboard, hearing the tonal movement as it forms beneath their fingers. Then go on to experiment with techniques and styles as with example 1. Also, once you have achieved the modulation to the dominant, you can return quickly to the tonic using the exercise 1 example above, or move out a few keys and then back a few keys, and thus we have wheels within circles....
For an extra 'jazzy' effect, try adding sevenths to the ii (formerly vi) chord, and even a major 7th to the I chords for that real cocktail hour feel!

MODULATION

Now that we have travelled forwards and backwards round the circle of fifths we have learnt how to step in and out of adjacent keys. We learnt in Part 5 about how relative major and minor keys are so closely related you can step in and out of each effortlessly.

With just the addition or subtraction of an accidental, and perhaps a pivot chord or two, you can move to adjacent keys easily too. This adds just another string to our bow, allowing us to change key (modulate) and then rework our musical material in the new key, perhaps with a change of texture. Or we can even change the musical material completely for the 'new' section, then return to the original key to 'recapitulate' the original idea. ABA. Just like we did with Adelita. Sounds complex doesn't it, but here is a simple example using the Pachelbel progression as a ground.

Pachelbel ABA

THE CIRCLE OF FIFTHS ANTI-CLOCKWISE IN MINOR KEYS

For minor keys we need to look to the inner part of the circle. We also need to remember the 'raised' seventh for each dominant chord as well as the key signatures. Essentially though, it is exactly like the major key version except to create a dominant chord from the existing tonic we need to change it from a minor chord to a dominant seventh (major triad with minor seventh) and that requires <u>two</u> changes:

1. The third must be raised a semi-tone to create a major triad (in A minor C= C♯)
2. A minor seventh from the root must be added to create the dominant seventh chord. (AC♯E**G**)

Then simply resolve the A7 to its new tonic D minor – which is the next stage anti-clockwise on the circle. Continue doing this until you arrive back at A minor.

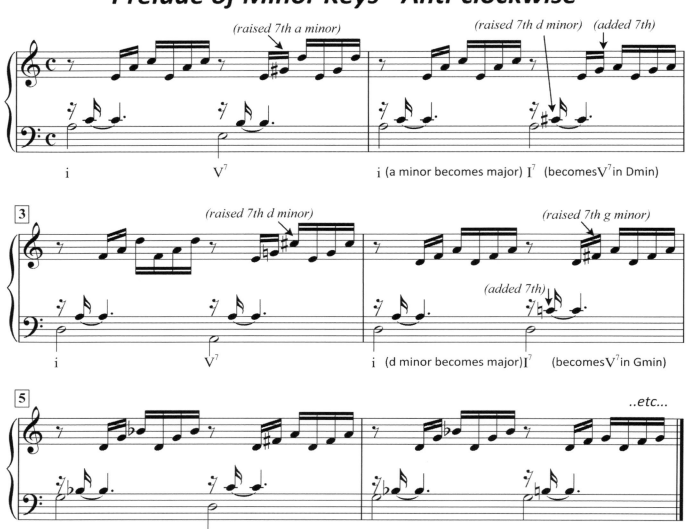

Prelude of Minor Keys - Anti-clockwise

THE CIRCLE OF FIFTHS CLOCKWISE IN MINOR KEYS

For minor keys clockwise, again, we need to look to the inner part of the circle and, of course, remember the 'raised' seventh for each dominant chord as well as the key signatures. It is a little easier than the anti-clockwise version requiring only a 're-interpretation' of the tonic as chord iv* which is followed by a V7 chord in the new (or target) key.

1. Chord i (a minor) becomes chord iv* in the target key – to be followed by...
2. Chord V7 in the target key (E minor) B D# F# A to create the dominant seventh...

Then simply resolve the B7 to its new tonic E minor – which is the next stage clockwise on the circle. Continue doing this until you arrive back at A minor.

*Chord iv could be made major here to accord with 'melodic minor' but it is optional…

Prelude of Minor Keys - clockwise

I hope that doing the exercises above has demonstrated how important the dominant seventh chord is for propelling you round the circle, but also for establishing key. Practise all four 'Prelude' exercises above and your 'practical' grasp of harmonic theory will have a solid foundation for what is to follow.

SECONDARY DOMINANTS

As we have discovered, the real power in the game of modulation lies with the dominant chord especially when adorned with a seventh. Bearing this in mind, we have seen how deploying a dominant seventh from an adjacent key leads us away from the home key to the target key creating a modulation.

Interestingly there is another use for the dominant which can be equally expressive. We call this a 'secondary' dominant and it is broadly all the other chords in a key except the primary dominant being used 'as a dominant' but not necessarily executing a modulation.

Play this: (Mediant (E) as Secondary Dominant)

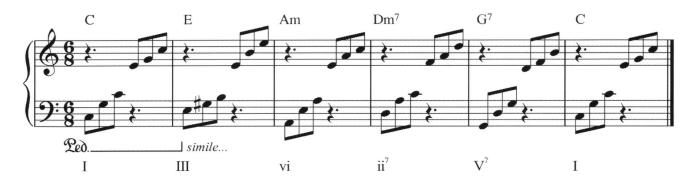

The E chord should typically be EGB, but by adding the G# to create a major chord, it is pulled towards the A (its usual 'tonic') by the 'gravity' of the circle of fifths. Now play again adding the seventh – EG#BD – the pull is even stronger.

...but we didn't modulate, we simply followed the A minor chord with a typical II7 – V7 – I cadence to bring us back 'home'. Can you spot the 'other' secondary dominant in the example above?

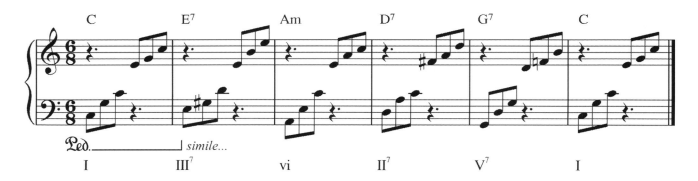

...we could have modulated if we'd established the key by emphasising the modulation like this....

Now do the above progressions in ALL keys: try different inversions, key signatures and styles, so you are fully conversant with the sound and shape of this progression. Do NOT use sheet music: if you must, use the triad hierarchy for each key, but where possible dispense with this too. Do a key a day and recap at the weekends.

SECONDARY DOMINANTS WITH AND WITHOUT MODULATIONS

The expressive nature of the secondary dominant is such that it 'sets up' an expectation that can then either be realised or denied. Try this exercise with all the chords of each hierarchy, turning them into 'secondary' dominants (with sevenths) and resolving them to their usual 'tonic', before returning to the 'home' key with a simple cadence.

Here they are in C:

Supertonic (D) as Secondary Dominant

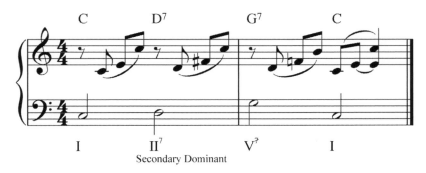

Tonic (C) as Secondary Dominant

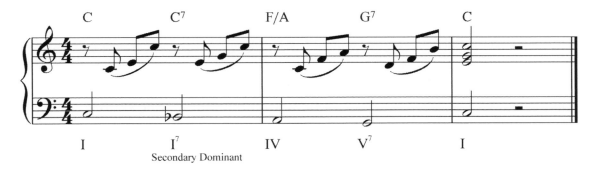

Submediant (A) as Secondary Dominant

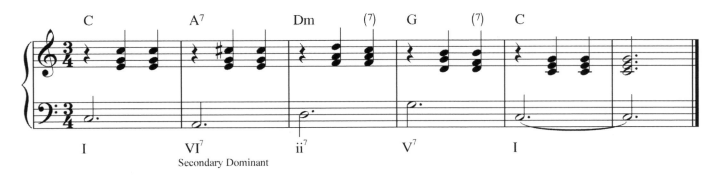

Subdominant (F) as Secondary Dominant

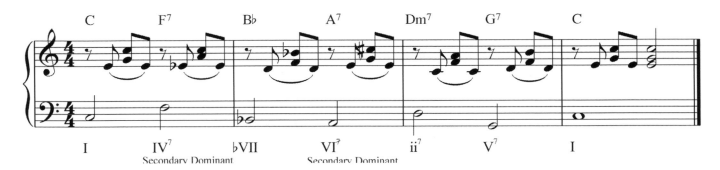

Leading Note (B) as Secondary Dominant

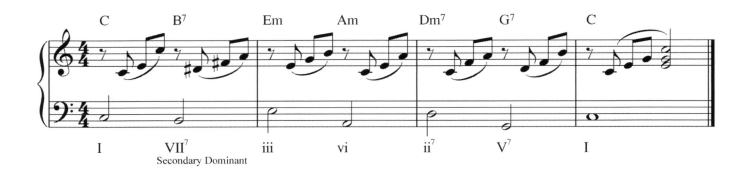

Now transpose these to ALL keys, and again vary the texture, time signature, style etc...it is very important that this retains an element of creativity because that is what makes it fun and ultimately satisfying... again do this perhaps a key a day and recap at the weekends.

Even though we remain within the triad hierarchy for each key, the harmonic variety and range is astonishing. We can move from chord to chord with purpose and momentum creating a variety of moods using the circle of fifths to develop a narrative. You will notice also that sometimes successive dominants occur, and this builds up the momentum so that when the 'resolution' arrives, the effect is more compelling. Wagner's Ring Cycle is based on exactly this premise as are all his late operas.

CONCLUSION

The completion of this chapter is a key stage in understanding practically, with your hands on the instrument and your ears carefully listening, the wondrous magic that is the 'circle of fifths'. You can hear clearly why invocations of the 'cosmos' are so appropriate where music is concerned for there are clearly 'orbits around planets' and their close relations; then movements between planets into different orbits.
There is also 'gravity' – the pull towards home through the dominant seventh and the pull away via the secondary dominant, as if a little force is injected to propel you out of your current orbit to planets new. All my life I have wondered at the music of the heavens and, when I play, I hear it, clearly and distinctly. The universe is beneath my fingers and in my ears.

CHAPTER NINE – EXTENSIONS AND SUSPENSIONS

SUSPENSIONS

Suspensions are a highly effective device. By introducing 'suspensions' the expected resolution of the 'true' chord is delayed, and this is doubly expressive because it not only delays resolution, but also the suspended note hangs over from the previous harmony like a memory or an echo, (called a preparation) adding more than a hint of melancholy especially when playing in a minor key like this:

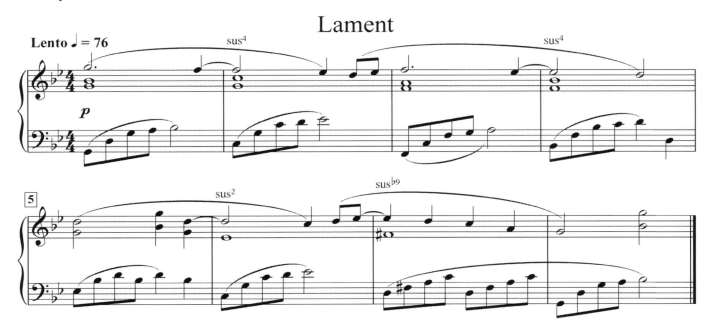

Did you notice the chord progression? – it was like an upside down version of the Pachelbel minor. Essentially there are three main suspensions:

1. Suspension of the Fourth
2. Suspension of the Sixth
3. Suspension of the Second (or Ninth)

In *Lament*, two of these feature; with a rather striking flat 9 (b9) suspension in bar 7. Suspensions can also be 'played' as well as 'suspended' so rather than the note hanging, it is repeated to create a subtle accent on the discordant note – like this;

There are one or two things to watch out for with suspensions:

1.   If the note of resolution is the third of a major chord, then do not resolve it in another part of the chord before the suspension – this will cause a discord (minor second) and ruin the effect of the suspension – play this....

* here the suspended B♭ clashes with the A in the tenor part so we lose the sense of 'hanging'
** here the A resolves the chord so the double suspension just sounds incorrect...

...remove the offending A's and you will hear the suspensions correctly – that is better isn't it?

2.   In minor keys this is desirable but not critical because the third is a whole step away from the fourth so not as discordant – play this excerpt from Beethoven....

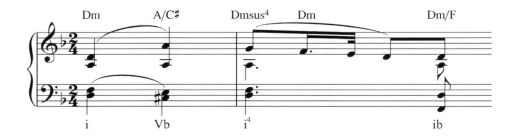

Here, the D minor chord with the sus4 is complete DFA, but it doesn't seem to affect the suspension in quite the same way. Beethoven is using it rather as a gentle discord with the suspension unprepared, so it is like an 'accented' passing note.

3.   Preparation is desirable, but not critical as you will hear below in bar 4 the A over the C7 chord.
     Now take a progression you know and include some melodic suspensions by hanging on to a note before letting it fall on to its resolving tone. Here is an example:

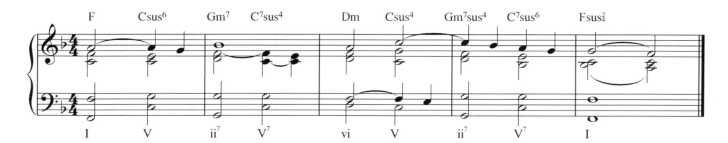

In each case I have only indicated the suspended chords – all resolve to their normal position; so Csus6 becomes C, Csus4 become C etc...

Play this example and you should notice the following 'events':

- Bar 1 – the A from the F chord suspends (sus6) before resolving to the G of the C chord.

- Bar 2 – the F from the Gm7 chord creates a suspended 4th, but also the B♭ is held to create the 7th.

- Bar 3 – Here the suspension is in the tenor part, the F is held to create a suspended 4th.

- Bar 4 – the top C from bar 3 is suspended to create a suspended 4th which resolves and then continues to fall to create a lovely discord on A – this is an 'unprepared' C7sus6 chord because it isn't held from a previous chord but resolves exactly like a suspension to the G. The discord created by the major seventh interval B♭ – A is a favourite of the romantic composers especially Chopin, particularly at the cadence.

- Bar 5 – this is a 'played' double suspension! The G and B♭ are suspended from the previous C7 chord resolving to the F and A on the third beat of the bar.

What is surprising is how much is going on in just these 5 bars. Admittedly we are deliberately emphasising suspensions, but it doesn't sound unmusical – it sounds hymn-like - it could easily be a chorale or an organ prelude. With practise these 'events' get wrapped up in the various textures a pianist uses so their effect is not so apparent, but this is a useful exercise to carry out on any chord progression because the hand shapes and resolutions become natural and effortless, which is necessary when harmonising a melody that has a lot of suspensions as part of its character.

Now apply this principle to the Doo-wop in other keys and, when comfortable, move to the Pachelbel in all the keys too
Here is the Pachelbel in F:

Try to do this from memory using a chord chart to guide you only when necessary – you should have the progressions under your fingers, so it is just a case of thinking about delaying resolution in one or more parts.

Take your time: perhaps do one key and one progression a day and become thoroughly versed in that key and progression. Then the following day revise it, and, if it is still fluent, start a new key.

RETARDATION

The opposite of a suspension is retardation: again very useful and expressive, and it allows the melody to 'float' above the harmony rather than 'hugging' too tightly to the harmony that underpins it. This is the expressive and dramatic nature of tonal music; a constant pulling away and pulling closer of the various voices until they all arrive at a harmonic resolution.

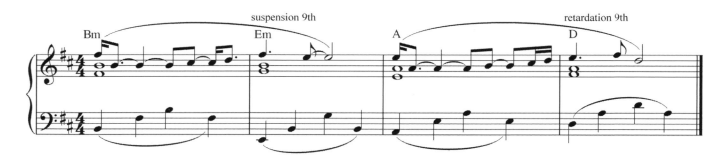

In both cases above the suspensions are unprepared – effectively 'appogiaturas' grace notes that fall or lean into the harmony or resolving note. For the improviser it is a useful device as it delays resolution so can turn a wrong note right: so long as you are in the correct key you can simply resolve the 'wrong' note!

Combined suspensions and retardations are the hall mark of the 'romantic' composer, try this example from the Chopin Ballade in A♭: here, he uses a suspension in his first rendering of the phrase, and then retardation on its transposed repeat:

Chopin's is a very sophisticated use of both suspension and retardation, here are simpler adaptations of the above that put the suspensions in sharper relief so their effect is clearer: play them.

Did you notice the bass note remains unchanged throughout each excerpt? We call this a 'pedal' point. Even though the chords are changing this note remains the same – we will learn more about pedal points as they are very effective devices for building tension.

I always think suspensions 'hang' where retardations 'lean' – it is hardly precise, but it helps.

The second phrase of the Chopin extract is in C, so, using the adaptation as an outline, try the following exercises:

1. Transpose into D and then G, and some other keys you know well too.
2. Add some new textures – perhaps play through the hands as arpeggios, or as a waltz.

APPLYING SUSPENSIONS AND RETARDATIONS

Now, bearing in mind the work we have done so far in this chapter, try the Doo-wop and add a suspension and retardation in each key: try the example in A Major.

See if you can spot the suspensions and retardations, but also identify the correct chords and harmony using whatever language you prefer.

You will also notice that using the descriptions for both styles (chord and Roman numeral) is getting a little complex – it can get unwieldy, but practitioners become very familiar with the changes as they have practised them so frequently and it all becomes second nature. There are also shorthand terms that can be useful: the term 'sus' for example refers to sus4, so for a chord of Csus it would always be CFG – where it isn't a sus4, it will be indicated like Csus9 which would be CED or Csus6 (CEA).

Additionally, the lead sheets become even more broadly descriptive allowing the performer to fill in the gaps using clues from the melodic line – so our Chopin might begin to look more like this:

Try the following exercise:

1. Ignore the chords indicated and, using the melody, create a chord progression that supports it.
2. Now create an accompaniment – does it change the nature of the melody?

Here is an example to give you an idea of what I mean:

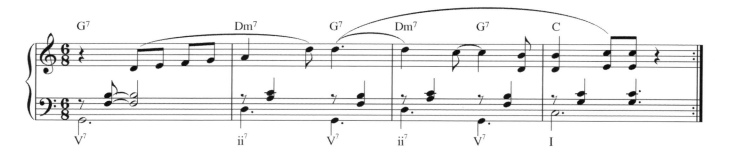

..it is almost a Chopin waltz now...

NEW CHORDS

The danger for any musical style is that previously effective musical devices – the cadence for example – lose their expressive power and become 'clichés', or they are used 'ironically' as a reference to the past. Here is an example of the iib – Ic – V7 – I cadence:

Clementi: Sonatina in F Op. 38, No. 3. (ending)

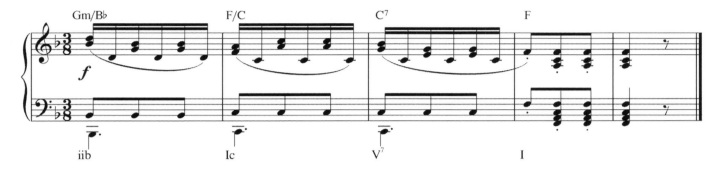

…this device works well enough in Haydn, Mozart and Clementi, but you find it less frequently in Beethoven and Schubert, and not at all in Chopin and Schumann, and yet all these composers are using a similar harmonic language.

To avoid 'cliché' and to 'renew' expressivity composers would 'decorate' or alter what had become standard devices in subtle and interesting ways; here are some altered cadences from the repertoire:

Granados: The Bell of the Afternoon from *Bocetos* (ending)

Above, what we see it is a perfect cadence (see the V7) except he inserts two further discords that descend to the final F. The clarity of the cadence is undermined and it becomes less defined, more 'romantic', also, two of the five chords have diminished qualities and only one is a clear triad, the final one.

Kabalevsky: An Old Dance Op.27, No. 7 (ending)

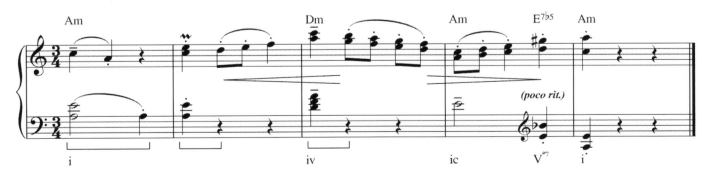

Above, we see how a very straight forward perfect cadence is given added spice by the E7♭5 chord instead of the conventional E7 – the expressive power of just one note.

Burgmuller: Angels' Voices Op. 100, No. 21 (ending)

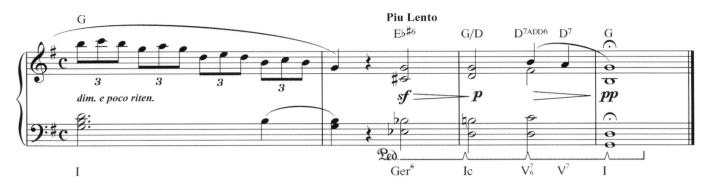

For Burgmuller, the emotional weight is in the 'pre-dominant' chord – the augmented (German) sixth – which he indicates SF. Also he adds a sixth to the D7 chord (DF♯BC) before falling to the D7 proper (DF♯AC) – this softens the cadence which contrasts with the more discordant German sixth making the ending more expressive than Clementi's traditional cadence.

Chopin: Etude in E major Op. 10, No. 3 (ending)

Here, Chopin uses the traditional 'plagal' cadence (IV – I), but flattens the third of the IV chord to make it A minor (iv - I) – thus adding a little 'pathos' to the close of this celebrated etude. This is characteristic of many of Chopin's works lending them an air of melancholy that helps explain their appeal.

AUGMENTED SIXTH CHORDS

Play the German sixth chord from the Burgmuller example above. What does it sound like?

On its own it sounds like a dominant seventh chord to me, and it would be if Burgmuller had spelt the C♯ as D♭. Eb-G-B♭-D♭ is about as dominant seventh as you could get, and ordinarily would resolve to A♭. Clearly, Burgmuller is approaching the end of a piece in G, and a cadence in A♭ would not do here, but it is the unexpected sound of the chord here that prepares for the resolution and close, and in order to indicate this on the score, he changes the flat to a sharp implying that rather than falling as a seventh should the sharp should rise: thereby becoming an augmented sixth chord. In this case, a 'German' sixth, which differs from the 'Italian' sixth (E♭ G C♯) and the 'French' sixth (E♭ G A C♯).

The Italian is merely minus the fifth, but the French sixth paves the way for the whole-tone harmony that was so much a feature of French music in the late nineteenth and early twentieth centuries. Here is the whole-tone scale with the 'French' sixth notes indicated:

Add this to the augmented chords that flow from the whole tone scale and we have the origins of modern music.

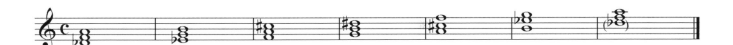

So now let's take our Pachelbel progression and this time make alterations to the cadence points and vary the qualities of the approach chords too…

Can you hear that although the underlying progression is maintained it has an altogether new sound? Work on this at the piano by either taking a progression from a piece you are currently playing, or inventing a new one from the hierarchy. Take it back to its essential harmony; play through the chords; altering some of the chords so that they offer a different sound. You will see how effective these subtle nuances are, and how much fun it is to experiment in just this way.

CHAPTER TEN – MORE ABOUT HARMONY

HARMONIC RHYTHM

At this point it is worth revisiting harmonic rhythm. So far, much of the work we have done has been rhythmically clear harmonically speaking. That is to say for each measure (bar) there is one clear harmony – much popular music sticks quite happily to this formula and it is fine to continue to do that. However, subtle changes in the rate at which the chords change can add enormously to the expressive content of the music.

Play this:

Now this:

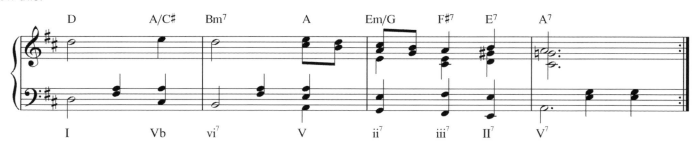

The music is essentially the same, but we have added some chord changes to give it a new harmonic rhythm. In the first case it is one harmony per bar; in the second, two per bar with a quickening rhythm for the third bar where there is a change per beat. The changing harmonic rhythm gives it added interest harmonically, but also propels the music forward because it suggests additional movement – like a dance – each chord being a step. Equally, harmonic rhythm can support subtle emphasis in melody, creating moments of drama within the phrase. Look at this version of La Folia and how it differs from its first appearance in Chapter 7:

The basic harmonic outline is unchanged, but additional chords 'pass' between them adding a different rhythm to the harmony.

Here is a melody – add the essential harmony as suggested by the bass notes; then see if you can add some 'passing chords' to 'vary' the harmonic rhythm. My example is at the end of this chapter – try not to look until you have made several attempts of you own – then you can see how my efforts compare.

PASSING CHORDS

Passing chords have a similar function, but are not so evenly rhythmic. They rather fill in the gaps between chords as opposed to creating a clear harmonic rhythm of their own: like the example below, where changes between tonic and subdominant, or tonic and dominant, in the blues just push the music forward:

Play this:

Notice how the chords change quickly at the end of each 'harmony' as they move towards the next harmony. This is a key feature of music (especially baroque music and jazz) – the idea that there is an 'underlying structural harmony' (chord C7) overlaid with faster changing smaller expressive alterations that lead to the next 'underlying harmony' (chord F7)…

Analyse the chords I use… you can see they are all from the hierarchy so not unusual in any respect, but they move towards the new chord adding extra momentum, making the music more expressive and interesting, especially when it is a slow blues. Try this idea in the key of G or F or any key – using the 12-bar progression, but adding passing chords.

Here is a bass line in a non-blues context – see if you can add some 'passing chords' and vary the harmonic rhythm to link the structural harmony: I've given very little detail so you have maximum freedom – take your time!
Again my response is at the end of the chapter – try not to look!

PEDAL POINTS

Pedal Points are a useful device for building tension. Chords can change over a pedal point without any reference to it other than that is belongs to the same key: like this:

You can see in the simple example above, all the chords are underpinned by the tonic note G except at the cadence – naturally this is known as a 'tonic' pedal.

Pedals can also work on other notes of the scale, especially the dominant, here is an example from Beethoven:

Notice how the key is D minor, but over a repeating A (the dominant) Beethoven plays a whole variety of harmonies before finally coming to rest on the dominant chord, which will inevitably bring us back to D minor.

Select a key and keep the hierarchy in mind or to hand, then, whilst running through the chords in the hierarchy in any order use:

- Tonic pedal point:
- Dominant pedal:
- Now perhaps add some suspensions too:

Here are some easy examples to help start you off......

EX. 1. Tonic Pedal:

EX. 2. Dominant Pedal: bars 5-7 (notice the secondary dominant on the tonic at bar 2)

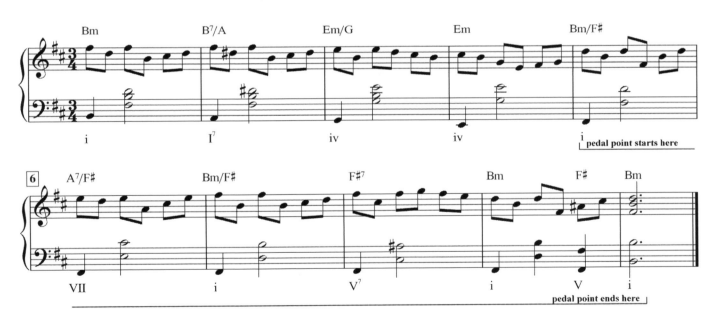

EX. 3. Mixture with suspensions: dominant pedal bars 1-6 – tonic pedal bar 7 (or this could be interpreted as a triple retardation!)

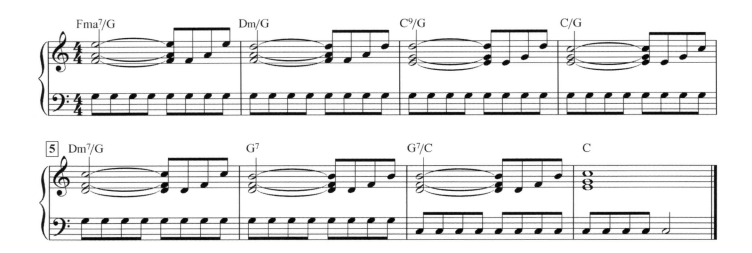

THE DIMINISHED SEVENTH CHORD

In the Beethoven example above, the chords he uses over the dominant pedal sound dramatic and discordant. The sense of harmony held together by the pedal tone A, whilst the chords above compete with one another for mastery of the tonal landscape. It sounds dramatic because it is: the two chords duelling for supremacy are GB♭C♯E and G♯BDF: play them now:

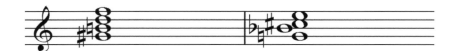

What do you notice?

- They both sound similar – transpositions of the same chord

- The intervals between the notes are identical in both cases; a minor third

- These intervals divide the octave equally – this means that for these chords there is NO hierarchy

- Any of the notes can be the root and any of the notes can be the leading note

- Because of the absence of hierarchy, these chords are atonal – without key

- Thus the diminished seventh chord is the most dynamic chord in tonal music

In the harmonic minor keys, diminished chords arise naturally out of the notes in the scale. So for D harmonic minor we hear:

So chord ii7 becomes especially effective as its notes comprise the diminished 7th.

As we have seen, each note can resolve the chord effectively, and any inversion has the same effect. Here is our chord iio7 E-G-B♭-D♭/C♯ resolving in several different ways, including D minor.

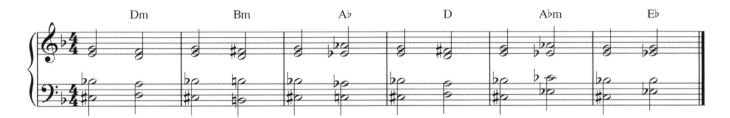

You can imagine what fun a composer can have with this chord! It was a staple of the 'silent' movie industry where successive diminished seventh chords in varying inversions could be used to heighten the tension before resolving. Here is a short example:

Scene 1: Lady on track with train approaching: moving chords using diminished 7ths for tension and alternating hands for rhythm and to simulate motion.

Scene 2: Fight between hero and villain: swirling arpeggios and dramatic octaves again diminished 7th chord implies uncertainty and drama. Closing bars, repeated octaves and shortened phrases to imply repeated blows and shortness of breath...

Scene 3: Villain defeated and hero rescues girl: C major triumphantly rings out with a standard use of diatonic (chords from the hierarchy) harmony, with just a hint of a minor, to add some character.

Trackside at the Silent Movie

A. Higgins

Now create your own story using the diminished 7th chord, and then chord progressions in major or minor keys to create a narrative. Keep it simple, perhaps three or four scenes, and try to use the diminished 7th chord, some major and minor key harmony, and vary the texture for each scene: sometimes it is useful to write out a short plot, add some general musical characteristics (loud, fast, tense, sad etc...) and then have that in mind while you experiment at the piano. I love telling stories through music and it makes my family laugh when I sit at the piano and make one up that suits something that has just happened!

Scene 1:

Scene 2:

Scene 3:

Scene 4:

SCALES AND THE DIMINISHED SEVENTH

Here is the scale harmonised using diminished sevenths – sounds rather more dramatic than the triad version doesn't it, and it never quite settles anywhere does it?

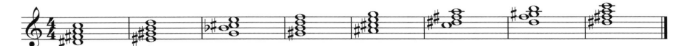

Also did you notice something else - there are only three diminished 7th chords. They each have 4 inversions, one per note naturally, and they vary in spelling based on the key you are in, but the pattern on the keyboard uses three chords only. Try it with the scale above – can you see the same four notes recur in different inversions. The 'spelling' can differ, when the inversions change, or depending on the key you are in – as follows:

As the scale suggests, too many successive dim 7ths and we lose sense of key completely and even this most powerfully expressive of chords loses its momentum and its expressive power as it starts to meander. Knowing when, where, and for how long, you can deploy its atonal effect is a question of taste and, in my opinion, too little is always better than too much.
It is a superb device for moving around the circle of fifths when you find yourself a long way from home. Beethoven was especially fond of this device when his explorations had taken him to the edges of tonality and it was time to bring back order and sanity. Even if you end up in F#major and your home is C, simple use of dim7 chord(s) followed by a V7 will bring you right back again.

If we analyse it, the F#o7 is acting like chord ii7 – which in C would be DF#AC – it 'slides chromatically' to a different version of chord ii DFA♭C♭ again a dim7th – and then resolves to chord V. Simply add the seventh to chord V and we can set up the perfect cadence to the tonic C.

The subtle science of harmony displays a curious logic, and yet to the ear it sings of the infinite.

CROSSING THE CIRCLE

Try this exercise: pick two keys on opposite sides of the circle of fifths and see if you can get from one to the other using chords that 'transition' between keys (dim7ths – secondary dominants).

Like this example:

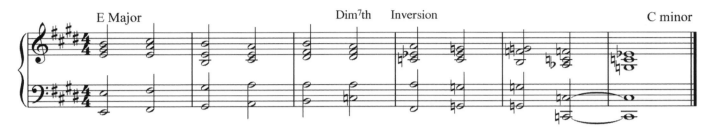

Did you hear how the music seems to shift direction but doesn't lose momentum or flow. The idea of a progression is to take you from one place to another (and back again in most cases), and this certainly happens here. We changed the spelling of the Dim7th but it is the same notes (D# = E♭). This is called 'Enharmonic' and you can see it moves us across the circle from the sharp to the flat side.

Having established an enharmonic route, lets make it more a piece of music than a progression by adding a melody, dynamics and texture. Like this:

Notice how we started with the chord progression. In the book so far we have focused on developing chords as a response to melody, and to add colour and texture, but there is nothing in music to say that chord progressions cannot be a starting point, and, in many cases, composers do have an overview of harmonic movement on to which they add the other elements. 'Sonata Form' exemplifies this.

The idea above is hardly a masterpiece, but it does achieve the goal in a musically effective way. The purpose of exercises like this is to sharpen the modulation tool box so you can manipulate harmony as and when you need to, and to facilitate greater concentration through goal directed practise rather than idle repetition.

But you can do it even quicker than that if you must:

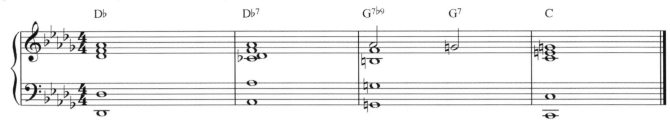

Now you choose any two keys from opposite sides of the circle and try and move smoothly from one to the other. Do this as an exercise every day, just like your scales or sight-reading. Put the circle chart in front of you, and choose two keys from each side.

THE TONIC MINOR

A particularly useful way of taking a leap round the circle is by using the tonic minor. Classical composers were especially fond of this device for their development sections. It took the theme at least a quarter round the circle, so the development section was essentially the journey back again. Clementi specialised in this technique, but Mozart, Haydn and Beethoven were also frequent exponents.

Here are the opening bars of the slow movement of Diabelli's Sonatina in F:

... the colour of the minor key transforms the music of course, but to get back, he simply uses a perfect cadence and resolves it to tonic major. This is a useful way of changing the mood without straying too far, but also avoiding the passagework that is necessitated by changing through all the keys like gears to get back home again.

Notice how important chord ii becomes: in the penultimate bar, it acts as a secondary dominant bringing us back to the dominant chord V (F) so resolution to I (B♭ - Tonic) is easily achieved.
Now you try using a familiar chord progression or invent a new one, or even take a piece you know well and transpose it to the minor key for an episode before returning back to the tonic 'proper'.

THE UNIQUE IMPORTANCE OF CHORDS TWO AND SIX

Chord II (two) cannot be overstated in its importance to musical harmony. As the 'pre-dominant' (the chord before the dominant) it is so often this chord that carries the 'emotional' weight of a musical phrase – it is this chord that hovers with uncertainty before the V7 that defines the key and the tonic that confirms it. It is no surprise that the most famous chord in classical music history – the 'Tristan' chord, is in fact chord iidim7.

The Tristan Chord:

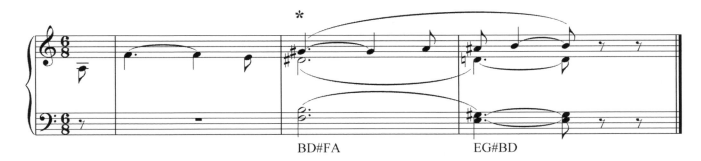

What should have happened is the V7 (EG#BD) should have resolved to chord i in A minor (ACE) – but it seems instead to resolve to the V7 and wait. In fact Wagner makes us wait a further four hours before he really resolves anything satisfactorily – but the revolution is that the dissonance of the ii chord is only partially resolved – this is where 'atonality' (no tonal centre) emerges. We, the listener, remain uncertain where the tonal centre of the music is.

Equally, in jazz, and, as we have seen with Doo-Wop, chord two, as the dominant of the dominant, plays a pivotal role in musical expression – it has a gravitational pull to the dominant, but the power to metamorphose into a chord that turns the dominant into a tonic, or at least threatens to. It is like a chameleon, it can change its colours and appear to be something it isn't, it teases the dominant in a way no other chord can, making the resolution of a piece stronger in the process.

Here is the Doo-Wop using sevenths on every chord:

The only other chord with anything like this emotional weight, is chord vi (six), but its power is more subtle and refined – both are very powerful expressive chords in the hierarchy and should be understood fully by any music student serious about playing effectively. It is useful to note that flat seconds (bII) and flat sixths (bVI) especially in first inversion (Neapolitan sixths!) are frequent substitutes for the more conventional standard chords ii7 & vi, and appear more often in 19th century (romantic) music, but, no matter the disguise they wear, their expressive power is derived from their substitution for the standard chords ii and vi we have used so far.

This flattening creates a tri-tone in the root between bii and V (so in C = D♭ to G) which is a very powerful effect: here it is in action...and it is very expressive:

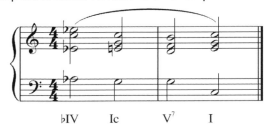

bIIb   Ic   V⁷   I

For chord six, the effect is also powerful, but more associated with the interrupted cadence type of expressiveness you might expect of chord vi. Here is an example…

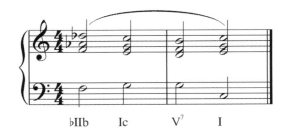

bIV   Ic   V⁷   I

Harmonic Rhythm Exercise (My Solution)

Passing Note Exercise (My Solution)

CHAPTER ELEVEN – RIFFS, REFRAINS AND OSTINATI

REFRAINS

A refrain is simply a repeating section of music – like a 'chorus' – it returns between verses or episodes in the piece. They are useful because they create a structure from which you can launch your next idea – thinking time if you like, but it is also a useful tool for memorising pieces.

STRATEGIES FOR MEMORISING

1)   Start with smaller repertoire (not Fugues or Sonatas)

      i)   Understand the harmony
      ii)   Play hands separately
      iii)   Understand the structure because you will memorise in sections

2)   Types of memory

      i)   Finger – this is the type often displayed by grade 1 students (it falls down when the pieces become longer and more complex
      ii)   Visual – this is remembering both – how the score looks and how your hands look on the keyboard – the 'shapes' you make
      iii)   Aural – simply put – how the music goes
      iv)   Analytical – understanding the musical signposts (modulations, cadence points, structural changes)
      v)   Emotional – the environment in which you learn – always change the environment and instrument to test your memory as it has a tendency to remember everything related to the piece including the room and piano used for practise, then, when you play it somewhere other, your memory fails.

3)   Test piece – **Eric Satie - Gnossiennes No. 1**

      i)   Key = F minor (play the scales: natural/harmonic melodic)
      ii)   Consider the structure – ABCBA'BCB (Rondo)
      iii)   Consider the Left Hand – analyse chords used and when
      iv)   Consider the melody(ies) – A B C & A'
      v)   Learn the refrain/Rondo theme (B) first.
      vi)   Now learn the C section
      vii)   Finally learn the A section(s) paying particular attention to the differences between A and A'
      viii)   The whole of this piece can be summarised in a few short phrases. Apply this to another short piece (a Schubert Waltz for example)

Eric Satie - Gnossiennes No. 1 – Memory Outline (80 bars reduced to 32)

Harmony: Three Chords: Fmin, B♭min, Cmin

Theme B: (refrain)

Theme C: (C major melody)

Theme A: (C harmonic minor melody)

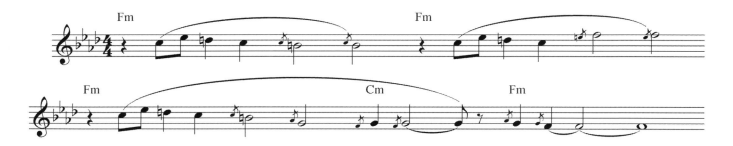

Theme A':

OSTINATO

Like refrains, ostinato are repetitive, only they can underpin whole section or even complete pieces whilst other parts of the music 'experiment'. For an improviser they are a useful practise tool. Here is a very famous example: notice too how the theme acts as a refrain to give the piece shape. Here is a useful guide building on the Satie on how we can approach the learning of a new piece that minimises the use of sheet music so that freedom at the keyboard is encouraged.

1)   Learning a new piece – Mouvement Perpetuel (Poulenc) Movement 1

    i)   What is the piece about – title – historical background – composer

    ii)   Use two hands to 'hear' the LH Ostinato

    iii)   Then transfer to LH only – then practise only this until it is fluent.

    iv)   Play and listen to the RH top-part only = descending scale legato

    v)   Add the 'inner part' and practise only this.

    vi)   Start the LH going, and drop RH onto its ostinato pattern

    vii)   Do this for each section then memorise as you did the Satie

    viii)   To add musicality and character, create a story. See how the use of modes and unexpected scales in the RH over the stubborn 'ostinato', gives the music a sense of moving through different scenes, while the theme acts as a 'refrain'

    ix)   Now you have grasped all the elements of the piece, it is yours to keep, but also as a starting point for experimentation. Using the LH ostinato, pick one of the scales or modes Poulenc has used and see what you can do with it…

Structure:
A
A
B
A
C
D
E
D : Repeat
A + coda & End

Mouvement Perpetuel (Poulenc) Movement 1 – Memory Outline

LH Ostinato – The Vicar's Bicycle

Theme A – The Vicar Whistles a tune (Bb)

Theme B: Child Practising (Lydian Mode)

Theme C: What's going on over there? (D♭minor)

Theme D: Up the Hill (B♭min)

Theme E: Down the Hill (E♭min)

Ending! (Cadence?)

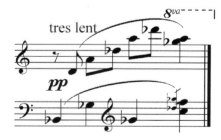

Now use Poulenc's ostinato figure and make up your own RH melodies. Use some of his 'modes' to help you. The five finger pattern in C really sets up the 'Lydian' mode – the theme itself is clearly B♭ major, and then he has excursions into B♭ minor and to the rather remote A♭ minor, all held together by the LH. Try them all, use his notes as a guide, but change their direction and order. At the very least it will be fun! My university professor gave us this as a composition exercise for two pianos, and the results were startling!

OSTINATO EXERCISE

An ostinato can be created from existing pieces for which they were not specifically intended. It is like those modern 'sampled' pop songs, where they take a very short fragment from a famous song from the past, and build a whole new song around it. Here we are taking a Chopin F minor Etude and mixing it with modal elements to create something more akin to Miles Davis. Here is the opening of the etude...

Here is the basic ostinato pattern:

Here is the adaptation of the melodic idea using a modal (dorian)/jazzy scale – we have reduced the tempo slightly to create a softer feel, and also to allow the right-hand 'riff' time to express itself.

Here are the notes of the dorian mode on F:

...the challenge is to improvise a new piece around this small extract using this mode: here is a fragment of an improvisation; work with this or devise your own.

Allegro Non Troppo

EXTENSIONS

An extension is simply an additional note a third higher than the top note of the chord. We have already met the 'seventh' chord which is an 'extension' of the triad = 135+7, (GBD-F) but theoretically we can keep adding thirds to the triad to create extended chords; like this....the 15th particle is back to C again.

Again, composers were looking for new ways to reinvigorate musical expression whilst holding true to the essential 'circle of fifths' notion of harmony. However, just as with sevenths, voicing becomes more complicated. Too many notes from an extended chord and it becomes difficult to tell which note is which, so the tendency was to drop the notes closer to the root but maintain the root itself, and favour the extended note; like this;

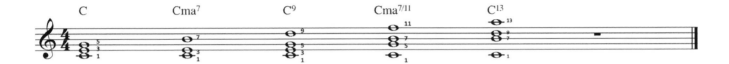

The next thing to consider are the accidentals: the majors and minors of each particle – you can see we are using the notes from the key of C, but extended chords can happen on any degree of the scale so we get major, minor chords emerging from these extensions. Like this:

So now we can add this technique of extension to one of the common progressions we know – let's start with the four chord Doo-Wop but this time I'm starting on the ii chord just as jazz would:

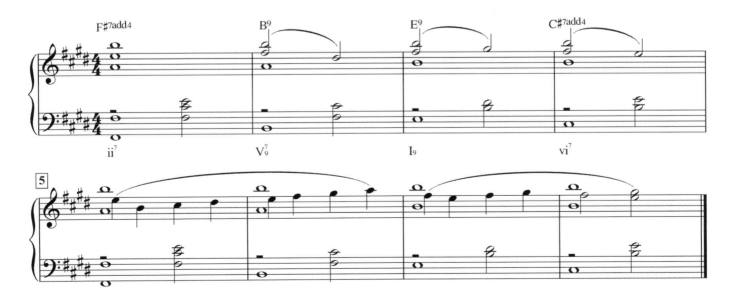

The harmony is less clear isn't it, more subtle and delicate. We know what the chords are, but they are not as distinct as they would be if we played standard triads – do a comparison…

If we always use extended chords we can lose the thread of the 'progression' so that the subtlety overwhelms the substance. The best practitioners use a variety of more or less extended chords so the progression retains momentum but carries a variety of harmonic expression. Here is a beautiful example.

Ravel Prelude in C (opening)

- Look at bar 2 & 3: right hand is GBD (G harmony) – left hand is ACEG (A min 7)
- Bar 4 is LH EGF♯B and RH BDF♯ and Bar 5 LH AEB (A9) and RH CEG (Cmajor)
- Bar 8 is LH Dmajor and RH is EGB (Emin)

It is almost as if Ravel is working in two keys, one per hand, but they work together because the right hand notes create extended chords from the root harmony of the left hand. Imagine if Ravel had harmonised this in a conventional way, without the extensions: it might have been like this?

In this version it sounds rather conventional doesn't it? That is the power of harmony – Ravel has transformed an ordinary tune into something hypnotic because the melody seems to float above the harmony supporting it. This would have been unthinkable in Mozart and Haydn's music as the classical ideal is firmly rooted in diatonic (of the scale) harmony where Ravel is toying with poly or bi-tonality (more than one key at a time). However, even in this rather sophisticated use of harmony, Ravel is still using the circle of fifths as the basis for his experimentation.

Using Ravel's model above, see if you can create a piece of music using essential circle of fifths harmony, but using extensions to expand the chords to create an impressionistic sound. Here is an example using a variation on the Doo-Wop, again starting with chord ii.

I Feel Inclined

A. Higgins

MELODIES FROM EXTENSIONS

Now we can try and combine all of the elements from this chapter. Below is a piece that uses an ostinato, extended melodies; transposition and extended chords: I have deliberately left a passage in the middle for improvisation. You really have a choice here – you can use the extended shape of the melody: the good old fashioned blues scale in G: or the scale/mode as you see fit. They all work, but will create different effects.

Notice the melody I deploy is based on a five finger position of D minor on a G minor ostinato. So the melody is working between the 5th and 9th degrees of the scale – an extended melody. The 'cool' or be-bop' movements in jazz favoured this technique – they used extended harmony upon which they built their melodic material. In my piece you can hear clearly in all the different versions of the melody that the five-finger position they occupy relative to the triad affects the mood – so imagine Miles Davis or John Coltrane taking a standard song melody and then applying it to the extended intervals rather than the triad and that is why their improvisations are often described as 'taking flight'.

In Chapter 13 there are some lead sheets and melodies to experiment with: try 'displacing' the melodies into different positions of the scale and see how effective this can be.

Walking Variations

A. Higgins

CHAPTER TWELVE – VARIATIONS

J.S. BACH – GOLDBERG:

Here is an example of an opening from: J. S. Bach's – Goldberg Aria:

Here is the harmonic progression with melodic outline for the first eight bars:

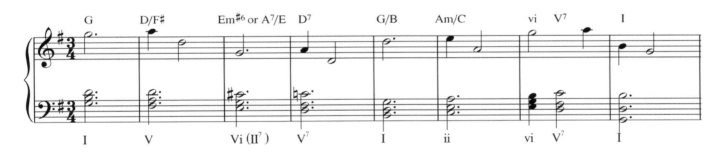

The underlying harmony is deceptively simple: do you recognise it? Replace the first chord V with vi and we have the four chords of the 'Doo-Wop'!

		TWO	FIVE	→I	TWO	FIVE	→I
I	V7	II7	V7	I	ii	(vi) V7	I
Gmaj	D7	A7	D7	G	Amin	(emin) D7	G

When harmony is reduced to its simplest form it really is all about tension and resolution. About the dominant and the tonic - chord ii holds a powerful position because it can turn dominant into tonic so it becomes the dominant itself. See how Bach makes II a major triad with a seventh so a 'secondary' dominant for the bar 4 imperfect cadence, but relaxes the impulse at the perfect cadence. It is too early in the piece for a full scale modulation so he cancels the C♯ of bar 3 with C♮ in bar 4, but doesn't resolve to a 'root' position chord I in bar 5, because it is too early to 'finish' the piece. Oh, the many decisions a composer has to make!

Now it is your turn to take this simple progression, play it through and elaborate on it....

MORE ABOUT MELODY

In my analysis of Bach's Aria, I deliberately included the melodic outline of the original. There are two reasons for this:

1. When improvising it is useful to keep a shadow of the original in the back of your mind. Not just the harmony, although that is certainly sufficient, but ideally the melody too.

2. Keeping the melody in mind gives you an opportunity to 'work the melody' in the same way we have the chords. Inversions; retrograde; substitution; transposition; can all apply to the melody. In this way we can use it as a starting point to invent our own melodic material. This is precisely what a good improviser, whether jazz, classical, rock or other style, does. The worst simply add standard hooks and licks out of jazz books practised over many years to every piece – each piece has its own possibilities and as creative musicians we should seek them out.

Here are some simple variations on the melody to give you an idea: add some of your own, and remember to think about changing the harmony; substitutions; using extensions; new chords; and exploring the rhythm too.

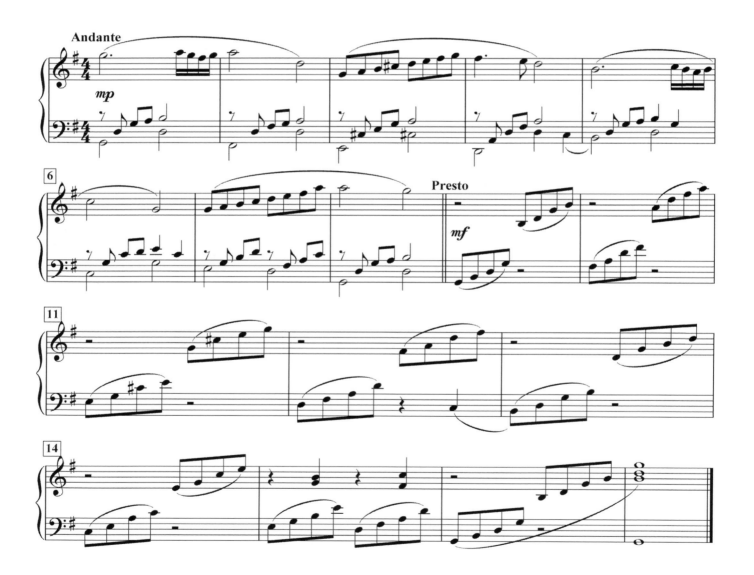

CHOPIN PRELUDE IN C MINOR: IMPROVISATIONS

Analyse   Harmonise   Improvise

EXPLORING CHOPIN... THE CHROMATIC DESCENDING BASSLINE

An extension of the 'ground bass' we studied earlier is this 'chromatic' version. Baroque composers would use this when the music was especially expressive. Dido's Lament from Purcell's great opera Dido and Aeneas is an especially good example, but also the Chopin above.

The descending bass line moves in half-steps (semi-tones) – below is just the bass-line in A minor (Chopin uses C minor and an alternate ending). I have indicated the chords – you need to supply the actual music. This was common practise in the baroque period so enjoy being a baroque improviser and remember to experiment with textures!

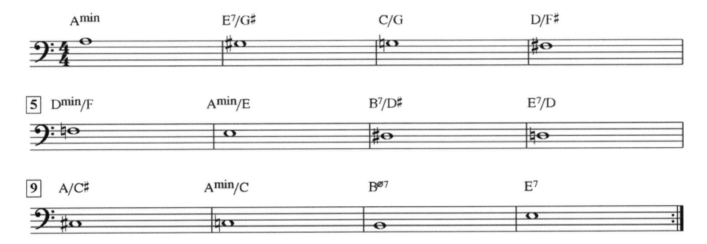

Did you notice the 'consecutive' dominant sevenths at Bar 7: B7 and then E7? This 'chromatic' harmony is highly expressive because the tonality (key centre) is very much in flux. We are heading for E, then for A, and the music is moving forward but without certainty. It could continue at bar 9 and 10 with A7/C♯ then D7/C, even bar 11 with G7, all following. Herein lies the key to Wagner's 'endless' melody – his huge opera's sustained their drama by moving unrelentingly through successive keys without resolution until arriving at their final 'tonal' destination. It is why the endings are so powerfully dramatic, and the music so restless and unique. It also presages the arrival of 'atonal' music (music without a key). Handle with care!

Practise this in all minor keys then transpose to the major key too – the effect is transformative.

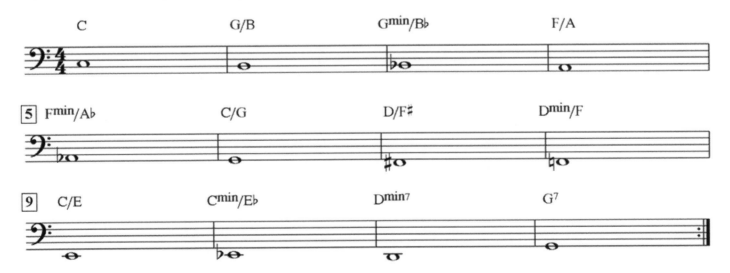

Now use this chromatic bassline and re-harmonise each time – this exercise is a real test of harmonic knowledge and very satisfying – I do this regularly just for the satisfaction of finding new chords that fit this ground bass:

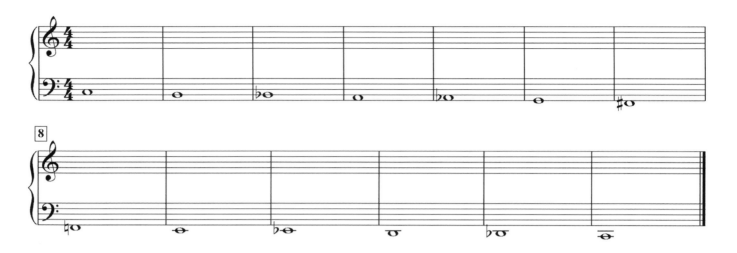

....here is an example to give you an idea:

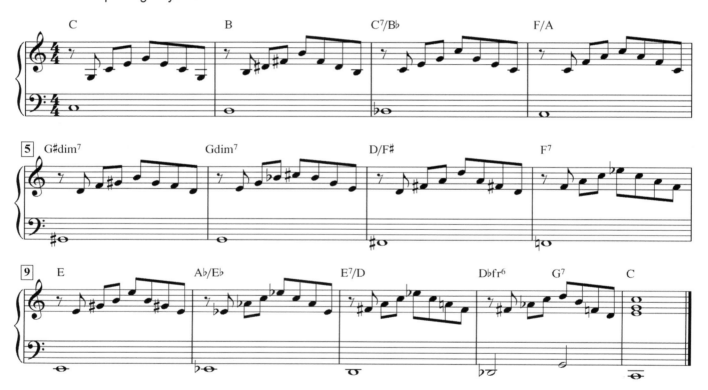

Now that you have established some interesting chords to fit this ground bass follow the usual steps:

1. Start to create new textures (waltz; arpeggios; Alberti basses; through the hands; polka) so you can hear the effect of one harmony moving to another.

2. Then use inversions of the chords above whilst keeping the ground bass – try to use the contrary rule where possible: that is: as the bass descends the music of the upper part ascends or remains constant. It helps the music breathe where having all parts going in the same direction can sound like a dirge.

3. Change the key and do the same exercise in all the keys you know. So much music for piano is based on the instrument itself and sometimes starting at a different point inevitably leads to a new solution.

Ground basses can also rise. Brahms Fourth Symphony features a very effective passacaglia fourth movement with a rising ground bass – have a listen to it when you can. Here is a rising sequence of my own for you to play and then one variation: add some more of your own.

THEME

VARIATION 1

A. Higgins

YOUR VARIATION(S)

Sibelius: Valsette Op. 40, No. 1 (Excerpt)

Consider this little waltz:

I have outlined the harmony above in chord form: it is unusual in some respects especially the return to E minor at bar 13: a perfect cadence just seems to appear from the previous Dminor chord preceding it, but Sibelius has set it up as a sequence: look at the melody from bar 9, then bar 13: it is transposed by a semitone from C7 to B7. It is still unusual, but not unmusical.

The harmony is full of interesting chords based on the circle. The bars 9 to 12 are simply V7 – I in F followed by ii – V – i in D minor. Sibelius steps round the circle through C to D minor rather conventionally, but the B7 at bar 13 is unexpected.

Using this as a starting point for improvisation opens up great possibilities: style; tempo; texture; melodic choices etc... and, of course as seasoned improvisers, we can choose a different style everyday. Today I have chosen a 'vamp' style: what will you choose?

Sibelius Valsette Vamped!

So what did I do?

- Changed the time signature to 4/4 but gave the rhythm a 'swing' feel
- Kept the pedal tone, but added the third to the B chord
- Extended the bars of G major harmony
- Introduced a new syncopated melody
- Added an ending

Throughout the book you may have noticed that I never ask you to 'play whatever you want'. We always have some ideas in our heads before we touch a key. This is Goal Directed Practise. Many times I hear students playing through their pieces endlessly believing they are 'practising' when in fact they are merely playing. Practise is about setting objectives and working towards them: in the case of improvising, we start with a theme, some chords, and existing piece, a story...anything that gives us a starting point then we try to express something musical using the elements at our disposal. With sufficient practise, it is possible to start with just the merest idea; four notes (like Beethoven's Fifth Symphony), but even the maestro himself had four notes and a very big idea!

IDEAS FOR PRACTISING

As much as we can use improvisation to modify and exploit pieces we have learnt and studied, we can also take the reverse approach and take out elements of a piece and turn them into miniature studies that give us the facility to overcome a technical difficulty. For example consider this etude from Chopin's second book of etudes Op. 25, No.1 'the Aeolian Harp'.

One of the key issues here is the left hand fluency over some rather awkward stretches. Chopin had an unusually extended fourth finger and many of his accompaniment figures take advantage of this creating a difficult stretch between fingers 3, 4 and 5 that needs a little practise.

To overcome this when I was learning the piece, I developed a simpler miniaturised study that focused on the same movement but without all the other difficulties of the Chopin. Naturally, because I wanted it to be fun, I turned it into a piece in its own right, and often give this to my students before they tackle the Chopin etude.

To make it more effective I changed the rhythmic emphasis: instead of the fluent 4-4 semi-quaver triplets, I added tenuto notes on the third and fifth semi-quavers, changed the time signature to 3-8 so it had a gentle lilt – (one and two, three) with a focus on the inner fingers. I did this for two reasons: to show the difference between the time signatures so the student would recognise how to play the correct rhythm even where the time value of the individual grouping appears the same, but also the emphasis on the middle fingers would strengthen them and keep the hand balanced.

Finally, I added a simple melody so the piece has a sense of itself.

APRIL SNOW

A. Higgins

(The musical box unwinds to a stop)

'I used to melt your heart like April snow'

CHAPTER THIRTEEN – PRACTISING

PHILOSOPHY

So much of learning to improvise is about a way of thinking, a philosophy if you like. To want to play Beethoven's Fur Elise, Scott Joplin's Entertainer, even Rachmaninov's Prelude in C#, inspires us to master the instrument and in the process we learn all the things necessary to achieve these noble and worthwhile goals. However, in all my years of teaching adults the most common theme that emerges from their many years of 'learning the piano' is the inability to just sit down a play a few chords or make up a tune or play by ear after hearing a melody: essentially, to improvise. Music is about expression and just as when we read a book we 'imagine' the voices of the characters in the pages, their thoughts and motivations, so we do with music. Often the trouble is that the score in all its glorious refined detail becomes the music and we lose sight of the fact that very often the notation itself is but a clue, a guide to the real meaning of the piece and we need to bring something of ourselves to the music. Perhaps by engaging more closely to the act of creation, we are, in the first place, better equipped to meet these demands, but also able to express something unique and personal in a musical way.

My contention is also that the ability to express oneself is in itself enough to justify the continuing place of music in a life. In such a competitive environment we are apt to think if we can't play Rachmaninov then we ought not to play at all and we set aside music as a thing tried but failed. But music is not exclusive, it is available at all levels – in the same way the delicate expression of a 9 year old reading out a self-penned poem always moves, then the first creative meanderings at the keyboard can do likewise. In both cases they start with some knowledge of the language and then reach out for a personal expression of that knowledge. As teachers we need to facilitate that desire to express not just with a diet of ever harder and more expressive pieces, but with a deeper understanding of the language they use so that the student can take the lessons from these great works and apply them anew.

PRACTISE

Now reader, it is your turn to seek out new musical worlds but to help you on your journey here are several exercises that will allow you to take all the concepts from this slim volume and apply them in all their rich diversity. Be patient and courageous, allow as much time as you might your scales or sight-reading on a daily basis and you will find your reward comes slowly at first but then easily.

When you have mastered your repertoire pieces, do not be afraid to unpick the detail and deconstruct their parts – it is only the analysis one would expect if one is to play convincingly, however through the exploration and elaboration, we come to a better understanding and knowledge of the composer's intentions.

Then, always accept the responsibility of creativity. Add an extra variation to the set; reshape a minuet; or a waltz; 'nocturnify' a polka; re-arrange a song; create a theme and compose a sonata. All of these activities will make you a better musician but will also help you understand just how music itself has evolved and diversified.

I have deliberately divided this chapter into sections appropriate to the skill acquired so we can recap what we already know and then apply it to the exercise given.

HARMONY

In part one we learnt to understand the triads and the harmony that make up each key. Exercises included:

- Using the Triad Hierarchy from each key and playing its chords progressively in 'any order'
- Focusing on some typical progressions that are favoured by composers (Doo-Wop and Pachelbel for major keys; Spanish and La Folia for minor keys)
- Harmonising the major scale and using substitutions
- Re-ordering the chords to create a 'B' section

In part two we learnt how to modulate through the circle of fifths and the added:

- Secondary dominants
- Extended chords (7ths, 9ths, 11ths etc..)
- Harmonic rhythm and passing chords
- New chords (augmented sixth, augmented triad, subdominant minor)
- Crossing the circle using 'chromatic' and 'enharmonic' harmony'
- The descending chromatic bass
- Bi-tonality

You should continue to work every day on these setting a goal every day for achieving a new and interesting chord progression in one or all of the above styles. Here are some examples as a guide and for you to work with:

8 Bar (16 chord) with Modulations and Inversions:

6 Bar with Chromatic chords:

8 Bar with Extensions:

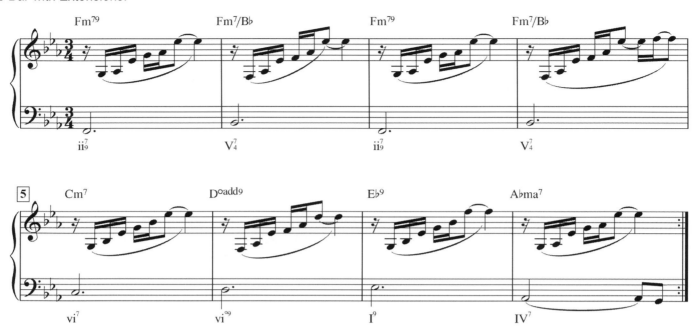

BEETHOVEN Variations on a Theme in C Minor (Ground Bass):

You will have noticed that on many occasions the harmonies that underpin melodies are very similar, hence the use of the 'classic' chord progressions. They have certain incidental changes like extra passing chords or an intensified harmonic rhythm, but what is striking is how the circle of fifths seems to underpin all of them. What makes the difference is the 'vernacular' or the style. Ravel simply extends his melodies so they hover above the rooted chords; where Mozart builds them from the diatonic scale; blues musicians use sevenths to 'colour' the music rather than as functional chords that establish or change keys.

MELODY

In part one we learnt to understand that triads and harmony underpin the melodies we invent and these are made up from the notes of the scales in which we are playing. Exercises included:

- Call and response to create a 'phrase' structure
- Inversions
- Identifying harmony notes (in the chord) and non-harmonic tones (passing notes)
- Four bar and eight bar phrases.
- The blues scale
- Reading a lead sheet

In part two we learnt how to modulate through the circle of fifths and the added:

- Suspensions and retardations both prepared and unprepared (appoggiaturas)
- Extended melodies (7ths, 9ths, 11ths etc..)
- Thematic variations
- Riffs

You should continue to work every day on these setting a goal every day of 'setting' a melody, either invented or from an existing tune and add a harmonic structure and texture to accompany it. Here are some examples as a guide and for you to work with:

The House Of The Rising Sun

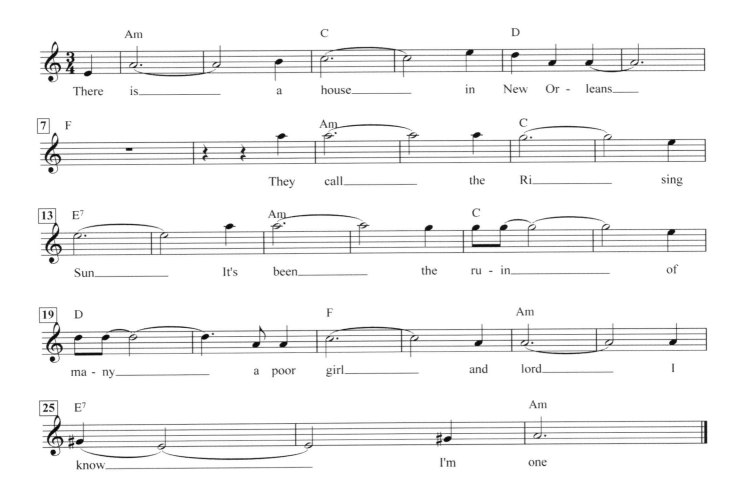

Scarborough Fair

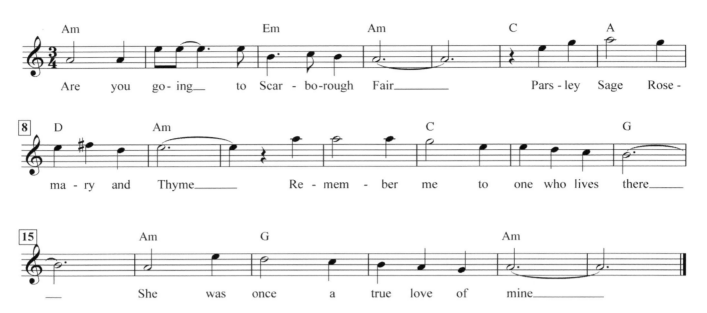

The Coventry Carol

N.B. The final chord of this haunting carol could be a D major chord. This closing a minor piece with a tonic major chord – suggesting hope in the face of tragic events – is commonly called a Picardy third or Tierce de Picardy. One must presume it was associated with composers from that area in France, although a colleague of mine once went to this region 'in search of the Picardy third' and came back disappointed by the lack of evidence to support this supposition!

STRUCTURES

In part one we learnt about simple chord progressions and how we can create pieces of music from 4 and 8 bar phrases which can be extended by repeats. We also learnt about:

- Call and response to create a melodic 'phrase' structure
- ABA (Ternery) structure
- Four bar and eight bar structures
- Repeats
- 12-Bar blues

In part two we learnt the following structural tools

- Refrains (Rondo or verse/chorus form)
- Ostinato and riffs
- Song form (lead sheets)
- Thematic variation form
- Variable bar phrasing

TEXTURES

In part one we learnt about simple textures so we could explore the chords and progressions we are working through including:

- Waltz/Polka/Minuet
- Arpeggios (separate hands and between the hands)
- Alberti's Bass
- Blocked chords (homophonic)
- Walking bassline
- Melody and accompaniment

In part two we developed the textures from part one to include:

- Suspensions
- Three-part stave
- Inner voices

Textures can also be used to delineate structures: they can be so variable as to make the same chord sequence sound utterly different and this skill is what creates the wonderful variety that emanates from the piano. It can be all things to all men. Percussive like a rhythm section; sustained like a string line; chordal like a hymn; cantabile like a song. The textures we have used in the book are just the tip of the iceberg and they can be combined and expanded in many thousands of ways to create new sounds and even techniques for the instrument. This structure through texture is at the essence of variation form and also jazz and blues improvisations: the chorus's as they are called repeat until the original theme re-emerges to signal the close of the piece.

132

Here is an example of a simple progression with variable textures that create a structure to highlight what I mean; use this to consider ideas on how you might vary your textures to create living, breathing structures that evolve – the very thing that makes music interesting and 'human'. In the example below we go from a 'chordal' (homophonic) texture, to an 'arpeggio between the hands' texture, to a 'melody and accompaniment'. The progression is essentially: i – III – V – vi – V – III – bii – i but by changing the textures; the order of chords and the mood, we have unity and variety within a single piece.

A. Higgins

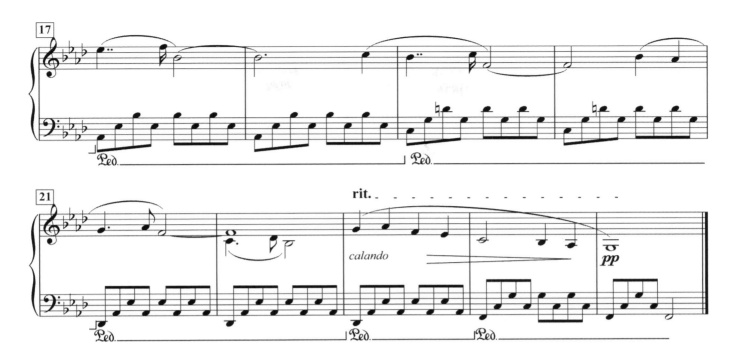

BLUES, JAZZ and POPULAR STYLES

We cannot justifiably leave a book about improvisation without at least a reference to styles of music that depend almost entirely on improvisation for their existence. Many times I have had the fortune to play with, and see in action, some of the best musicians in these areas, and, without exception, the key to their astonishing vibrancy is their understanding of harmony and then their own particular stylistic 'vernacular'. It was with this in mind that I specifically planned a book that did not specialise in any style that represents the peaks of improvisational prowess, as there are so many of these in existence, rather I concentrated on a book of essentials that would facilitate departure into any of the possible forms of music that uses 'harmony' in its widest sense thereafter.

That said, the very use of extended harmony, of the blues scale, and of the familiar 'doo-wop' progression, leads us into the territory of popular music, so here are a few examples of the style from which you can expand or invent your own 'improvisations'.

Jazz Prelude

Amazing Grace (excerpt from Alfred's Basic Adult Book 1)

This famous hymn can easily be jazzed up using seventh chords: analyse the chord structure and create a jazz improvisation using the melody and its patterns. Remember to try inversions, diminution (shorten the note values), augmentation (lengthen the note values) and you can hear traces of the blues scale in this extract so test your blues scale knowledge at the same time!

... this extract from Amazing Grace is incomplete. As an extra exercise work out the rest of the melody and harmonise it appropriately to complete the piece. Then you start to pick it apart and create some improvisations: here are some clean staves so you can do this in your own time:

STRIDE BLUES